CW00345854

PURE
WIT

PURE WIT

The Revolutionary Life of
Margaret Cavendish

FRANCESCA PEACOCK

An Apollo Book

First published in the UK in 2023 by Head of Zeus Ltd,
part of Bloomsbury Publishing Plc

Copyright © Francesca Peacock, 2023

The moral right of Francesca Peacock to be identified
as the author of this work has been asserted in accordance with
the Copyright, Designs and Patents Act of 1988.

All rights reserved. No part of this publication may be reproduced,
stored in a retrieval system, or transmitted in any form or by any means,
electronic, mechanical, photocopying, recording, or otherwise,
without the prior permission of both the copyright owner
and the above publisher of this book.

Epigraph from *If Not, Winter: Fragments Of Sappho* by Anne Carson,
reproduced with permission of Little Brown Book Group Limited.

Epigraph from *The Hearing Trumpet* by Leonora Carrington, reproduced
with permission of *The New York Review of Books* and Paul De Angelis,
Paul De Angelis Books.

Lines from *The Complete Poems* by Philip Larkin, reproduced with
permission of Faber & Faber.

Extract from *Art on My Mind: Visual Politics* by bell hooks,
reproduced with permission of The New Press.

9 7 5 3 1 2 4 6 8

A catalogue record for this book is available from the British Library.

ISBN (HB): 9781837930173
ISBN (E): 9781837930142

Printed and bound in Great Britain by
CPI Group (UK) Ltd, Croydon CR0 4YY

MIX
Paper | Supporting
responsible forestry
FSC
www.fsc.org   FSC® C171272

Head of Zeus Ltd
First Floor East
5–8 Hardwick Street
London EC1R 4RG

www.headofzeus.com

For Margaret Cavendish, and Elizabeth Peacock.

My ambition is not only to be Empress, but Authoress of a whole world

Margaret Cavendish, *The Blazing World* (1666)

someone will remember us
    I say
    even in another time

Sappho 147.1, trans. Anne Carson,
If Not, Winter (2003)

Miracles, witches, fairy tales, grow up Darling!

Leonora Carrington, *The Hearing Trumpet* (1976)

Contents

Author's note

In her 1655 work *The Worlds Olio*, Margaret Cavendish memorably declared "it is against nature for a woman to spell right". She was railing against the printers who had sent her previous book to the press without correcting her "hundred" faults of spelling and grammar, and, in a metaphor typical of her, she argued that her book-baby had been "lamed" by a bad "midwife and nurse".

So as not to further anger Cavendish, I have altered her (and other authors') idiosyncratic or historic spelling at points where it might prove an impediment to understanding and engaging with their work. But, in the spirit of protecting women's rights to spell as they wish, I have left Cavendish's distinctive orthography untouched in places where to chaing it wold bee to risk losing something vitall from the original text.

Introduction

The empress and authoress of a whole world

IN APRIL 1667, Margaret Cavendish was the talk of London society. At the first performance of *The Humorous Lovers* – a play everyone believed was by her though it was, in fact, written by her husband, the Duke of Newcastle – she had chosen an extravagantly provocative outfit. Sitting in the audience, she wore a dress so low-cut that "her breasts" were "all laid out to view". As if that boldness were not enough, she had even completed the look with "scarlet trimmed nipples". In a riotously bizarre letter to his father, the young man-about-town Charles North described the situation succinctly: "the Duchess Newcastle is all the pageant now discoursed on". In North's rather fantastical account, she had apparently tried to enter the playhouse in either a "triumphal chariot" pulled by two horses, or an even more glamorous one pulled by "8 white bulls", before then sneaking in "incognito".[1]

That same spring, the Restoration diarist Samuel Pepys recorded his attempts to catch a glimpse of the now-famous Duchess of Newcastle. "The whole story of this lady is a romance, and all she do is romantic", he wrote in early April when Cavendish was visiting court.[2] Pepys hoped to be able to see her in Whitehall, when she would be there "to make a visit to the Queen". But, for Pepys, she was herself a kind of royalty: that evening, so many people had heard she was coming to court that she was beset by crowds as if she were the "Queen of Sweden". Two weeks later, he managed to catch sight of her as she rode past in her coach, which was decked out "all in velvet". He describes her appearance in brilliant, obsessive detail – she was wearing a "velvet cap", "black patches" on her face to disguise her pimples, and was "naked-necked" down to her "black just-au-corps", a type of knee-length jacket that was normally reserved for men. "All the town-talk is now-a-days of her extravagancies", he huffed.

Pepys was hardly immune to the general fascination with her. "I hope to see more of her on Mayday", he wrote. He was not the only one who had that idea: on the first of May, Margaret was "followed and crowded upon by coaches all the way she went", to the point that "nobody could come near her".[3] Ten days later, in an image reminiscent of David Bowie being mobbed by adoring fans in the 1970s, or the Beatles being hotly pursued in the 1960s, she was chased by "100 boys and girls running looking upon her". There is something slightly fantastical about these partial sightings: at one moment, all Pepys could see was a "black coach, adorned with silver instead of gold" and everything inside was a dizzying monochrome mix of "black and white".[4] Cavendish was a mysterious, enchanted creature.

But, if much of London thought Margaret was some strange combination of a costumed actress, unreal goddess, and magical princess, not everyone was so convinced. Mary Evelyn – wife of the diarist John Evelyn – visited her at her London home of Newcastle House, Clerkenwell and came away believing that she was insane: "I was surprised to find so much extravagancy and vanity in any person not confined within four walls." She even feared her unnaturalness would be contagious: "I hope, as she is an original, she may never have a copy," she wrote. Mary left in a hurry to avoid "infection".[5] The fact that her husband could not stay away from Margaret could hardly have helped stem her displeasure. In another nugget of gossip, the Lord Chamberlain even had to tell Cavendish to stop dressing her servants at court in "affected velvet caps".[6]

* * *

Who, or what, was this woman? A fairy queen, or insane whore? It wasn't until the end of May 1667 that Pepys had his chance to make Margaret's acquaintance and make up his own mind.

The Royal Society had been founded in 1660, and counted John Evelyn, the chemist Robert Boyle, and the architect Christopher Wren amongst its founding members: it was, unequivocally, the home of male Restoration scientific and scholarly endeavour. Having attacked two of its leading members in her recent publication, *Observations upon Experimental Philosophy* (1666) just a year earlier, and having satirised the Society as a whole in *The Blazing World* (1666), Cavendish decided that the time was right to press her case to attend a meeting of the Society. "After much debate, pro and con" and a ballot – many of the eminent men of the Society were against the idea, and feared "the town will be full of ballads" mocking the visit – an invitation was extended to Margaret, the first woman to be welcomed into the Society's then home at Arundel House.[7]

Margaret's visit proceeded in typically dramatic fashion. She wore a decadent dress, and was followed by her troupe of attendant ladies as crowds clamoured to see her. But for all the excitement, Pepys's assessment was damning: she was little more than "a good, comely woman" whose "dress so antick" made her little more than an amusing spectacle. She may have made it into the building of the Royal Society, but the men at its heart were all too quick to show her the door. After she had left – with an "elaborate curtsey", of course – the Society returned to their usual preoccupations: they made plans to measure the earth in St James's Park on Monday morning.[8]

* * *

The men of the Royal Society and all the hangers-on who had stood by to watch her visit did not quite understand Margaret Cavendish. Pepys's assessment of her as a "good, comely woman" – with all the normality that that description implies – is laughably meaningless when applied to her life. This was a woman who lived at the forefront of the turbulence and disorder of the seventeenth century: who went into exile with Queen Henrietta Maria; who associated with Ben Jonson, Thomas Hobbes, and William Davenant; and who published poetry, fiction, prose, and philosophy at a time when an infinitesimally small number of women were writing at all, and an even smaller number dared to use their own name on their published works. She wrote about feminism, lesbianism, and cross-dressing – alongside discussions about the right form of government, the working of microscopes, and how atoms move. The life of Margaret Cavendish – born Margaret Lucas in 1623, to a wealthy but not aristocratic Royalist family – is anything but ordinary.

Why, then, have few people outside academia and dusty archives heard of her? In her own lifetime, she wouldn't have countenanced this as a possibility. She was remarkably confident about her aims: "All I desire is fame, and fame is nothing but a great noise, and noise lives most in a multitude, therefore I wish my book may set a-work every tongue."[9] A bold statement – made bolder by the fact that it is found in the preface to her first printed work; the first non-anonymous published work of literature by an aristocratic woman since 1621, and one of a mere handful of signed works by women published in the first six decades of the seventeenth century. But, as Cavendish would later write in one of her plays, "fame is a double life, as infamy is a double death".[10] Sadly, much of her later critical reputation has been shrouded in infamy.

In her ground-breaking feminist essay *A Room of One's Own* (1929), Virginia Woolf set Cavendish up for this second death. Woolf famously wrote the story of "Shakespeare's sister", Judith – a woman who was "as adventurous, as imaginative, as agog to see the world" as her brother, but was denied any of his chances and education because of the accident of her sex. Judith ends up dead: she "killed herself one winter's night" when the heartbreak of not being able to fulfil her talent and genius got too much for her. But not content with an imagined, frustrated female talent,

Woolf turned her critical eye to the pages of literary history to find the female writers who were also "born with a great gift" and, as a result of being unable to use it, found themselves "crazed", dead, or spending their days "in some lonely cottage outside the village, half witch, half wizard, feared and mocked at".[11]

Woolf kindly dismissed the poet Anne Finch, Countess of Winchelsea – "her gift is all grown about with weeds and bound with briars" – and lauded the Restoration playwright Aphra Behn ("for here begins the freedom of the mind"; she showed women they could "make money by [their] pen[s]") before she lit upon "hare-brained, fantastical" Margaret Cavendish. Some of Woolf's comments on Cavendish are so damning they are almost the platonic ideal of insults: she is "crack-brained and bird-witted"; a "giant cucumber" in a rose garden who chokes the other plants; and she "frittered her time away scribbling nonsense and plunging ever deeper into obscurity". Few readers in the twentieth century could, in good conscience, pick up a Cavendish volume after reading such excoriating words. And, in Woolf's view, nobody did: her books "moulder in the gloom of public libraries".

But there's every chance that Woolf wouldn't have wanted to insult Margaret quite as much as she did. Her brilliantly catty comments are contained within a much more nuanced reading. Woolf writes sensitively about how Margaret's burning "passion for poetry" guided her life, and her critique of Cavendish's writings is not so much concerned with their content as with their execution. Her intelligence "poured itself out... in torrents of rhyme and prose, poetry and philosophy which stand congealed in quartos and folios that nobody ever reads". In *The Common Reader*, Woolf even went as far as to admire "something noble and Quixotic and high-spirited" in Cavendish.[12] Woolf did, then, follow this up with the verdict that she had the "freakishness of an elf, the irresponsibility of some non-human creature, its heartlessness and its charm".

*

There is a moment in the introduction to many academic works about Cavendish when the writer suggests that, whilst Woolf's accusations are cruel, there is some truth in them. What follows is often an *apologia* for focusing on Cavendish – a disclaimer for the more difficult parts of her writing, her difficult style, or her contradictory beliefs. As one scholar has put it, "perhaps more than any other early modern woman writer Cavendish has prompted critical disclaimers, qualifications, and apologies".[13] There is no getting around the fact that some of Cavendish's writing is hard going: too niche for modern readers; too rooted in a philosophical context that feels too distant from us; and too divorced from modern concerns about plot, realism, and concision. But for every moment of heavy-going philosophical argument, there is a spark of wit or satire so sharp that it feels it could have been written yesterday. And, more importantly, no academic or writer ever makes such an apology for some of John Dryden's duller works, or Ben Jonson's more obscure, boring plays. This is not to say that Cavendish is a female Donne, or a feminist, royalist Milton. But her work does deserve to be read seriously – without a pre-emptive apology about its quality or the gender of the author, and with true engagement with her ideas. Margaret Cavendish was a virtuoso; a radical; and one of those historical figures who seem to be spectacularly out of joint with the century into which they were born.

And her life, as well as her writing, deserves to be remembered. Everything Margaret did, from her birth 400 years ago in 1623 to her premature death in 1673, was striking, genre-defying, and – in the true, non-hyperbolic sense – awe-inspiring. In 1653, when Cavendish published her first book, *Poems and Fancies,* women simply did not write and publish books of poetry under their own name. If they did write, they circulated their work in manuscripts. If they did decide to publish, they would do so anonymously, under their initials or the ever-prolific title,

"A Woman". If they did decide to print a book under their own name, it would overwhelmingly often be something on a "safe" subject, such as a book of advice to mothers or a work of religious piety. Margaret – having written her poems whilst she was penniless, stranded without her husband, and in the midst of petitioning the Interregnum government to allow her access to some of the proceeds from the estates Newcastle had owned prior to the war – did none of this: her book went to press with her name dominating the title page. And the subject of her poems? How atoms function, the destruction wreaked by civil wars, and elements of her own autobiography. Over the next twenty years of her life and in her twenty-three books, Cavendish tore up the rules of what was expected of seventeenth-century women and rewrote them on her own terms.

The subjects of her writing are hardly what any reader would associate with the seventeenth century. Her interests are radically, preternaturally modern. She wrote about women who cross-dress in order to fight in wars, travel more safely, and experience adventure. She wrote repeatedly about her antipathy to marriage, and why any wedding is a considerably better deal for a man than a woman. She was intrigued, if not obsessed, by the idea of a women-only separatist utopia – and even wrote about the possibility of lesbian love. "But why may not I love a woman with the same affection I could a man?" asks one of her remarkably forward-thinking characters.[14] She was, despite her contradictions, a (proto)-feminist*: she truly believed that women should have access to a world beyond childbirth, housework, and – for aristocrats – needlework and dancing. She was a talented scientist and philosopher, and was not afraid to disagree with the received opinions and maxims of the day. She even wrote one of the earliest works of science fiction. She did not have children, but she did bring a new genre into the world.

---

* This is a difficult term, and one that will be discussed further on.

With her uncompromising desire for fame and power, and her (apparent) refusal of traditional roles for women, it seems hardly flippant or historically illiterate to argue that Cavendish's sensibility and writing have as much relevance to our century as they did to her own.

* * *

But history withers if we only consider the parts of it that feel relevant to our own predicaments, and Margaret Cavendish's life sheds light on the weird, and often under-appreciated, world of the seventeenth century.

It's all too often said that England escaped the revolutionary fever that raced through America and France in the eighteenth century, but a revolution which was just as violent and bloody – and, in its own way, as historically significant – had happened a century before. The English Civil War broke out in 1642 and, by 1649, the autocratic King Charles's head was no longer attached to his body. Everything changed – from how the country was governed to how the population prayed – and many of the transformations lasted long after the Restoration in 1660. Cavendish was at the centre of this disturbance: she was a member of a Royalist family and was a lady-in-waiting at the royal court. She was forced into exile in France, and did not live permanently in England for sixteen years. Her life and writing are a brilliant prism through which to view this period, and to ask new questions about early modern women's lives. Margaret was groundbreakingly radical, but she was not alone in transgressing gendered expectations and pushing at ever-flimsier boundaries. In many ways, the tumult and turbulence of the seventeenth century provided new possibilities for women. The wars gave them political roles as petitioners, and, in some cases, active roles in the fighting. And the changes in religion, with the growth of Nonconformist and Quaker communities, gave an ever-growing number of women the chance to prioritise their intellectual, spiritual life. Women in the seventeenth century were far from the silent, submissive stereotype that has persisted in popular thought.

But for a woman who delighted in bold, attention-grabbing stunts and was so preoccupied by the lure of fame, Margaret was near-debilitatingly shy: she struggled to speak when at Queen Henrietta Maria's court as a young girl, and, three decades later, she would fight the same tongue-tied "bashfulness" when meeting the beau monde of London in her triumphant spring of 1667. And it was not mere shyness that marked Margaret out and prevented her from enjoying society: her life was plagued by periods of "melancholy", and she was equally troubled by the unsavoury cures she prescribed herself to overcome this condition, and by other ailments. Purging, fasting, and potions of all kinds composed of foul-sounding ingredients formed part of her diet from her late teens onwards.

At the centre of Margaret's life – and at the centre of this book – is a difficult love story: Margaret Lucas met William Cavendish, the 1st Duke of Newcastle, when she was twenty-two, and he was thirty years her senior. The slightly unsavoury nature of their age gap (although common for the period) pales in significance when considering the strength of their love. Given her extreme shyness, it is surprising that their courtship prospered. But William was one of the few people that Margaret could speak and open up to. He was unfazed by the ambitious, intelligent woman he married, and tirelessly supported her publishing career: he wrote prefatory poems (in one, he lauds her "pure wit"), collaborated with her on writing projects, sent copies of her books to his well-connected friends and acquaintances, and helped with her day-to-day tasks.[15] His only worry about his wife being a writer – unlike the many critics who damned her as a mad whore – was that she spent too much time sitting down. And the relationship ran both ways: Margaret married William despite knowing that he was a disgraced Royalist commander without a penny to his name, and despite her belief that marriage trapped a woman within the submissive half of a union. This love story has been placed on a pedestal in studies of Cavendish: as a sign of her husband's goodness for dealing with her "eccentricities", and a sign of her feminine dutifulness, despite the wilder sides of her character. But it was certainly more complex than some historians have argued: in later years, their relationship seems to have faltered and Cavendish's tirades against marriage would increase. Nonetheless, their letters and poems open a window into a wonderfully intimate, passionate, and tumultuous seventeenth-century relationship.

* * *

In 1666, Cavendish published her most famous, and now most anthologised, work: *The Blazing World*. Part scientific treatise, part utopian philosophy, and part proto-science fiction, it was wholly radical and marked the indisputable high point of her literary career. It ends with a predictably modest note:

> By this poetical description, you may perceive, that my ambition is not only to be Empress, but Authoress of a whole world; and that the worlds I have made... are framed and composed of the most pure... parts of my mind; which creation was more easily and suddenly effected, than the conquests of the two famous monarchs of the world, Alexander and Caesar.[16]

She goes on to write that her creation caused fewer "disturbances" and "deaths" than these two famous titans. Not content with mere world domination, or near-divine world creation, Cavendish insists upon proving that she can complete this universal triumph better than any man – or woman, for that matter – who came before her.

Margaret Cavendish was the Empress of her own literary world, and did achieve fame in her lifetime – and for nearly a century afterwards. But in our own, she is far less known than other Restoration literary figures like Lord Rochester,

John Dryden, or Aphra Behn. Nor does she have a place within the canon of female writers who fought for women's writing to be taken seriously, from Mary Sidney, Countess of Pembroke, to George Eliot, Jane Austen and, of course, Virginia Woolf. But, four centuries after her birth, it's time for that to change. Woolf once wrote that "the crazy Duchess became a bogey to frighten clever girls with": what better time to prove that we're not scared?

1

The monstrous regiment of women

O N THE DARK, cold evening of 7 January 1674, Westminster
Abbey received a very special visitor. In a hearse decked
out in luxurious black velvet – and as a part of a full heraldic
ceremony complete with processing nobles and her coat of arms
held aloft – the body of Margaret Cavendish entered its final
resting place. It was a sombre service, lit only by the torches of
the mourners, but one seemingly more befitting a queen than a
woman born to a gentry family from Colchester.[1]

As with every other aspect of Cavendish's life, her funeral
was a moment of extraordinary theatre: the procession had
only begun after her body had been laid out in state for four
days in her family's London residence, Newcastle House, after
having travelled down – complete with her retinue of servants
– from Welbeck Abbey, where she had died a few weeks earlier
in December 1673. Servants were mounted on horseback and
attired in long black coats; the six horses that pulled her coffin
were also draped in black fabric; and her coronet was carried
into the abbey on its own black velvet cushion. The inclusion
of her heraldic insignia embroidered on the black velvet pall –
ever dramatic, it featured her own coat of arms impaled upon
her husband's – cost her husband William as much as £90.[*]

---

* Some of the costs of the funeral came to £130, as seen in *BL Add MS
12514*, ff. 282/90. This was an extraordinary expense: just a decade earlier,
Samuel Pepys had only paid £11 6s for the funeral of his brother, Tom.

The richly decked pageant, accompanied by the velvet-covered coaches of noble mourners, made its way to the abbey through Smithfield, past the Old Bailey, down Fleet Street and then along the Strand. Anyone who was in London that evening could not fail to have missed the significance of what had occurred. An Empress – "the most high, mighty and most noble Princess" – had died.[2]

After her remains were received by John Rosen, the Dean of Westminster Abbey, and followed by two of her sisters and a fleet of attendant earls, dukes and lords, Margaret was laid in a vault beneath the abbey's north transept; the tomb that William, thirty years Margaret's senior, had prepared in the expectation that he would enter it first. A simple epitaph, which can still be seen today, was inscribed beneath a sculpture of her body: "This Duchess was a wise, witty, and learned Lady, which her many books do well testify."[3]

* * *

How *did* Cavendish come to be the recipient of such pomp and adulation? Her funeral was just one outward show of the mark she had made on the seventeenth-century English world. In the years after her death, and before his own demise in December 1676, William organised the publication of a laudatory volume for his late wife: *Letters and Poems in Honour of the Incomparable Princess, Margaret, Duchess of Newcastle*. Cavendish was praised by everyone from the rectors and principals of colleges at Oxford and Cambridge to the leading intellectual and poetic figures of the seventeenth century, Thomas Hobbes, George Etherege, and Thomas Shadwell amongst them.

But Cavendish had not been born into this world of intellectuals, dramatists, poets, and well-connected aristocrats. Born Margaret Lucas in 1623, she was the last daughter of the eight children of Sir Thomas Lucas and Elizabeth Leighton. Thomas Lucas was a wealthy landowner in Essex – Margaret grew up in a large, luxurious house on the site of the former St John's Abbey – but this wealth had little to do with his own efforts: he was the son of the lawyer and politician Sir Thomas Lucas, and had come into money and land after his father's death, but not before he had spent nearly seven years in exile after an ill-fated duel with a young courtier.[4] Cavendish's mother, Elizabeth Leighton, was the daughter of a city gentleman, and had met Thomas whilst he was in his early twenties and dandying around London society. The couple had encountered a typical problem: Elizabeth became pregnant with Margaret's older brother, Thomas, before they could have a chance to marry. The scandal of an illegitimate child only became worse after the duel. Elizabeth gave birth in ignominy when she was only thirteen, and with her beloved Thomas miles away and unable to return from Europe. Thomas – who was some twelve years older than the teenage girl he had got pregnant and then abandoned – only met his son after a pardon was granted in 1604, when the boy was six. The couple did not marry until August of that year, and even then, given Thomas's father's disapproval, only in secret.

By the time of Margaret's birth, this scandal was confined to history. Margaret's father, Thomas, had died in 1625 when she was only two, and in her autobiography, *A True Relation of My Birth, Breeding, and Life,* Cavendish recasts the disgrace of his exile as something honourable: "my father by honour challenged him, with valour fought him, and in justice killed him".[5] Even later, Cavendish would use the example of the duel to suggest that she had always been surrounded by particularly masculine, virile men: like her husband, who "hath been a general of an army", she writes, "my father was a swordman, who was banished for a time... Thus have I been born, bred, lived, and married, all with sword-men".[6]

In drawing a likeness between her father and her husband, Cavendish was ever-so-subtly eliding many of the differences between the two men. Whilst both may have been "sword-men" (although to what extent a single duel which resulted in an awfully timed exile allows one to use this title is dubious), Sir Thomas Lucas and William Cavendish were rather different characters. To modern, democratic ears, the title "Sir" implies the pomposity of the nobility and gentry, but the Lucas family's wealth was far from the splendour of the Cavendishes (William was the grandson of Bess of Hardwick, who is now most famous for her construction of Chatsworth House in Derbyshire).

The Lucases had come into their money through the modern professions: Margaret's great-grandfather, John Lucas, had acquired his riches through marriage, law, and politics, while his son, Margaret's grandfather Thomas, had been knighted by Elizabeth I in 1571. John Lucas had bought St John's Abbey in 1548: he had a privileged position overseeing the "Court of Requests" which received all requests and messages directed to the king, and he had been well rewarded by the monarch for his service. He was granted former monastic land in 1548, and made his home amongst the ruins of the Abbey and its 200 acres. Lucas built a manor house on the site and, by the time of Margaret's childhood, it would have had the feel of a well-established gentry seat, complete with formal gardens, a grand hall, and rich furnishings.[7] Margaret's grandfather, Thomas, further consolidated the family's position: he, too, sat in Parliament and had a role at court as a favourite of Elizabeth I, who even visited the Abbey on a number of occasions. But as quick as the Lucas family had risen, their fall would be equally swift. Margaret's aunt, Anne, was a maid of honour at Elizabeth I's court, and angered the queen by marrying without her permission (an error Margaret would echo in her own life). But still more damaging was Thomas's duel: by the time Margaret was born, the Lucases were not a well-connected court family but were, instead, the kin of an outlaw who had only been allowed back into the country after Elizabeth I had died, and James I had granted him a pardon.

Margaret did not grow up in penury – far from it, she tells her readers that she grew up not just with "plenty" but "delight and pleasure to a superfluity"; the income from the Abbey's land would have made the Lucases one of the wealthiest families in Essex.[8] But she was emphatically not a society daughter who would be courted on the marriage market; nor was she connected to the intellectual, aristocratic seventeenth-century world. Instead, her childhood was both secluded – her widowed mother lived an extremely cloistered life – and unconstrained: Margaret could read, write, and wear what she wanted.

One answer to the question of how a "bashful", "melancholy" woman from a wealthy but not particularly influential family came to be honoured with such a funeral and to have been at the centre of such an intellectual web is simple: she married a man who was well connected in the Royalist Restoration world, and who doted on her ceaselessly. William did, after all, pay the great sums her funeral required, assist with her writing and ensure the publication of her posthumous tribute, and commission a memorial for her in Westminster Abbey.

But there's also a far more interesting reason. Cavendish was not just the over-indulged wife of a duke: she was the epicentre of a new wave of women's writing, education, and thinking.

* * *

In the summer of 1673 – just six months before Margaret died – Bathsua Makin (her unusual name comes from the biblical figure of Bathsheba) published an essay which was part call-to-arms, and part advertisement: she had "lately erected" a school for "Gentlewomen" at "Tottenham-high Cross", and wanted to enrol new pupils. Makin was a well-educated woman: she had been the tutor to the daughter of Charles I, Elizabeth Stuart, and was proficient in classical languages Cavendish could only dream of reading. Her pamphlet, *An Essay to Revive The Antient Education of Gentlewoman*, name-checks everyone from Sappho to the seventeenth-century Dutch painter and scholar Anna Maria van Schurman in her argument for the "abused Sex" to "set the right value upon themselves" and seek education for both them and their daughters. She writes:

> The barbarous custom to breed women low, is grown general amongst us, and hath prevailed so far, that it is verily believed (especially amongst a sort of debauched sots) that women are not endued with such Reason.[9]

Makin did not pull her punches (she expects "to meet with many scoffs and taunts from inconsiderate and illiterate men") but she was not alone in her calls for the education of women.

Mary More's *The Woman's Right* – a defence of the legal rights of women in marriage and a call for their greater intellectual instruction – is thought to have been written at some point between 1674 and 1680. Not published, but circulated in manuscript, More's text argues that "whenever women give themselves to study", they "prove as learned... with as much (or more) ease than men". She cites the examples of "Deborah and Boadicea" and "Queen Elizabeth ... who was also so expert in Tongues", and gives her call for learning a consciously erudite, logical air when she declares that the examples of historical women give hope to contemporary women: "what hath been done may be done is a rule in philosophy".[10]

Two decades later, in 1694, Mary Astell would publish *A Serious Proposal to the Ladies* (anonymously, under the name "A lover of her sex"). Astell's proposal was not just for greater education of women, but for women to retire – wholesale – to a "monastery" of "religious retirement" where they would obtain the "right ideas and be truly acquainted with the nature of those objects that present themselves to her mind".[11] There are aspects of Astell's proposal which sound more like a hippy commune than a schoolroom – "here are no serpents to deceive you, whilst you entertain yourselves in these delicious gardens" – but the call for feminine intellectual improvement echoes those of More and Makin.

These women scholars – they are joined by Anna Schurman, whose book, *The Learned Maid*, was translated into English in 1659 – were a brilliant late seventeenth-century phenomenon. Noble, wealthy women had been writing and reading since the Middle Ages (the historical image of the illiterate noble wife is a persistent, insidious fallacy), and had even received some fame and respect for their work. Mary Sidney, Countess of Pembroke, had continued her brother Philip Sidney's work on translation of the psalms after his death and had been lauded for doing so, and the intellectual brilliance of Elizabeth I was indisputable (even if women rulers had savage detractors like the Calvinist John Knox, the author of *The First Blast of the Trumpet Against the Monstrous Regiment of Women*, written to excoriate the regimes of Mary Tudor and Mary of Guise, Regent of Scotland). But these women writers and intellectuals were relatively isolated examples, rather than part of a trend.

During his reign, James I feared educated women (it's not too much to draw a link between this and his persistent terror of witchcraft). When asked if his daughter should be educated classically, he quipped that "to make women learned and foxes tame has the same effect – to make them more cunning". The result of his disparagement was a court, and a court life, which did not value educated women: they were a curio, an oddity, and fundamentally distasteful. One anecdote recalls how, upon being presented with a woman who could speak Latin, Greek, and Hebrew, the king replied "But can she spin?".[12] Makin may well have had a point when she wrote that "a learned woman is thought to be a comet, that bodes mischief".[13]

* * *

Makin wrote her famous call-to-pens mere months before Margaret died – suddenly, and of unknown causes – at the age of fifty. But Cavendish had been born a generation before, when King James was still on the throne and women's education was not the heated subject of pamphlets and debate. Instead, the favoured topic was women's moral and spiritual inferiority. In the decade before Margaret's birth, a pamphlet war had started in response to Joseph Swetnam's *The Arraignment of Lewd, Idle, Froward and Unconstant Woman* (1615). Swetnam's title accurately suggests the pamphlet's contents, and his beliefs about women are far from complimentary:

> ... there are many young men which cudgel their wits, and beat their brains, and spend all their time in love with women, and if they get a smile or but a favour at their loves hand... they think they have gotten God by the hand, but within a while after they will find that they have but the Devil by the foot.[14]

Outrage was expressed in response to Swetnam in pamphlets by Rachel Speght (*A Mouzell for Melastomus*, 1617), Constantia Munda (*The Worming of a mad Dogge*, 1617), and Ester Sowernam (*Esther Hath Hang'd Haman*, 1617). These pamphlets focused less on high-blown ideals of improving women's literacy and access to education so that men could no longer see them simply as evil, inferior, devious wretches – "her breast will be the harbourer of an envious heart, and her heart the storehouse of poisoned hatred, her head will devise villainy" – than they did on trying simply to prove that women were not inhumanly cruel.

This was the debate at the moment of Cavendish's birth: she was hardly the poster girl for women's education, but, for some historians, a symbol of the tragic denial of such opportunities. Aside from her denigration of her as a "giant cucumber", Virginia Woolf was cutting about Cavendish's lack of schooling. Her "wild, generous, untutored intelligence" poured itself out "higgledy-piggledy", she wrote.[15] Makin's comment was undoubtedly kinder, and arguably more insightful. She lauds Margaret – "the present Duchess... overtops many men" – but admits that her success is unusual. She triumphs "by her own genius, rather than any timely instruction".[16]

This claim of "self-education" and individual genius is one that persists throughout Margaret's work. In the preface to her first published work, *Poems and Fancies* (1653), she claims she "never read nor heard of any English book to instruct [her]" scientific beliefs. And in her later work, *Philosophical Opinions* (1655), she claims that she had "never conversed with any professed scholar in learning". These claims would come back to bite her, as scholarly friends railed against the insinuation that she had either never "conversed" with them, or that they were not her friends – but it is clear that she was insistent upon presenting herself as a natural, unschooled, and untaught genius.[17]

This claim to ignorance might have been part safety mechanism (nobody could accuse her of being uneducated if she admitted it first), and in part a desire for attention as the miracle-writer ("learning is artificial, but wit is natural" she remarks in the preface to *Observations Upon Experimental Philosophy*), but there is a grain of truth to it when talking about her early years. In her autobiography, Cavendish goes into detail about her education as a child. She shows no hint of displeasure about how she was raised by her mother (her father "died peaceably" when she was very young): she was bred "according to [her] birth, and the nature of [her] sex" – "virtuously, modestly, civilly, honourably, and on honest principles". In practice, this meant "all sorts" of tutors for "singing, dancing, playing on music, reading, writing, music, and the like". But even this distinctly feminine education was not strictly enforced: "my mother cared not so much for our dancing and fiddling, singing and prating of several languages, as that we should be bred virtuously", repeats Cavendish. For a mother who had been so damaged by scandal in her own youth, Elizabeth had no stronger desire than to prevent it for her daughters. Cavendish even writes of how her mother refused to allow "vulgar serving-men" to court the nursery maids "lest their rude love-making" might give the children all sorts of wrong ideas.[18]

Cavendish evidently did receive slightly more education than her self-presentation might suggest. By the time she was a young child, her older sisters and brothers had grown up – and two of her sisters had married. The older couples "read, work[ed], walk[ed]" with each other, whilst the young Cavendish lived in her own indulged, imaginative seclusion. She was "addicted from [her] childhood to contemplation rather than conversation, to solitariness rather than society, to melancholy rather than mirth, to write with the pen than to work with a needle". She was wrapped up in worlds of her own creation, and sought education where she could find it. Writing when she was a grown woman, she reminisced about the "several sheets of paper" she folded into "little baby-books" that she filled as a child: "unlegible letters" – covered in "blots" so large they formed "broad seas" of ink – recording all her childhood stories, concerns, and thoughts.[19] These sixteen books are now lost, but their existence shows that Cavendish, from a young age and despite her meagre instruction, could not resist the urge to write.

Books were prohibitively expensive in the early seventeenth century (although this was unlikely to have posed any difficulty for the wealthy Lucas family), and there was very little literature specifically targeted at children. But Margaret must have had access to enough books to be able to pronounce, some years later, that as a girl she was "in love with three dead men... The one was Caesar, for his valour; the second Ovid, for his wit; and the third was our countryman Shakespeare".[20] Her schooling was erratic – she was clearly dedicated to reading, writing, and discovery, but she did not receive a fraction of the dedicated and stringent humanist tuition that was provided for boys in the grammar and public schools of the time.

This education of shreds and patches was not unusual for wealthy women in the early seventeenth century. If the idea of schooling was not dismissed out of hand, as it was for James I's daughters, then the process was likely to be something cobbled together from individual reading, whatever tutors could be hired, and – perhaps most usefully – the dutiful smatterings gleaned from brothers who had been to school or had far better instructors. (In her autobiography, Cavendish recalls how if she read anything she "understood not", she would ask her "brother, Lord Lucas" to aid her with his greater learning.)

Lucy Hutchinson – Cavendish's contemporary, born in 1618 and the wife of the Puritan Colonel John Hutchinson – was the exception, not the rule, when she triumphantly wrote in her autobiography that "by the time [she] was four years old, [she] read English perfectly".[21] Hutchinson's "eight tutors" in multiple subjects and languages – particularly unusually, her father even desired her to learn Latin – was indicative of her Calvinist upbringing, rather than a widespread desire to educate well-read women. Lady Ann Fanshawe (later the author of the first recorded ice-cream recipe, and Cavendish's contemporary during her Civil War exile in Oxford), is far more representative of the general spirit of women's education when she records how she had "all the advantages that time afforded": she learned "fine works with [her] needle", along with "singing, lute, the virginals and dancing".[22]

* * *

Whilst Cavendish's education may have had much in common with that of Ann Fanshawe, there was one aspect of her early interests that was certainly out of the ordinary.

It was taken as a given that wealthy noblewomen would be interested in the clothes they wore – in his 1688 tract, *Advice to a Daughter*, Lord Halifax counsels his daughter against being too "proud of her fine gown" – but Cavendish took this interest to a rather different level.[23] Rather than just desiring the finest materials (although, of course, she never struggled to have these: her mother kept her children in "rich and costly" clothes), she also developed an interest in her own inimitable style.[24] She preferred clothes to toys – "toys as... were to adorn my person"

– and took "great delight in attiring, fine dressing, and fashions". But she was not content merely to wear the best dresses and gowns: she desired "fashions" she invented herself, and took no pleasure in "such fashion as was invented by others". In her later years, this habit of designing her own fantastical wardrobe (nipple tassels; cross-dressing; black velvet philosophers' hats) would result in some none-too-kind comments from men and other women at court ("report did dress me in a hundred several fashions"), and even an apocryphal cruel aside from Charles II who, upon catching sight of what he thought was a "devil in phantom masquerade" with a "pyramid on her head" is said to have remarked "I am ready to wager that it was the Duchess of Newcastle".[25]

But for the young Margaret, it is yet another sign of her individuality: her clothes, as she claimed of her ideas, came from herself rather than any external influence. And, indeed, it was also at odds with other women who were self-consciously trying to promote their intellectualism. Lucy Hutchinson, writing in her memoir, stresses her "negligence of her dress and habit, and all womanish ornaments" in favour of dedicating herself "wholly up to study and writing".[26] Margaret did not see the point of such piety and asceticism. In a forthright expression of her unreformed, anti-Calvinist spirit, she declared she "always took delight in a singularity, even in accoutrement of habits".[27]

* * *

As much as Cavendish courted originality throughout her life – in her dress; in her education; in her writing – she was simultaneously delighted by and afraid of the attention it could bring. Her childhood years in St John's Abbey were marked by something that would plague her throughout the rest of her life: she was unremittingly and debilitatingly shy. In her autobiography, she describes it as a "bashfulness". Her nervousness not only causes "blushes", but "contracts her spirits to a paleness". She was so shy she could barely function when she was beyond her "mother's, brothers', and sisters' sight" – it was only their presence that gave her "confidence" she could not "do amiss".

This description of nervousness, anxiety, and sadness – a self-described "melancholy" nature – makes Cavendish's recollections of the closeness of the Lucas family particularly poignant. During her childhood, many of her siblings were already married or taking part in public life: two of her elder sisters, Mary and Elizabeth, had married Sir Peter Killigrew and Sir William Walter respectively, and her three brothers had long since gone out into the world. Her eldest brother, Sir Thomas Lucas, could not inherit his father's wealth because he was illegitimate, and became a professional soldier instead: he served with the Dutch States Army, and then later fought in Ireland against the Irish Catholic Confederates. Her two other brothers – Sir John and Sir Charles – also became soldiers on the side of the Royalist cause after the outbreak of the Civil War, a cause for which Sir Charles would later die. Despite the fact that many of the Lucases were married or engaged in public life during her childhood, Cavendish recalls how the family still very much operated as a close-knit unit: her sisters "had no familiar conversation or intimate acquaintance with the families to which each other were linked to by marriage" but instead went about "in a flock together".[28] In a later letter about the perils of marriage, Cavendish would write that "daughters are but branches which by marriage are broken off from the root from whence they sprang and ingrafted into the stock of another family".[29] The opposite of this cruel transplantation was true for the Lucases: the "root" of their family remained strong. And it was within this unit – formed by friendship, understanding and "harmless recreations" without "strangers" – that Margaret truly felt comfortable, and unconstrained by her shyness.

Yet even with her family, Cavendish's debilitating anxiety did not disappear completely. Her third sister, Catherine, married the wealthy heir Edmund Pye in 1635, and Margaret would often stay with the couple in London. It was Catherine who she loved with a "supernatural affection", and Catherine who gave her so much anxiety: she was continually afraid that some "evil misfortune or accident" might befall her – or, indeed, anyone she loved.[30] She would wake Catherine in her sleep if she was breathing too quietly, for fear she "had been dead"; would lay her face over her mouth to "feel if [she] breathed"; and would knock on her door if she felt she had been praying "longer... than usual".[31]

For Cavendish, love was not something easy and comforting – it was an all-consuming desire to guard, protect, and ensure the safety of the beloved. It is, perhaps, easy to see Margaret's anxious devotion as something neurotic, pathological, and unnatural (she would even inspect Catherine's food, for fear it would "kill" her). But given the tribulations that were to befall the Lucas family in the coming years, her caution seems remarkably, and tragically, prescient.

2

This unnatural war came like a whirlwind

O N FRIDAY 7 July 1648 – nearly a month into an eleven-week siege of Colchester, and at the point where food other than the town's limited supply of cats and dogs was beginning to run out – Margaret's childhood home of St John's Abbey was stormed by the Parliamentary army led by Sir Thomas Fairfax. The soldiers battered and assaulted the house until, using some well-timed hand grenades, they found themselves within its bare walls – already scarred and pockmarked by six years of war and the blind fury of the fighting.[1]

Not content with simple destruction, and finding the provisions and furnishings of the grand house depleted and hardly worth plundering, the marauding soldiers made their way to the chapel, and the vault that lay beneath it. It wasn't long before the soldiers reappeared, now wearing hair cut from the un-decomposed corpses of Margaret's dead mother and sister. They scattered the bones of Margaret's other ancestors about, and made merry with their new wigs: St John's Abbey hadn't seen such jollity since the earliest days of the Civil War in 1642.

This gruesome merriment could not last, as the realities of siege warfare were not kind to either side of the conflict. The Royalists trapped inside Colchester had it worse: they were reduced to eating horse meat, boiled-down soap, and rats and mice; and they had to deal with the anger of the (often Parliamentarian) townspeople with whom they were trapped.[2] Cruelty and inhumanity became almost routine. When some women complained to the Royalist army that they were starving, the commander Lord Norwich told them to eat their children.[3] But, outside the town's walls, Fairfax's army was also struggling. After nearly a month's siege, Royalist newspapers mocked them for having achieved little more than capturing a handful of windmills and refusing passage to two women who wanted to travel to London. As one wit put it, there should be "a day of Thanksgiving, for these glorious victories at Colchester, over Petticoats and Windmills".[4]

By the end of August, however, not even the resolutely Royalist newspaper *Mercurius Pragmaticus* could pretend that the situation in Essex was anything other than dire. As late as 22 August, Royalist propagandists were still claiming that the doom-laden reports from five men who had swum over the river away from the besieged town about the state of the starving population were not to be believed (a reporter summoned up an imagined feast of stores of corn, rice, and cheese which would have surely made the besieged drool if they could have read it).[5] But, on 24 August, news of the Royalist surrender of Preston reached the town when Fairfax had the details of the victory flown over the besieged walls on kites. As a result, discussion of surrender began in earnest and, by 26 August, a letter was read in the House of Commons about the conditions for ending the fighting: all that remained was to discuss the terms of the treaty.

But if any Royalists expected the demise of Colchester to be just another sad, but ultimately unimportant, defeat in the second Civil War (1648–1649), they would be sorely mistaken. In a move which was distinctly unusual for the time – captured soldiers were rarely killed – some of the Royalist army leaders were sentenced by a military court to death by firing squad. As recently as June 1648, Parliament had voted to condemn all those who participated in the second Civil War (on the Royalist side, naturally) as traitors guilty of "high treason". The aristocratic army leaders were handed over to Parliament, but the other four were condemned to die in Colchester on 28 August.

As it happened, only two of the men were shot in the castle yard at Colchester in the early evening, after the other two escaped. To Royalist eyes, the execution was an act "so unsoldierlike, unworthy and barbarous, that it will heap eternal infamy on the heads of their brutish executioners".[6] One of the men is said to have spoken just as the guns were being raised:

> ... But seeing *I* must dye and that there is no way to obtaine mercy, but that I must now finish my course in this way, to which I beseech Almighty God to assist me, to dye with comfort in my Saviour.[7]

Without further ado, he was shot to pieces and carried to his resting place: the Lucas family vault in St. Giles's Church, Colchester. The victim of the firing squad – the man who had led the fight against Fairfax's besieging army and had, by all accounts, been particularly harsh in suppressing Parliamentarians – was Sir Charles Lucas, Margaret's beloved brother.[8]

* * *

How did the woman who had struggled to sleep without checking whether her sister was alive, and only ever felt comfortable in the presence of her family, come to be absent when her brother was shot, and her mother and sister's corpses were desecrated by out-of-control soldiers? And how did the Lucas family come to be at the centre of this turbulent new world of Civil War England with all its violence, political machinations, and divided loyalties? The answer to this lies in another uprising in Colchester, six years earlier, in August 1642.

By the summer of 1642, it was clear that England was about to collapse into serious civil disturbance, if not all-out civil war.

Charles I's eleven years of personal rule – the period in which the king had governed alone after the short-lived Parliaments of 1628 and the escalating criticism of his policies – had come to an end in 1640. Charles I had been obliged to call the Short Parliament (so called because it only lasted three weeks) to try to fund the Bishops' Wars in Scotland, wars which had begun after the king had attempted to reform the Church in Scotland. As part of his High Anglican reforms to the Church led by Archbishop William Laud, Charles I had attempted to reintroduce the *Book of Common Prayer* – the prayer book of England – to a Scottish congregation who were attached to John Knox's Presbyterian *Book of Common Order*. The reforms had gone down spectacularly badly, sparking rioting and widespread dissent, and, by 1638, much of the population had signed a "National Covenant" agreeing to oppose further changes to the Scottish Church. The Bishops' Wars were the king's attempts to reassert his power: there was fighting in 1639 and 1640 and a third scuffle the same year in which the Scots had occupied Northumberland and Durham. Charles called the Short Parliament in an interlude between the bouts of fighting, but dissolved it as soon as it became clear that the debate the MPs wanted to have was less about financing the king's wars than it was his abuse of royal privileges.

The Long Parliament – called in 1640, the same year as the Short Parliament – was the result of Charles I's ever-present money problems: he could not finance a war without Parliament's assent. But, once again, the king's financial woes were ignored by MPs more concerned with the overreach of royal power: the members passed laws against the Laudian reforms, laws which made it illegal to levy taxes without Parliament's consent, and, perhaps most importantly, the Triennial Act of 1641. Parliament now had to be called at least once every three years, and could even meet without the king's summons. This was a fight for an early form of parliamentary democracy, and in all aspects of life – from different types of communion tables to laws determining how a Parliament could be dissolved – battle lines were rapidly being drawn.

These disputes reached a head in May 1641, when Parliament passed the Protestation: an act which was notionally designed to avert a civil war by asking all men over the age of eighteen to sign an oath affirming their allegiance to the king and the Church of England. Its declarations – "I do... vow, and protest to maintain... the true Reformed Protestant religion" – suggest harmony, and it was signed by all members of both Houses of Parliament before it made its way to each parish. Just months before the wars begun, each person who signed it pledged allegiance to the king.

But the Protestation's implications were more unsettling than they might seem: the very act of declaration implied that the king's power came from public assent. Moreover, its divisiveness (it was designed to "weed out" Catholics who would refuse to sign it, and it suggested that Laud's reforms were "Popish innovations") did little to foster national unity, or allegiance to the king (whose own wife, Henrietta Maria, was a Catholic). But by January 1642 – before the Protestation lists had even been returned from the parishes – it seemed all but meaningless. Ireland had dissolved into war (and the Lord Deputy of Ireland, Thomas Wentworth, Earl of Strafford, had been executed for high treason after it was alleged he had tried to use the Irish army to threaten England) and on 4 January 1642, Charles I made his fatal mistake. Angered with the continuing tensions, and the failure of the Protestation, the king wanted to arrest the five prominent MPs who he believed had encouraged the Scots to invade England, and were continuing to undermine his power. He marched into Parliament accompanied by armed soldiers, and attempted to arrest the politicians – but they had been warned, and had already escaped. It was the king and his family who came off worse from the attempt: they fled to Hampton Court, in the first of many dramatic journeys and exiles that would continue for the remainder of the war.

It was in this feverish period that, as one historian put it, Margaret's oldest brother Sir John Lucas "stepped out of his back gate shortly after midnight on 22 August 1642" and "stepped almost immediately into the pages of history".[9] The Lucas family were devout Royalists and Sir John Lucas, a constant supporter of the king, had begun to make preparations: he had ordered weapons to be packed up and sent to the Abbey so that they, along with his horses, could be sent to help the Royalist forces.[10] Unfortunately for John, his preparations had not been subtle: the townspeople had noticed the movement of arms, and had petitioned the wonderfully named Harbottle Grimson, Recorder of Colchester, to enter and search his house.

Grimson refused, but allowed a watch to be set up: it was this eagle-eyed group that spied the horses and Sir John leaving the Abbey by the back gate, and responded by entering and ransacking the house. Some contemporary reports put the number of marauders – or "trained band and volunteers" – at upwards of a hundred people, with "five thousand men, women, and children" who stood by and watched. The house was invaded, and the horses, armour, weapons and "other warlike furniture" were duly seized – they would, later, be used by the Parliamentary forces. The house and gardens were ransacked, and the livestock were either killed or driven away. And, in a move that would be repeated only six years later, the family vault was opened and the coffins stabbed with swords.

John's moment of Royalist heroism was not yet over: he was taken to London and imprisoned, but he was released on bail in time to fight with the king at Newbury. But for the other members of his family, the violent attack would have rather more long-lasting effects. At the time of the siege, Margaret's mother Elizabeth was in the Abbey, along with John's wife and child Anne Nevill and Mary Lucas, and one unmarried daughter – either Margaret herself, or Anne. For a woman like Elizabeth who, as Margaret's autobiography records, prided herself on her righteousness and honour and held herself above the manners of the servants or common townspeople of Colchester, being paraded through the streets on her way to captivity at the town's common jail must have been beyond mortifying. Indeed, she was nearly saved the embarrassment: as she was walking to her captivity, she was attacked by a man wielding a sword. If someone else had not stopped the blow, she would have died in the street. The women remained in jail for three days, whilst St John's Abbey was looted of everything from crockery to blankets and candlesticks.

The violence against the Lucas family is now known to historians as part of the "Stour Valley Riots": an outbreak of Puritan violence directed against mainly Catholic families in the East Anglia region at the beginning of the Civil War. The Lucases were one of the first families to fall foul of this movement. They weren't Catholic, and nor could all their thousands of persecutors have been Puritan – but the broad-brush analysis of political and religiously motivated violence holds true. Just 13 miles away at St Orsyth Priory, Countess Elizabeth Rivers – whose family had strong Catholic links – also became a victim of the violence, as a "rude multitude... threatened her life, carted away her goods, digged up her corn, drove away her cattle, and destroyed her gardens".[11] She was left without so much as a change of clothes. The people of Colchester did not attack St John's Abbey purely because they resented Sir John stockpiling weapons and armour, but because they felt involved in something larger: violence – and the political engagement that preceded it – was spreading rapidly across the country.

For the nineteen-year-old Margaret, it would have been impossible to avoid the significance of these political changes and difficulties. It is difficult to know whether Margaret was at St John's Abbey – and witnessed the violence and humiliation that befell her mother – or was, instead, safely ensconced with one of her married sisters. The sources that record the episode were written in a hurry, with the threat of mob violence hovering over their writers, and at least one source refers to "sisters" in the plural being present.[12] The absence of this traumatic episode from her autobiography is notable – but it is far from the only moment in her life which is not mentioned in that account, and, perhaps, it was simply too distressing for her to remember and record. Whilst she may never have written about it directly, her later prose-romances are full of tales of sudden wars and disturbances, and young women being uprooted from their homes and all they hold dear.

* * *

The Civil War would define much of the rest of Margaret's life. It would lead her to join Henrietta Maria's court as a lady-in-waiting, remove her to France as an exile, see her married to a disgraced Royalist commander some thirty years her elder, and would be the constant focus of most, if not all, of her writing in the decades to come. From her discussion of atoms, to her theories of government, all the genres with which she experimented would be touched by martial metaphors and concerns. The conflict would also bring about the destruction of her family: her brothers would be wounded, executed, or imprisoned; her mother and sister would die before she could return to England to see them on their sick beds or bury them; and the family wealth and land would be seized and run into ruin.

But Margaret could hardly have been aware of the significance these early days of siege and mob violence would have for her and those she loved. Whilst the newly impoverished and chastened Lucas family made its way to London and then to Oxford, two of the major figures in Margaret's later life were already deeply involved with the war effort. Henrietta Maria – Charles I's French Catholic wife – was never content to let her husband manage his campaigns alone and corresponded with commanders and generals herself, sometimes directly contradicting the king's wishes.

In early 1643 – just five months after the young Margaret had been rudely ejected from her childhood home – her future husband and the queen were conspiring to ensure the safe passage of a flotilla carrying a cargo of weapons and armour from Holland. Henrietta Maria had already attempted the passage, and had been frustrated by a storm so dramatic that she believed she – and her ladies-in-waiting who were also recruited for this mission – would die. (Ships full of noble ladies beset by storms becomes something of a literary motif in this period; it is tempting to think that the meteorological conditions reflected the country's political turbulence.)[13]

The then Earl of Newcastle – later to become the Marquess, and then the Duke – was fighting in the North, taking part in battles in York, Tadcaster, and Leeds in 1642. In January 1643, he was working with Henrietta Maria: her flotilla needed somewhere to land, and the key northern port of Hull was under the Parliamentarian rule of Lord Fairfax. Henrietta Maria, pursued by ships sent by the Puritan naval commander, Robert Rich, the 2nd Earl of Warwick, made her way over from Holland and, after the wind changed, landed at Bridlington Bay, a town on the coast just south of Scarborough and north of Hull. In a small thatched cottage overlooking the quay, the fifty-year-old earl and the thirty-three-year-old queen had dinner. By the following morning, the same quay was under violent bombardment from Warwick's ships. The queen only survived – having taken the lead in directing her ladies and the troops around her – by sheltering in a ditch for two hours. In a moment of extreme bravery and folly, she had returned to her bedroom during the attack to rescue her little dog, Mitte, who was still sleeping on her bed. Both she and Newcastle made it out alive, and she would later march the weapons down to Oxford.

* * *

The relationship between Newcastle and Henrietta Maria is fascinating. Henrietta Maria was an active participant in the war – gathering weapons; holding war councils; and advising her husband on which diplomatic path to take – but this did not win her many favours from contemporary commentators who believed she was power-hungry, domineering, and far too masculine. She was accused of having an affair with Newcastle's distant cousin, Sir Charles Cavendish, and was caricatured as a "Popish" whore who was out to destroy England's religion, and who must be stopped at all costs. In one 1644 pamphlet, *The Great Eclipse of the Sun*, Henrietta Maria was described as a "Popish planet" who had "persuaded [the king] that darkness was light" and plunged the nation into the burning "combustion of a civil war".[14] Not content with this brand of astrological insult, other pamphlets leaned on a more classically sexist trope, and implied that she was unduly masculine in her power: "she is the man, and *reigns*".[15]

But Newcastle had no problem with the queen's assumption of male roles. She, however, took umbrage with his dramatic ways and his fondness for the pomp and rank of his status as a general. He would regularly retire after fighting to an evening of music and congenial company, and would not allow himself to be interrupted. Henrietta Maria, perhaps rightly, pronounced him "fantastic and inconstant".[16] In June 1643, the king wrote to Henrietta Maria ordering her to instruct Newcastle to march his army to Oxford. She disagreed – she was engaged in fighting in the North and the Midlands – and wrote to Newcastle instead that she would *not* instruct him in the king's wishes "since I have taken a resolution with you that you remain".[17] In a move that could, potentially, have been dangerous for the earl, he sided with the queen.

Whilst Margaret's future husband was involved in the war at an extraordinarily high level – he regularly held councils of war with the queen – her brothers were also fighting for the Royalist cause. Her eldest brother, the illegitimate Thomas, was a career soldier and had been fighting for many years. In the early 1640s, he was in Ireland, helping to negotiate a ceasefire with the Irish Catholic Confederacy. John Lucas, her second brother, had fought at Newbury after his imprisonment, and Charles Lucas – her youngest brother – was beginning his career as a colonel in the king's cavalry. He fought at Powick Bridge, near Worcester and, in October 1642, would fight in the first "pitched battle" of the war – a battle carefully planned by the opposing forces, rather than being the result of a chance skirmish – at Edgehill.

* * *

Margaret's fate while these swordmen – and, in Henrietta Maria's case, swordswomen – fought in the early stages of war is not entirely clear. It is likely that the Lucas family took refuge in the comparative safety of London after the attack on St John's Abbey, where they might have stayed with either Margaret's sister Mary Killigrew, who lived in court lodgings at Whitehall, or her favourite sister Catherine Pye who lived in Covent Garden. (Mary's husband, Peter, would work for Parliament during the war, and held a government role during the Protectorate – the Civil War divided the country, and tore apart families.)

Though it was a refuge from the riots they had escaped in Colchester, London was still a Parliamentarian stronghold. As Charles I's advisor and chronicler, Edward Hyde, the Earl of Clarendon so succinctly put it, London "was the sink of all the ill humour of the Kingdom".[18] Charles I had left the city in a hurry following his failed attempt to arrest the five MPs he had accused of treason in January 1642, and would not return for seven years, until his trial and execution. After a spell at Windsor Castle, a trip down to Dover to wave his wife off, and a tour of the North – including setting up court in York – he established himself and his loyal Royalists in Oxford. The university town was no longer a peaceful home for students, but a fortified military barracks, with strengthened walls, the king's army camped out and drilling in what is now University Parks, and the Exam Schools transformed into a noisy, dusty conglomeration of storehouses and workshops. The gothic splendour of New College housed a military arsenal, and other colleges were hosting blacksmiths, stables and sentry posts. The Restoration diarist Anthony à Wood was a scholar in Oxford at the time, and records how the students were moved into a "dark nasty room" which was "very unfit for the purpose" so as to make way for yet more of the king's retinue and war machine.[19] The king himself set up his court in the grandiose scenery of Christ Church whilst, when she arrived some months later, Henrietta Maria would enjoy the spacious quadrangles and gardens of Merton College.

But for the other Royalists who followed the court, life was not quite so splendid. Ann Fanshawe – Cavendish's direct contemporary – moved to Oxford with her sister after her father had been captured and imprisoned in his house in Bishopsgate Street, London. Oxford seemed, to them, the only place of safety left, but that did not mean that it was by any means comfortable. Ann and her sister had "till that hour lived in great plenty and great order" and, in the muck, disorder, and chaotic living arrangements of a wartime city

> … found ourselves like fishes out of the water, and the scene
> was so changed, that we knew not at all how to act any part
> but obedience, for, from as good a house as any gentleman
> of England had, we came to a baker's house in an obscure
> street, and from rooms well furnished, to lie in a very bad
> bed in a garret, to one dish of meat, and that not the best
> ordered, no money, for we were as poor as Job, nor clothes
> more than a man or two brought in their cloak bags[20]

The poverty and disruption were made worse by the fact that the city was beset by illnesses resulting from the cramped conditions – the records mention typhus, smallpox, and the plague – and the constant spectacle of injured soldiers. The city's previously beautiful rivers ran with muck and butcher's blood, and corpses were quickly buried on "Jews' Mount", now the site of Oxford Castle.

It was to this city of extraordinary divisions – where the gilded spectacle of court life went on within earshot of drilling soldiers and preparations for war – that Margaret made her way in the summer of 1643. She would never see her mother again.

* * *

In her later writings about the war – both her fictionalised accounts and her political writings about the nature of monarchical rule – Margaret is remarkably opaque (her harsher critics might claim obtuse) about the origins of war. Her prose-romance "Assaulted and Pursued Chastity", published in *Natures Pictures* (1656), begins with the remarkably fairy-tale like sentence: "In our Kingdom of Riches, after a long and sleepy peace, overgrown with plenty and ease, luxury broke out into factious sores, and feverish ambition, into a plaguey rebellion, killing numbers with the sword of unjust war."[21] Its fantastical tone – and the fact that she sees no nuance in the causes of the war beyond "factious sores" – could be explained by the fact that this is fiction, but it is also a reflection of her Royalist outlook and upbringing.

Cavendish, like Charles I, and his father James I before him, believed in the divine right to rule, and the royal prerogative. Dissent from this could not, for her, be a product of rational political thought. It was nothing more than a rejection of the instinctive principles in which she believed: she did not so much disagree with the anti-Royalist side, as utterly fail to understand them. This strain of Cavendish's arch-conservatism appears elsewhere in her work: she frequently adheres to a belief in the "great chain of being" – that is, a strict hierarchy of the world and of all the living things it contains – and her later radicalism mixes with an almost visceral reluctance to deviate from her beliefs in monarchic government and society as it was before the Civil War.[*]

Cavendish's simplified, black-and-white approach to the outbreak and causes of war finds echoes in her non-fiction

---

[*] Her deviation from this hierarchy is found in her writings about animals, and her belief that they should not necessarily be subjugated by humans. This is discussed more fully in Chapter 11.

works. *A True Relation of My Birth, Breeding, and Life* – Cavendish's autobiography – was initially appended to the 1656 edition of *Natures Pictures*, and then removed from the second edition. A broadly historical document – although there is some cause to think of it as an exercise in "self-fashioning" – it, too, adopts the language of romance when describing the outbreak of the Civil War. Cavendish writes:

> ... this unnatural war came like a whirlwind, which felled down their [her siblings'] houses, where some in the wars were crushed to death, as my youngest brother Sir Charles Lucas, and my brother Sir Thomas Lucas[22]

And, in her biography of her husband – *The Life of William Cavendish*, published in 1667 – she insists that the causes of the disturbance lay in Parliament's "unjustly and unmannerly" treatment of the king.

A spontaneous outbreak as a result of too much luxury; a whirlwind; a result of impolite treatment; or "the greatest storm", as she described it in *The Worlds Olio* (1655): Cavendish has a trunk full of metaphors and fantastical descriptions for the causes of war, none of which seem to touch on the actual origins of the conflict. She believed the violence had emerged inexplicably from perfect peace:

> *A Kingdom which long time had lived in Peace,*
> *Her People rich with Plenty, fat with Ease,*
> *With Pride were haughty grown, Pride Envy bred,*
> *From Envy Factions grew, then Mischief spread;*
> *And Libels every where were strew'd about,*
> *Which after soon a Civil War broke out*[23]

It would not be unreasonable to think that, having seen the anger of the crowd in Colchester as they stormed her house, or heard of it from her traumatised family, she would be attuned to the demands of those who wanted greater religious freedom, greater political engagement, and a new style of governance. But as this poem shows, she believed war had erupted, shockingly and suddenly, in a land where everyone lived with "ease". And even when she does delve deeper into the causes of "rebellion", she still turns a blind eye to the political causes. She would later write:

> There is nothing causeth rebellion so soon as the unequal living of the subject; as for a Noble man, who strives to live like his King, a Gentleman to live like a Noble man, and a Peasant, or a Citizen to live like a Gentleman; For every man living not according to their quality, will in short time think his quality according to his expense, which must needs make a disorder[24]

Her snobbery – the insistence that all must live to "their quality" – is typical of Cavendish: her radical flair is shot through with an extraordinary conservatism. It is also wonderfully hypocritical: what were her family if not "gentlemen" who had aspired to the aristocracy? By the time she wrote this, Margaret Cavendish was already a marchioness.

Her ambivalence and ambiguity about the outbreak of the war are in sharp contrast to Lucy Hutchinson, the Puritan wife of Colonel John Hutchinson. Writing in her biography of her husband, Hutchinson did not believe that the violence emerged from a kingdom at peace, but instead had come from an uneasy, temporary calm. She describes how she was born when "the land was then at peace... if that quietness may be called a peace, which was rather like that calm and smooth surface of the sea, whose dark womb is already impregnated with a horrid tempest".[25] With her Puritan upbringing, Hutchinson was able to see the turbulence of religious differences and repression – and the desire for greater political representation as a check on royal power – that was bubbling under the surface of a superficially peaceful country. Cavendish and Hutchinson would not have agreed on much, if anything, but they might have bonded over their fondness for the metaphor of the storm.

Cavendish and Hutchinson may have been divided by their beliefs about the outbreak of war, but they were united in the strength of their allegiance. What made individuals, families, and communities choose sides in the war – and what motivated them, as in the case of both Cavendish and Newcastle, to go through so much hardship for their cause? In the case of the Parliamentarians, the cause is more readily definable: Charles I had, in their view – and, quite clearly in the case of his attempt to arrest the five MPs – overstepped the limits of his royal privileges. From dissenting Protestants and Puritans to newly wealthy and powerful mercantile families, the anti-Royalist side had something clear to fight for, be it for religion and the repeal of the Laudian reforms to the Church, or a desire for greater involvement and power in public life. On the Royalist side, however, the cause was often rather less consciously thought out: it was support for the established way of being; a hierarchical society with the king – as chosen by God – at the top. But if the society they were fighting for was more traditional, their support was no less strongly felt: as the Royalist propaganda newsbook *Mercurius Aulicus* (printed in Oxford and smuggled into London) made clear, the Royalists believed they were, paradoxically, fighting for peace – a society in which the recent "unhappy differences" could be forgotten, and "all tumults, affronts, and violences" laid to rest.[26]

If Cavendish leaves something to be desired in her analysis of the outbreak of the Civil War, she makes up for it with her eloquence about how all-consuming the fighting was. In *The Worlds Olio* – some of her earliest writing – she constantly refers to the war. It is a touchstone for everything else, including the descriptions of how women change their appearance with makeup ("she must put on as many several faces, and behaviours as a State doth; for a state in time of war puts on a face of anger"), and a mark of distinction between different types of fame (always a favourite subject for Cavendish): fame "that is gotten in the wars, sound[s] louder than those that are gotten in peace".[27]

Nor was she reticent about its horrors. In *Natures Pictures*, she reaches for regal constitutional authority when, in "The She-Anchoret", she depicts moral philosophers questioning a wise woman who has dedicated her life to contemplation. They ask "what government for a commonwealth was best", and her reply is unequivocal:

Monarchical; for as one sun is sufficient to give light and heat to all the several creatures in the world; so one governor is sufficient to give laws and rules to the several members of a Commonwealth; besides, said she, no good government can be without union, and union is singularity not in plurality; for union is drawn to a point, when numbers make Division, Extraction, Subtraction, which oftentimes brings distraction, and distraction confusions.[28]

Having lived through the "distraction" and confusions of the Civil War, Cavendish had no wish to see it happen again. But, more than that, she considered herself a philosopher who could couch her really quite authoritarian beliefs in rational, scientific terms.

This abstract description of division and disorder pales in comparison to her poem "A Description of the Battle in Fight". Here, she writes:

Some, their legs hang dangling by the nervous strings,
And shoulders cut, hung loose, like flying wings.
Here heads are cleft in two parts, brains lie mashed,
And all their faces into slices hashed.[29]

It's a poem which rivals Wilfred Owen for battlefield brutality; there is no question of Cavendish not having experienced the horrors of war, even if her age, gender, and status would have shielded her from much.

But away from such vivid wartime scenes, it is her description of how civil wars "may be compared to a pack of cards" that is among the most moving of her conceits.[30] In Cavendish's metaphor, the cards are "made up in order, every... suit is by itself, as from one, two, and three, and so to the tenth card, which is like the commons in several degrees in order." (Once again, the snobbery is obvious.) "The coat cards by themselves... are the nobles", but war sets "life at the stake" and "shuffles them together":

intermixing the nobles and the commons, where loyalty is shuffled from the crown, duty from parents, tenderness from children, fidelity from masters, continencies from husbands and wives, truth from friends, from justice innocency, charity from mystery.

In this topsy-turvy world, "chance plays and fortune draws the stakes".

Cavendish's vision of order is a stringently hierarchical one, and it was especially out of place at a time when new ideas about the franchise and the involvement of the commons in the government of the country were being seriously debated. But, despite her commitment to unadulterated kingship, there is true drama to the image she creates: a shuffled pack of cards which turns children against parents, friends against friends, and wrecks the whole machinery of the country. By the end of the war, Cavendish would be no stranger to any of the situations she describes: her sister would be married to a Parliamentarian, she would not see her mother again before she died, her husband would face the wrath of his so-called friends who blamed him for a dramatic military failure, and she would risk her life in a storm-tossed journey to exile in France.

3

Generalissimas and she-soldiers

IN THE LATE summer of 1643, Cavendish made a journey fraught with danger. At the age of barely twenty, and travelling without her mother, she left the Parliamentarian stronghold of London for the Royalist camp at Oxford: a dangerous journey of more than 50 miles, at a time when marauding highwaymen and bandits – often disaffected and down-on-their-luck Royalists, or hungry soldiers who had taken to pillaging and thieving to top up their meagre wages – had become a constant presence on the roads.* What she was doing – joining the Royalist forces – was illegal. Her sex, and the fact that she was unlikely to be joining the king to help with the fighting, would not have protected her given she was travelling with her brother, a Royalist soldier.

When Cavendish later wrote about why she made this journey, she made herself sound like the paragon of virtue – the young Royalist daughter who could not bear not to be a part of the wartime community. She had heard that the queen did not have "the same number" of maids of honour "she was used to have" (presumably far too many of her ladies were trapped in besieged castles, or did not want to uproot themselves to live

---

* The threat of highwaymen would get so bad later in the century that it began to resemble something of a farce. Everyone was at it: as legend would have it, the aristocratic Lady Katherine Ferrers would rob her dinner guests after a quick change of outfit.

in the picturesque squalor of Oxford), and "wooed and won" her mother over until she was allowed to make the journey. Her mother and siblings, rightly, thought that Margaret would be too "inexperienced in the world" and too shy and "bashful" to survive the gossip-filled life of court, but they allowed her to go all the same – and refused, on the grounds of propriety, her wish to return when it became clear that her anxiety and nervousness were all but debilitating.[1]

But was Cavendish really just as she liked to describe herself: a loyal subject who had "a great desire to be one of [the queen's] maids of honour"? There is an element of truth to her self-presentation. Margaret had grown up in a distinctly Royalist household, and would have seen something of the pomp and circumstance of court life when, at the age of fifteen, she witnessed the queen's mother Maria de Medici – accompanied by her carriages full of *filles d'honneur* and *femmes de chambre* – visiting England. Maria stayed in Colchester, at St John's Abbey.[2] Such an event (there was a banquet, chattering in French and much entertainment of the royal visitor) must have terrified the achingly shy Margaret. Yet she must also have enjoyed the spectacle it presented – if it had been too overwhelming, why else would she, a mere five years later, have so wanted to join Henrietta Maria's court?

On a more prosaic level, there was surely a desire to be involved and, in the language of more recent wars, to "do her bit". All three of her brothers were, by 1643, either fighting for the king (in Ireland or England) or trying to rejoin him. Her middle brother, John, had been declared a "malignant" for his involvement in the war – which meant that all of his land and property (including St John's Abbey) was now liable for confiscation by the Parliamentarian army. Margaret really had very little choice: her home had been ransacked and could now be confiscated, and London was a Parliamentarian stronghold which didn't look too kindly on its Royalist inhabitants, no matter how shy, quiet, and dedicated to their writing and reading they were. The year of Margaret's flight had seen the city begin to construct its own defences against Royalist armies, and, by the summer, control of the Tower of London was transferred to the Parliamentarian Lord Mayor, Isaac Pennington.[3] Entering the court was, also, one of the few "careers" open to women of Margaret's social position – the job description of being an "Empress and authoress of the whole world" was yet to be invented.[4]

* * *

But as her willingness to make the perilous journey shows, Cavendish certainly had an interest in a life beyond the normal routines of a woman of her station. Could delight in danger be another possible explanation as to why Margaret was so keen to make it to Oxford?

Henrietta Maria's daring journey to Holland to buy weapons, her tempestuous passage back to Bridlington, and her march back to Oxford had been much reported in the mass of newspapers and newsletters – both Parliamentarian and Royalist – published since the outbreak of the war. There were reports of the cannons she'd imported – "the Queen's pocket pistols" – and breathless descriptions of how she had managed to escape the naval bombardment at Bridlington.[5] Parliamentarian papers were able to argue that the nation was being destroyed by the queen's masculine power – "this Kingdom is woefully ruined by a... conjugal conspiracy, by a plot in matrimony" – and could even suggest that the king was being cuckolded (there was some speculation over who "sleeps best in her lodgings at Oxford").[6] Henrietta Maria herself was unfazed by this rather prurient interest in the masculine aspects of her character, and not only wrote to the king that the army would "go on better than it does" if she had more power over it, but also described herself as the "she-majesty generalissima".[7]

Living in London – where the printing presses for the Parliamentarian paper *Mercurius Britannicus* were based, and where she would have also had access to smuggled editions of the Royalist paper *Mercurius Aulicus* – Margaret could not have been ignorant of the power and strength of Henrietta Maria. She esteemed the queen: in her later life, she would write proudly of her husband's role in smuggling the weapons and money from "her Majesty the Queen, out of Holland".[8] Ever contradictory in her extreme shyness and paradoxical bravery, Cavendish made her decision probably as much out of passion for the Royalist cause and a desire to see the world outside the shelter of her family, as from a wish to be in close proximity to this strong, powerful woman who seemed to have whole armies and nations at her command, and had already risked her life for her husband and adopted country.

* * *

If Margaret had expected she-soldiers, female generals, and a life of buccaneering danger and delight, she was sorely disappointed by the court at Oxford. Back in James I's day and until his death in 1625, life at court had been one long riot of illicit sex, drunkenness, and neglecting government business in favour of hunting trips (all punctuated, of course, by routine bouts of the bubonic plague and the necessity to escape from London). But, after his ascension to the throne, Charles I had encouraged a rather different way of life: excessive drunkenness was replaced by a delight in the arts (he commissioned Van Dyck and Rubens, and bought works by Raphael and Titian), and bawdy ribaldry was replaced by Anglican piety and sober enjoyment of poetry. Even the resolutely anti-monarchical Lucy Hutchinson was able to praise the king in this respect: she wrote that the court of James I was "a nursery of lust and intemperance", and, in a brilliant image, that the "treasure of the kingdom" was "wasted by court-caterpillars". But she noted approvingly that "the face of the court was much changed in the change of the king, for King Charles was temperate and chaste and serious, so that the fools and bawds, mimics and catamites of the former court grew out of fashion".[9]

By the time that Margaret arrived at court in late summer 1643, Queen Henrietta Maria's life was nothing like it had been during her daring tour of the country when she had ridden astride her horse "without the effeminacy of a woman" and had lived with her soldiers as if they were her "brethren".[10] Instead of soldiers' camps, ships' cabins, and borrowed cottages, she spent her days inside the lavishly decorated rooms of Merton College, where a replica of her Royal Household had been constructed. Descriptions of her pre-war household reveal the level of formality of day-to-day life: the queen moved between her Presence Chamber, Privy Chamber, Withdrawing Chamber, and Bed Chamber – all of which were under the protection of the only chamber that had access to the outside world, the Guard Chamber, where the door was "carefully kept" to prevent the entry of "any lackeys, footmen, or any other unfit persons". Servants and the maids of honours' ladies were left in this room, and only those who had been sworn into the queen's other chambers were allowed to pass through. The rules were rigid and pedantic: "no women under the degree of a baroness" were admitted into the Privy Chamber; it was only possible to enter into the Withdrawing Chamber with the express permission of the queen's chamberlain; and only the ladies who attended the queen were allowed to use the "privy closet" – that is, the loo – in the suite of rooms. They were expressly anxious that no servants use this loo when they were away "at prayers or sermon" and not present to keep a watchful eye over it.[11]

But these rules pale in comparison to those that governed mealtimes. The queen ate at a raised table at one end of the Presence Chamber, and only those who were serving her food were permitted to stand upon the carpet that surrounded her chair. The food was served by carvers and a cupbearer, and dinner was only eaten after all persons who were "not of good quality" had left; those who remained had to eat some metres away from the queen, at the lower end of the chamber. And for the assembled ladies-in-waiting, this was hardly a relaxing meal: they had to remain on duty to entertain the queen.

But it was the endless standing and sitting around that would come to grate on Cavendish the most. As a maid of honour, her job was to be "in presence". She would arrive in the Presence Chamber before 11 o'clock in the morning, and would stand or sit around the sides – waiting to entertain the queen or relay news about someone who had come to visit – until accompanying the queen to morning prayers, and sit in presence again until the queen's lunch time. The maids would then remain in presence until supper time, at which point they had the respite of returning to their own chamber, where no man could be admitted. To ensure all these edicts were followed, the maids of honour were watched over by the "mother of the maids", who had the right to report them to the Lord Chamberlain or Vice Chamberlain if they disobeyed. Being a maid of honour was a more political, high-stakes, and tedious appointment than is often realised.

The shy, anxious, and family-minded Cavendish had gone from a world in which she could retreat into hidden corners and write imaginatively about what struck her receptive and impressionable mind – all with the safe knowledge that her siblings were never very far away, or that her indulgent mother was nearby – to a world in which she was continually on show and surveilled by more senior courtiers. She had no time or space to write, and no outlet for her creativity other than the endless gossip of the court; gossip which had, presumably, only become more introverted and sterile as the realities of being trapped in a fortified city began to set in.

In her later life, Cavendish was excoriating about the difficulties she had experienced. She was, in her own words, "like one that had no foundation to stand [on]", and was so beset by fears that she would do or say the wrong thing that she instead retreated into silence: she would rather be "accounted a fool than to be thought rude or wanton". One can only imagine what the other noblewomen made of this small, nervous creature who had made such a treacherous journey to join the court, and then all but refused to become involved in its life.[12]

Cavendish's best writing on this part of her life is her play *The Presence*, published after the Restoration in her collection *Plays, Never Before Printed* (1668). Writing long after her days as a courtier had ended, Cavendish was able to be honest about the vapidities and oddities of the entire Royal Household. She – like Ben Jonson, and other playwrights of the period – was a fan of typological names that told her readers all they needed to know: she describes a "Monsieur Mode", Ladies "Quick-Wit" and "Self-Conceit", and the thinly veiled autobiographical "Lady Bashful". Her send-up of the stupidities of court life is amusing: "we courtiers have little time to pray; for what with dressing, trimming, waiting, ushering, watching, courting, and the like, all our time is spent", complains one courtier, whilst one lady equates being "a very fine person" with wearing "fine clothes".[13] And her description of the endless rules and formalities – "The Princess keeps to her Chamber today. / Yes, but she has permitted them into her Presence" – confirms that wartime did not put a stop to the formalities described at the beginning of the queen's reign.[14]

In the midst of a frankly bizarre plot that sees the princess fall in love with an "idea" of a man who she then sets about trying to marry, whilst alternately believing that he is a poor sailor, a princess, and finally a prince, it is Cavendish's description of the alienation, isolation, and despair felt by Lady Bashful which is most resonant with her own life at court. The other ladies describe her as "so bashful" that it dims "what beauty nature hath given her", and she does not speak an entire word in the whole first scene where she is introduced.[15] (As Cavendish states in the prefaces to her plays, she never expected them to be performed, as they were written when the theatres were shut. This non-speaking role, then, lacks even the presence of having Lady Bashful visible on stage.) But when she does speak for the first time, it is oddly self-assured. A courtier called "Spend All"

– one of a number of veiled portraits of Newcastle, Cavendish's later spendthrift husband – compliments her by saying his eyes had searched for her in the Privy Chamber, and her reply is the rather rebarbative "It seems that either you were blind, or that I had not any Beauty" before she affirms that she would "rather be a Meteor singly alone, then a star in a crowd".[16] Shy and confident; stone silent and cruelly witty – the contradictory Cavendish escapes from any easy analysis, or empty pity.

* * *

The Presence wasn't the only play that Cavendish wrote about her wartime experiences. *Bell in Campo*, published in her earlier collection *Plays* (1662), seems to take its inspiration from the military exploits of Henrietta Maria. It opens with the discussion of war between the "Kingdom of Reformation" and the "Kingdom of Faction" (no prizes for guessing which name Cavendish gave the Royalist side), and a description of the "General" who is "to command in chief":

> He is a man that is both valiant and well experienced in wars, temperate and just in peace, wise and politic in public affairs, careful and prudent in his own family, and a most generous person.[17]

There is only one problem for this upright man of military prowess: when he tells his wife, the Lady Victoria, that he is "commanded to the wars", and even waxes lyrical about how much he will miss her ("to leave you is such a cross as my nature sinks under"), she has absolutely none of it. She tells him that she must be "but second place" in his affections, because he prefers his "honour" over her. In answer to his declaration that their "honours" are intertwined, she offers this exchange:

> LADY VICTORIA: Then I must partake of your actions, and go along with you.

LORD GENERAL: What to the wars?
LADY VICTORIA: To any place where you are.

No descriptions of the hardships of camp-life – "long marches, ill lodgings, much watching, cold nights, scorching days, hunger and danger" – are enough to dissuade Lady Victoria and, before the General knows it, she has assembled a whole troop of wives to accompany her into camp, and later into battle.

Bell in Campo takes elements of Henrietta Maria's 1643 military campaign, and lightly fictionalises them. Henrietta Maria never fought, as the women – "the noble heroickesses" – of Lady Victoria's army do, but she did make use of military language that subverted the expectations of soldierly and army life. As Henrietta Maria was the "generalissima", Lady Victoria is the "generalless... instructeress, ruler and commanderess".[18] She orders her women to put on armour, imposes strict rules on camp watch ("whosoever drinks anything but water... shall be punished"), and even sets about imposing the rules of military rank: "no Captains or Colonels, shall advance beyond their company, troop, regiment or brigade".[19] This "warlike body" is different to Henrietta Maria's – they fight, rather than gather weapons – and, after the male army "begins to flag", they step in to save the day, and end up winning the battle for the weaker men. The commanders of the General's army write a letter to Lady Victoria and her women, in which they call them "goddesses on Earth, who have the power and dominion over men".[20]

Cavendish's play is a riot of imagined feminism and, quite literally, a call to arms. Her Lady Victoria rails against the "masculine sex" who believe that women "are only fit to breed and bring forth children", and lays waste to the beliefs that women have

... no ingenuity for inventions, nor subtle wit for politicians; nor prudence for directions, nor industry for execution; nor patience for opportunity, nor judgment for counsellors, nor

secrecy for trust; nor method to keep the peace, nor courage
to make war[21]

As the events of the play make clear, and despite the inevitable
"mirth" of the male commanders, the women's army *did* have the
"courage to make war". In Cavendish's imagined world, women
overcome the fact they are "kept as slaves forced to obey",
and "make [them]selves free". The rhetoric and drama of the
whole text – complete with women dressed "like Amazons" and
marching "by the sound of flutes" – makes it uncannily radical.
Cavendish wanted nothing to do with the women who believed
themselves too "tender" to go to war with Lady Victoria, and
establishes a coherent alternative to a male-dominated society:
this play is not a mere protest, but a call for wholesale revolution.
But this call for revolution is paradoxically expressed in terms
of Cavendish's authoritarian monarchism: Lady Victoria's
female soldiers are fighting on the side of the "Kingdom
of Reformation" not the destabilising, more radical "Kingdom
of Faction". Cavendish seems to believe her feminist revolution
can take place within the existing order of society despite the
fact that her women set up their own army camp; a separate,
independent society. Indeed, many of her later works rely on a
dream of a separatist utopia for feminist or lesbian radicalism.
These multiple contradictions – between Cavendish's liberatory
instincts, her belief in the existing structures of hierarchy and
power, and her imagined desire for separatist communities –
will be discussed further in Chapter 8.

Cavendish took elements of Henrietta Maria's strength, and
emphasised and enlarged them until she had written a work
of proto-feminist political rebellion. But *Bell in Campo* also
contains tantalising elements of truth. When one captain in
the army asks his wife to accompany him, she replies that she
would rather not "disquiet [her] rest with inconveniences".[22] His
reply – "Faith wife, if you will not go, I will have a laundry-
maid to ride in my wagon, and lie in my tent" – describes the

far more widespread role of women in camp life. Many women *did* accompany men on their campaigns around the country: as dutiful wives, women who cooked, cleaned, or mended, or as the Captain's comment makes clear, as prostitutes. And life in camp was as horrible as might be expected: one Royalist woman who followed the king's army in 1642, Dorothy Leeke, wrote about the day-to-day worries of how the "weather grows cold", and how she wanted more clothes to keep her warm. Aside from freezing limbs and rainy weather, there was the more all-pervasive threat of danger: in Leeke's words, if the army loses a battle, "what will become of us, I know not". She was, perhaps, hopeful when she wrote "I trust I shall not live to see it".[23]

And, as depressing as it might sound, Dorothy Leeke was right to hope she would not live through a Royalist defeat. The women who had followed the Royalist camp to Naseby in 1645 suffered terribly. As hundreds of infantrymen and camp-followers fled from the New Model Army, the Parliamentarian cavalry launched a brutal attack on the Royalist women, who they believed were Irish Catholics. They cut and slashed many of them to death, and those that lived were hardly luckier: their faces were cruelly cut at either the mouth or nose; a mutilation designed to render them "marked for whores".[24]

* * *

If the reality of life for women who followed the men into battle was so gruesome, was Cavendish's *Bell in Campo* nothing other than a fantasy of female military prowess and feminine power? Not quite.

In recent years, there has been a growing historical debate about the extent to which women – as cross-dressed soldiers, soldiers who fought "as women", and women who resisted sieges – were involved in the Civil War.[25] As so much of this fighting activity (especially for the women who cross-dressed) depended upon secrecy, there are frustratingly few documentary sources. But, the undeniable truth is that women, across all classes, in all capacities, and on both sides of the conflict, played a far greater role than most conventional military history has ever given them credit for. Indeed, for some women, the very nature of the conflict was something to be described and explained in explicitly gendered terms. The Baptist prophetess Elizabeth Poole spoke to the inner sanctum of the Parliamentarian army in 1648, when the subject of discussion was whether the king should be executed. Poole was against killing him, but still declared that Charles I had done grave wrong. In her words, he was a "father and husband" but, because he had taken the English people as "a wife for his own lusts", the "yoke" of subordination had been "taken from [their] necks".[26] In Poole's rhetoric – and it is important to distinguish between her emotive language, and the realities of the conflict – the king's oppression was inherently patriarchal.

When it comes to women who partook in actual fighting, they fall broadly into four distinct categories: those who resisted a siege or violent assault (that is, not so much fought as declined to surrender); those who fought whilst making no secret of their gender (the *Bell in Campo* school of violence); those who fought whilst dressed as men; and, lastly, those who spied.

* * *

The rules of seventeenth-century siege warfare sound cruel to modern ears, but they did follow an internal logic. Once a house or castle was besieged, the commander of the besieging army would invite the inhabitants to surrender. At this point, the women and children could leave the town or fortress peacefully, and with an honourable guarantee of their safety. If the place refused to surrender – and the women and children remained – they became as legitimate a target as the men and soldiers; the division between "civilian" and "soldier" was dissolved. This stemmed in part from a desire to balance the asymmetries of siege warfare: if a city or house had a water source, good provisions, and strong fortifications, it could conceivably hold out for months. It was the besieging force, stuck outside in the elements, that was on the back foot.[27]

It is against this background of rules and expectations that the 1644 siege at Lathom House against Charlotte de la Trémoille, Countess of Derby, must be understood. Charlotte's husband, the Earl of Derby, was a leading Royalist in the north of England, and had been sent to fortify the Isle of Man. In his absence, the Parliamentarian commander Sir Thomas Fairfax saw an opportunity to strengthen his position, and set out to conquer the house. Unfortunately for him, he had dramatically underestimated the countess's strength. As early as May 1643, the countess had been asked to "yield", and had refused, citing her inability to "purchase her peace with the loss of her honour". From May onwards, she lived as a prisoner under house arrest: the house was not being bombarded, but she could not go beyond "her gardens and walks". After a "skirmish" between her soldiers (estimates put the size of her garrison at 300 men) and the Parliamentarian troops in early February 1644, she heard of plans to besiege her house once more, and set about preparing her fortifications, provisioning, and recruiting more soldiers. Just two days into the siege, Sir Thomas Fairfax sent a letter, as the rules of siege warfare required, asking the countess to surrender.[28]

Charlotte played for time, and asked Fairfax for a week to consider his proposition – a week in which the besieging force would be stuck outside in the wind, rain, and cold, and she and her soldiers were safely ensconced in her large demesne. Fairfax refused, and the countess's reply was scathing. With icy haughtiness, she reminded him that because of "both her Lord's honour and her own birth", it was more fitting and "knightly that Sir Thomas Fairfax should wait upon her, than she upon him". History does not record what Fairfax's face looked like as he opened this letter.

After further failed negotiations (the countess asked for a month in Lathom House before she would decamp to the Isle of

Man), the siege lasted three months and ended when, at the end of May, Prince Rupert came to her rescue. During this ordeal, the countess had not mellowed or weakened. Nothing – from chaplains likening her to the whore of Babylon, to neighbours begging her to consider the damage the fighting was doing to the countryside, and promise after promise of a safe passage and an honourable surrender – would persuade her to give up her house. When, at the end of April, one more missive asking her to surrender arrived, she responded with the comment that the commander of the besieging force, Colonel Rigby, should be hung from her gates. The letter she sent back deserves quoting:

> Tell that insolent rebel, he shall neither have persons, goods, nor house: when our strength and provision is spent, we shall find a fire more merciful than Rigby, and then if the providence of God prevent it not, my goods and house shall burn in his sight: myself, children, and soldiers, rather than fall into his wands, will seal our religion and loyalty in the same flame.[29]

The lady was not for turning. The countess was, undoubtedly, less bothered about her up-ending of gender expectations than she was about protecting her house and her family, but her example demonstrates the surprising roles women often played in the Civil War, and the fact that they were not, by any means, neutral actors.

The Countess of Derby was hardly alone in her staunch defence of her house. With husbands and sons away fighting, women up and down the country were besieged, from Lady Cholmley in Scarborough Castle, to the brave defence of Corfe Castle by Lady Bankes who held out against a Parliamentarian force with only five soldiers. Margaret's future step-daughters – Jane, Elizabeth, and Frances Cavendish, the daughters of the Earl of Newcastle and his first wife, Elizabeth Basset – were besieged at Welbeck in 1644. Abandoned by their father and brothers, and with their mother having just died, the young women surrendered the house, but not before trying to ensure the safety of some of their family's belongings.[30]

Women loyal to Parliament were also frequently trapped inside their castle walls. Lady Brilliana Harley was besieged in Brampton Bryan Castle in the summer of 1643. Her letters to her son ("My Dear Ned") are more plaintive and vulnerable than any of the surviving documents relating to the fiery Countess of Derby, but they still reveal a quiet strength in the face of being surrounded by Royalist soldiers in the absence of her husband. Writing nearly a month after the siege had begun, Brilliana's letter to her son makes no mention of surrender, and only asks that he "pray for me that the Lord in mercy may preserve me from my cruel and blood thirsty enemies". A month later, in September, she appears more equivocal when she writes "My dear Ned, let me know your mind whether I had best stay or remove" – but she did remain in the castle until, presumably under terrible stress, she died of a cold in October.[31]

* * *

But what about the women who, rather than just refusing to surrender, actually took up arms?

The tensions that would spark the Civil War in England began to cause problems earlier in Scotland, as Charles I's desire to spread Anglicanism throughout the broadly Presbyterian country resulted in outright rebellion and the First Bishops' War of 1639. It was in this war that Anna, Lady Cunningham led a mixed-sex regiment at the Battle of Berwick. Her son had joined the king, and was nearing the coast by ship, but she decided to organise a force to resist the landing. She "animate[d] all other ladies and gentlewomen to make all possible resistance" and set about "carrying earth and stones" to make fortifications. Not content with this, she found herself a pistol and "vowed to discharge upon her own son" if he landed.[32]

And, when he did land, Lady Cunningham literally stuck to her guns: she, along with her male and female allies, marched under a banner which showed a hand repelling a prayer book (it was the introduction of the new prayer book that had caused such resentment in Scotland) and led "her own troop of horse". In a brilliant image, she even had her "dags" (a type of gun) dangling from her girdle and silver bullets reserved for her son.[33]

Lady Cunningham's defence was well chronicled at the time because it was something of a novelty: an aristocratic woman was so willing to defend her faith that she would, in a complete inversion of everything expected of a mother, even be willing to kill her own child. Letters at the time seem almost prurient in their interest in her warlike attire, and laud her as a "notable virago!".[34] It is, however, rather harder to find details of the military efforts of women who were not so well-born: they are less likely to be chronicled in state papers, and also less likely to be literate enough to write their own letters or keep diaries. Yet in the 1643 siege and capture of Bristol by Royalist forces, the efforts of two women, Dorothy Hazard (sometimes spelled "Dorathy Hassard") and Joan Batten, were at least partially recorded.

Bristol came under attack in July 1643, when Prince Rupert and the Royalist forces approached the city. The Parliamentarian Colonel Nathaniel Fiennes capitulated almost as soon as the prince had breached the city walls. Fiennes (he was the father of the diarist and travel writer Celia Fiennes) was later tried for his perceived cowardice. The testimonies and depositions of these two women were made at this trial by the Council of War.

Dorothy Hazard – a dissenter who was married to a grocer before her second marriage to a Church of England clergyman, whom she later separated from to set up Bristol's first dissenting church – was desperate to defend the city. As she testified at Fiennes's trial, she had sent three months' worth of food for her and her family into the castle at Bristol in expectation of a siege, and upon hearing that the Royalists had begun to enter the city had joined with "diverse other women and maids" to fortify the gate. Not content with building fortifications, she was one of a group of women that went to the army and told the troops that they would "stand by them" as they fought.[35]

But it is the testimony of Joan Batten, about whom even less is known than Dorothy Hazard, which reveals the sheer commitment of these women to fighting for the Parliamentarian cause. In her deposition, she recalled how some 200 women begged Fiennes not to surrender, and told him that they would not only "work in the fortifications in the very face of the enemy", but would go with their children "into the mouth of the canon to death and keep off the shot from the soldiers". Like Lady Cunningham, these women put the demands of war and political allegiance above motherhood. Fiennes did make use of the women, but not quite in the way they suggested, when he asked them to continue fortifying the Frome gate. Their efforts were in vain: Bristol remained in Royalist hands until Prince Rupert surrendered to Lord Fairfax in 1645.

* * *

These women who fought whilst making a spectacle of their femininity and their subversion of maternal expectations were not quite the women that Charles I had in mind when he was penning a draft text for a proclamation governing his army in 1643. In one draft, he angrily wrote "Memorandum: that no woman presume to wear man's apparel under pain of the severest punishment". This was crossed out, and then the following was written in its place:

> Lastly, because the confounding of habits appertaining to both sexes... is a thing which Nature and religion forbid, and our soul abhors... [&] yet the prostitute impudency of some women... have... thus conversed in our Army, therefore let no woman presume to counterfeit her sex by wearing man's apparel under pain of the severest punishment[36]

49

"Prostitute impudency"; "women... conversed in our Army"; and women "counterfeit[ing]" their sex – what on earth was Charles I referring to? Some clue lies in an anonymous seventeenth-century ballad that dates from the same period as Charles's angry tirade. It is sung from the point of view of a woman, who joyfully declares:

> *Put me on a man's attire,*
> *Give me a soldier's coat.*
> *I'll make King Charles's foes*
> *Quickly to change their note!*[37]

Despite this she-soldier's avowed Royalist beliefs, the king was evidently not an admirer of this new breed of cross-dressing warriors. Nor would he have been a fan of Mary Ambree, the heroine of a ballad that had been circulating since the 1620s. The ballad made much of Mary's change of clothes – "she clothed herself from top to the toe, / with buff of the bravest and seemly to show" – and then goes on to describe her extraordinary bravery:

> *The sky then she filled with the smock of her shot*
> *And her enemies bodies with bullets so hot*
> *For one her own men a score killed she,*
> *Was not this a brave bonny Lass Mary Ambree*[38]

Margaret Cavendish also described a cross-dressing warrior. Lady Orphant, in her play *Loves Adventures* (published in 1662, but written before that date), dresses up first as a beggar, and later as a soldier as part of a plan to marry the man to whom her dead father had betrothed her. But if cross-dressing soldiers were the nightmare of Charles I and the vogue of popular ballads, how many of them were there? And how many of them successfully fought with their sex undetected?

Given the level of deception implicit in this undertaking, it is understandably difficult to find sources that record female soldiers dressed as men. One recent historical study identified only five references to cross-dressed women on either side of the conflict: an "infinitesimal figure".[39] One such woman is the rather tragic Nan Ball, who had followed her "beloved Lieutenant" into war dressed in men's clothes. She was discovered, and turned out of the army without any record of her ever fighting. Other stories tell of prostitutes in male clothing in the army camps, and even a cross-dressed Royalist prisoner of war who had such a "fair countenance" that she had caught the eye of Oliver Cromwell. He suspected that she was the mistress of Lord Percy – the Royalist soldier she had been captured with – and asked her to sing to blow her cover.[40]

All of these stories – from the ballad's lyrics which focus on the cross-dressed woman's clothes and her "true love" at her side, to the continual emphasis on disguised prostitutes and courtesans – suggest that the figure of the cross-dressed woman soldier was more of a titillating imagined fancy than it was a historical reality. But there were still *some* women who took to men's clothes in their bid to fight for their beliefs. In December 1645, *The Scottish Dove* ran a report on a "young man" who was in the Parliamentarian army for "twelve months". Her true sex was only discovered when, on leave in Shropshire, she asked a tailor to make her a "petticoat and waistcoat" and asked him to take her measurements, averring that it was for her "sister, which is just of my stature every way". The tailor was suspicious, and reported her. After investigation, it was discovered she was a woman. She had fought for a year, had been "very active and well exercised in arms" and had avoided detection by refusing to share a bed with any other soldier.

This example, and that of Ann Dimack (or "Anne Dymocke") who joined the army in the 1650s after the young man she had wanted to marry was "cast away", suggests that there may well have been more women in the army than historical documents have recorded. After all, during life at war – when clean changes of clothes were hard to come by, and daily washes were a thing of dreams – it would have been none too hard to conceal a woman's body.

* * *

But if these women soldiers were either not that common, or were good, diligent soldiers who caused no difficulties, why was Charles I so anxious to suppress them? As his proclamation (which he eventually did not issue, perhaps for fear of mockery from the Parliamentarian press) suggests, it was not so much the women fighting that angered him, as it was the "prostitute impudence" and unsavouriness of cross-dressing – a sin outlawed in the bible, a fear of women out of their proper subordinate place.[41]

The truth is that cross-dressing had been a widespread vogue since the days of James I. Back in 1620, James I had asked his bishops to preach against the new vogue for masculine dress. And even Charles I's own wife was up to it: just three years before this draft proclamation, she had acted in a court masque in which she had been dressed in a martial "Amazonian habit" (although, of course, he would have seen a dramatic difference between high-born women's stage antics and the daily clothing of female commoners).

The most famous story of early modern cross-dressing is that of Mary Frith: the early seventeenth-century actress, pickpocket, and pimp who haunted the underworld of London, wearing men's clothes and smoking cigars. Thomas Middleton and Thomas Dekker's 1610 play *The Roaring Girl* is based on her exploits, but even the decadence of the Jacobean stage could not do justice to the bare facts of her life: she had a sham marriage to minimise the number of court cases which could be brought against her, once did penance for a charge of prostitution whilst blind drunk, and was even temporarily committed to Bedlam.

If Mary – "Moll" – Frith was at one end of the cross-dressing scale, then many other, respectable, women were not so radically different from her. In 1616, Barnaby Rich published a pamphlet entitled *My Ladies Looking Glass* which railed against the "folly of new fashions". Rich's tirade attacks a broad range of transgressions – wigs and "paint" on the face are, according to him, evidences of sin – but he is fascinating on the subject of early seventeenth-century style. After proclaiming that "new invented vanities came from hell", he utters the sentence "I know not what to say, or whether I should accuse men, for suiting themselves in women's apparel, or whether I should accuse women for suiting themselves in men's apparel."[42] Under the rule of James I, when women began to wear looser clothes, with more manly shapes, one visual barrier between the genders began to weaken.

In the post-Restoration world – when women could act on stage, and could play the "breeches part" of men – this titillating interest in cross-dressing would become more and more dramatic, and Margaret would make use of it in many of the brilliantly bizarre outfits she designed for herself. But it is fascinating that Charles considered it important enough, in the midst of a war that threatened his rule and his very existence, to spend his limited time and resources worrying about women dressing as men.

* * *

For some of the women engaged in the violence and deceptions of the Civil War, cross-dressing as a man would have provided little help. In the post-Restoration years, Aphra Behn, Cavendish's direct contemporary and fellow career writer, was a female spy: she worked briefly as "Agent 160" or "Astrea" in the late 1660s when she was recruited by Charles II during the Second Anglo-Dutch War. Her task was to turn her rumoured former lover William Scott – who was working for the Dutch – into a double agent for the English. She failed in her mission, and was no more successful in making money out of the enterprise: she was forced to pawn her jewellery, and returned to England in debt – debt that would force her to turn to writing for money. But she was only the latest in a long line of women who spied during the Civil War and the years afterwards, none of them as well known as the poet and playwright.

On the Parliamentarian side was the agent Elizabeth Alkin (who was given the imaginative name "Parliament Joan" by the propagandists). Making use of an unassuming appearance, she was employed by different Parliamentarian generals to expose those who were supplying much-needed resources to the Royalist forces. Her most interesting work was her self-appointed mission to seek out and shut down the Royalist printing presses churning out their weekly propaganda. She did manage to make one arrest of a monarchist printer, and otherwise succeeded in raising the hackles of those she pursued: *Mercurius Pragmaticus* attacked her for her femininity, and called her an "old bitch".[43] In later years – after her husband had been hanged as a spy by Royalist forces, and she had herself spent time in a "house of correction" – Alkin also went on to write her own propagandist newsbooks, using names which subversively implied that their contents were Royalist.

Alkin's gender can't have done much to protect her: female spies abounded on both sides of the conflict. In the Royalist camp, there is the miraculous story of Jane Whorwood. By all accounts more beautiful, with her "deep red coloured hair", than poor old "fat" Elizabeth Alkin, Whorwood had a rather more glamorous job than shutting down printing presses. She had worked for the Royalist forces for three years before the king was imprisoned on the Isle of Wight in 1647, and whilst he was there, she was one of his few and most trusted confidants. She devised ingenious plans to get him off the island. Using coded letters to communicate with other spies, the king, and dedicated courtiers, she launched a number of escape attempts – including one in which she smuggled in nitric acid in order to dissolve the bars on the king's windows.

The escape attempts failed, but the coded letters from the king to Jane offer a fascinating insight into the life of a man who had, until recently, been seen as a devoted husband: in one letter, which was only successfully decoded in 2006 by the historian Sarah Poynting, it becomes clear that the king was devising ways that Whorwood could "get a swiving from [him]".[44] Swiving is, of course, seventeenth-century slang for "shagging". This moment of indiscretion on the king's part (and it doesn't appear to have been a short affair) sheds some light on Charles I's view of female combatants. He had no problem with Whorwood's involvement – but her femininity was not hidden, especially not when she was in his bed (or, as one letter reveals, in his loo). It was only those women who fought while testing the limits of their sex that angered him.

Unfortunately for Charles, his complaints had little effect. Women, from countesses to clergymen's wives, and from spies to soldiers, had a far greater role in the Civil War than is often supposed. They strained so forcefully at the expectations of their sex that the popular image of the quiet, docile early modern women seems to disintegrate as soon as any pressure is applied to it. It may not have quite been the dramatic triumph of *Bell in Campo*, but women were involved in all levels of the conflict, and not all stayed at home to avoid "the least puff of wind".

4

On sorrow's billows this ship was tossed

IN HER 1656 collection of poetry and prose, *Natures Pictures*, Margaret Cavendish wrote the sorry tale of "Travalia": a woman who, as her name suggests, is not allowed to stay in one place for long. The story's title – "Assaulted and Pursued Chastity" – gives some clue as to what this lost daughter of a war-ridden kingdom goes through.[1] After a storm casts her ship aground in the "Kingdom of Sensuality", she is promptly sold into prostitution, shoots her would-be customer, and cross-dresses as a young page to escape by boat. The not inconsiderable drama of the story is only heightened by the sheer number of storms this young woman must suffer. The first storm begins her crisis, but the second is no less intense:

> Fortune... irritated the Gods against them... making the clouds and seas to meet them, showers to beat them, winds to toss them, thunder to affright them, lightning to amaze them, insomuch as they had neither strength to help themselves, nor sight to guide them, nor memory to direct them, nor courage to support them[2]

There is more than a hint of Shakespeare's *The Tempest* in this description – Cavendish was a great admirer of Shakespeare, and even wrote criticism of his plays.[3] This is an all-consuming hurricane: it leaves nothing standing, and allows its victims no respite or calm to reassemble themselves. "The rudder was broke, the masts were split, the sails all torn, the ship did leak… Nothing was left but black despair", wrote Cavendish.

Travalia and the captain of the boat – who becomes her adoptive father – do, eventually, find something other than black despair when they land on a tropical island, only to discover that they are being kept alive as human sacrifices. As is the way with Cavendish's fiction, this difficulty is quickly overcome, and it isn't long before Travalia and her father are being worshipped as gods. But after they "began to grow weary of their divine honours", they take to their boat again. By now, the cyclical structure of the story should make the next storm seem less of a surprise, but the description of "storms of fears" which take hold of the boat when "a great whale" of a group of marauding pirates seize the ship is still dramatic.[4] This storm is metaphorical, but the dangers of the sea and maritime travel are a constant. Every distressing element of the story – from the "shipwreck" of sexual assault, to "rough thoughts" which move Travalia like a "ship at sea, that is not anchored or ballasted" – is told through a nautical metaphor.

Why, in one of her most well-structured and diverse stories, does Cavendish keep returning to the same image? What is it about a storm-wrecked ship that seems, to her, to be the perfect metaphor for everything from physical danger to emotional tumult? This fixation is not limited to one story. In *The Blazing World* (1666) it is a "tempest" that picks up the ship and causes the Lady to find herself in the brave new world beyond the North Pole, where the rest of the story takes place. It is no coincidence that the wonderful utopia she finds herself in is a world in which ships are resistant to wind and waves, and where storms can be defeated.

In *Poems and Fancies* (1653), Cavendish uses the image of a ship to describe her own life:

A ship of youth in the world's sea was sent;
Balanced with self-conceit and pride it went
And large sails of ambition set thereon,
Hung to a tall mast of good opinion.[5]

This metaphor of the young Margaret as a "balanced" ship is touching: it is equal parts fragile and delicately poised, and majestic and powerful. She describes how it had "winds of praise and beauty's flowing tide". But the calm doesn't last: just a few lines later, "rebellious clouds foul black did grow, / And showers of blood into those seas did throw". Margaret, like Travalia, found herself in the middle of a tempest.

* * *

The storm Margaret was caught up in during the summer of 1644 could not be resolved in one hastily written sentence, or skipped over with a turn of the page. That spring, Henrietta Maria had begun to worry about the safety of her court in Oxford. She was heavily pregnant, and the continual noise and muck of the city were becoming intolerable, while her soldiers were hardly the most comfortable neighbours. Her apartments in Merton formed a part of the city's outer walls: she had no respite from the war in which she had been such an active participant, not even when she was ill with her pregnancy.

And so, on 3 April, she and her ladies began their journey – a journey that would take them out of England for the duration of the war, and away from their families who were still in the thick of the fighting. They first went to Bath, where Henrietta Maria was treated by the royal physician, Theodore Mayerne, and then proceeded to Exeter, where the queen gave birth to a daughter with the assistance of a midwife sent by her sister-in-law Anne of Austria, the queen of France. Still ill from the birth – and half-blind from post-partum complications, by some accounts – Henrietta Maria did not have long to recover: the city was threatened by rapidly advancing Parliamentary forces, and the queen's letter begging for clemency in her illness was met only by an assurance that she would be escorted to London if she gave herself up.[6] Unwilling to do what amounted to little more than surrender, she left her new-born daughter, Henrietta Anne, and fled the city. She hid "under a heap of litter" in a hut for three days without food or water, and reunited with her other ladies-in-waiting – who had escaped in various disguises – at Falmouth.[7] The she-generalissima had been momentarily weakened by her pregnancy, but she was not going to let it endanger her further, or hinder her commitment to the Royalist cause.

The ship at Falmouth that was to carry Henrietta Maria and her ladies to France – Margaret amongst them – endured considerable trials before it reached its destination. No sooner had the vessel left the port than a Parliamentary ship began to fire its cannon at their "little bark".[8] There was an imminent danger of being sunk or, worse, captured. Faced with the prospect of falling into Parliament's hands, and the humiliation that would bring, Henrietta Maria took charge. She forbade her ship from firing back, as it would delay their progress, and set them on a high-stakes course for France, with "every sail set for speed".[9] Her terrified ladies were already cowering when the queen upped the stakes once more: she told the captain that, in the event that escape became impossible, he was to blow up the ship, killing her with the explosion. At this point, her ladies let out "piercing shrieks". Henrietta Maria – still suffering from her pregnancy and having just left her new-born baby in the arms of her godmother, Anne Douglas, Lady Dalkeith – remained stoically silent.

The ship was pursued and attacked until it neared the coast of France, and was hit by one or more shots until "everyone on board gave themselves over for lost". Just as it seemed the trial might be over and they were within sight of Dieppe, a "furious storm" pushed them away again and extended their journey. They did, eventually, make it to Brest, 350 miles to the west

– where the queen, unrecognised, laid herself down to sleep in a peasant's cabin.

In her own autobiography, Margaret makes no mention of the storm, the attack by the Parliamentary navy, or even the ship. She writes only that she "continued almost two years" at court, with no description of the dramatic journey from England to France.[10]* But as her other writings show, these were moments of sheer terror, desolation, and loss of hope she would never forget. It was, perhaps, too painful and emotional an odyssey to recount in the personal voice of her autobiography, but that did not stop her from using it for her other characters. Every storm, civil war, and uprooted heroine is a nod to Margaret's own life, and a hint of how comfortable she was mixing fact and fiction, romance and history.

* * *

France was, at least, dry land, but it was by no means a paradise for Margaret. The court first made their way to the spa town of Bourbon l'Archambault to help the queen recover from her illness (reports make much of Henrietta Maria's loss of beauty, and of her looking "more like one of the miserable heroines in romance, than a real Queen"), before they travelled up to Paris.[11] The queen was well received by the French court (this was, after all, her family) and was given lodgings at the Louvre, with a country house in Saint-Germain. The grandiosity of these addresses belies the disorder within: the court – Henrietta Maria's ladies were joined by large numbers of Royalist exiles – could not move around their apartments without meeting piles of excrement at every turn. The French courtiers and servants

---

* The absence of discussion of this dramatic storm in her autobiography lends credence to the fact that Margaret may well have been present in the 1642 siege of St John's Abbey (see Chapter 2) – the fact that she did not write about it does not suggest it did not happen, or did not have a great effect on her.

were in the habit of relieving themselves in odd corners. By the beginning of 1645, Margaret had the "purging flux" – dysentery. She was only saved by a strong course of laudanum.[12]

Dysentery – "the stomach in an unnatural fire" – was the most dramatic and life-threatening of Margaret's woes in France, but it was by no means her only trouble. By her own admission, Margaret had no talent in the "prating of several languages" but here she was, aged twenty-one and without a relative or friend to look after her amidst a foreign court.[13] Henrietta Maria returned to speaking French, and openly practised her Catholicism. Unable to speak the language and wrenched from any of her family ties (when in Oxford, she could occasionally see some of her sisters), it is no surprise that the already anxious Margaret fell into a period of "melancholy" depression – one of many that would haunt her for the rest of her life. Cavendish would not return to England until 1651, and would not live there permanently until after the Restoration in 1660. She would not see her mother, two of her brothers, and her sister again: they would die before she returned from exile.

* * *

Still, in April 1645, Margaret had some cause for amusement. In the middle of one of their interminable days of being "in presence", the ladies-in-waiting were presented with something worth waiting for: one of the king's lords of the Privy Council made a dramatic entrance at court, in a decadent coach pulled by no fewer than nine horses. Not content with this display of grandeur and wealth, he then gave seven of the horses to the queen mother, despite the fact that he had been offered outrageous sums for them, and had dug himself into considerable debt to afford them in the first place.[14] Ever fond of theatrics, Margaret must have enjoyed this spectacle. And it was as well she did: this flamboyant man, William Cavendish, the then Marquis of Newcastle, would become her husband before the year was out.

William's theatrical entrance into court – which was designed, in part, to trick creditors into lending him more money – belied the reality of his situation: he had been on the continent since July 1644, after his embarrassing defeat at the battle of Marston Moor. A disagreement with the cavalry general Prince Rupert led to organisational chaos on the battlefield when the Parliamentary army attacked. On a battlefield just outside York, William became the de facto leader of a group of volunteer troops, only to see them surrounded by Parliamentary forces. Regiment after regiment surrendered, until only his own personal infantry, the Whitecoats, remained: their bravery did not save them, and they were "killed in rank and file".[15] Fewer than thirty survived, and estimates put the total deaths at 4,000 soldiers. This was William's first – and last – significant defeat in battle, but it was one defeat too many: he saw that "all was lost" and left for Hamburg from Scarborough.

Newcastle's self-imposed exile did not go down well: he had been a popular general, but now he was seen as little more than a coward who had given up at his first defeat. Other Royalist commanders – Margaret's brother, Sir Charles Lucas, amongst them – who had been captured at the battle went on to fight again rather than retreat across the Channel. William's war record suffers in both the Earl of Clarendon's account, and in contemporary reports. Sir Philip Warwick, the writer and politician, fancied himself something of a wit when he wrote that Newcastle "had a tincture of a romantic spirit, and had the misfortune to be somewhat of a poet". He sums up the general's contradictions accurately: he was "a gentleman of grandeur, generosity, loyalty", but this failure meant he could never be seen in the same light again.[16]

Cavendish's later account of her husband's wartime service does not downplay the destruction and defeat, but maintains that he had little choice but to go into exile. Newcastle's one-time friend and supporter Henrietta Maria (all her letters to him begin, affectionately, "cousin") wrote to assure him "of the continuance of my esteem for you, not being so unjust as to forget past services upon a present misfortune".[17] The letter is signed "your very good, and affectionate friend" – and Henrietta Maria does offer assistance – but the very fact she had to write it at all reveals the precarious position William was now in.

Margaret cannot have been unaware of William's disgrace – her own brother had been held in the Tower of London until December 1644 as a result of the battle – but that did not stop her from becoming interested in this man of a "stature of a middle size" and "courtly, civil, easy and free" behaviour who visited the court repeatedly in the coming months.[18] Nor was the attention one-sided: William "pleased to take some particular notice of me, and express more than an ordinary affection for me" wrote Margaret in her autobiography.[19] In her memoir, Cavendish's description of the passion of their relationship is understated – she is unconventional for including it at all; Lucy Hutchinson's comparable biography and description of her courtship with her husband was not published during her lifetime – but "more than an ordinary affection" is quite the understatement when describing the relationship between William and Margaret. Between 10 April and 20 December 1645, when Margaret's mother, Elizabeth Lucas, wrote to congratulate the pair on their marriage, Margaret wrote William at least twenty-one undated letters of affection, love, and courtship. In response, he penned more than seventy poems: an incredibly prolific rate of more than one every two days.

* * *

Cavendish's letters – the originals can be found in the British Library, for anyone brave enough to attempt her handwriting – begin *in media res* with the spiteful, gossipy world of court: "others foresee we shall be unfortunat, tho we see it not our seleves", she writes, with her typically idiosyncratic spelling.[20] If the pair were already discussing their future, and the relationship was well known enough to be discussed by "others", then they must have met more than just once, and there must have been other letters which are now lost. From this early point in the relationship, it is clear that not all was running smoothly: "good frindes" were counselling both parties to "take heed" before they committed themselves any further, and were trying to "unty the knot of our affection". The gossip was, as ever, indiscriminate and cruel. Margaret's friends told her that William was something of a ladies' man: "you had ashured your selfe to many and was constant to non" (there were rumours of his interest in the Countess of Rutland some years before). In William's ears were constant reminders of the illegitimacy of Margaret's oldest brother. Margaret was afraid to write anything that could cause a "scandall of [her] reputation", and told William it was "imposabll to keep out of the rech of a slandering tongue".[21]

The heaviness of the subject – "St Germain is a place of much censure" – is lightened by Margaret's clear affection ("tis the natur of those that cannot be happy to dessir non else should be so, as I shall be in haveing you") and her evident embarrassment at her youth and lack of polish: the page is covered in crossings out, uneven lines, and pools of ink. On the reverse of the envelope of the first letter, she has written "pray let the falt of my wrighting to my pen". The pen was obviously not to blame – the rest of the letters are rarely more readable, and, in her later writing, she would often expound upon her difficulties with handwriting and spelling. But the figure of the young Cavendish, hurriedly writing these letters in secret and worrying how an older, established man of the world would read her haphazard script, is touching.

Her nervousness was not limited to the faults of her handwriting: as the letters progress, there is a palpable sense of how vulnerable she was, alone at court, the subject of gossip, and falling for a disreputable exile who was more than double her age. She is scared of openly admitting her affection for William, and is aware that she cannot write all she feels: "I am sory you should think your love so transends mine" she writes when he has evidently complained that her letters lack the passion of his.[22] But just a few letters later, she anxiously backtracks when she believes she has gone too far: "I am a lettel a shamed of my last letter... for wemen must love silently".[23] Her reticence is all the more poignant when it is compared to the poems William was sending her: he lauds her as "graced like a goddess, born by angels' wings", with beauty that makes "all your sex else, such wretched mortal things".[24]

Overblown, dramatic, and borrowing heavily from the tradition of courtly love poetry he would have read when he was younger, William's poems make up for their lack of skill with their demonstration of feeling. He thought Margaret was beautiful, had resoundingly fallen in love, and wanted to marry her. The growing relationship between them has all the speed and urgency of a fictional prose romance. The pair exchanged portraits and love tokens, and, in one letter, Margaret upbraids William for having "a plot against my health" in writing so early in the day. The letter she writes in response – by "candell light" as she would rather "read your leter than slepe" – is chaotically illegible: she writes with winding lines, hectic crossings, and uses every possible part of the page. On the envelope, she wrote "if you cannot reed this letter, blam me not for it was so early I was half a slep".[25]

William's poems have an incessant physical focus. He went so far in imagining the night of their wedding ("now you're in bed / with trembling maidenhood") that Cavendish had to reprimand him and remind him that they were not yet married: "there is a customary law that must be signed before I may lawfully call you husband".[26] And, not content with just correcting his lustfulness (there is, in more than one letter, a sense that William has asked Margaret to do something she felt she could not do prior to marriage), she even went as far as to add a postscript to one of her letters of "my lord lett your ear limit your poetry". When reading some of William's poems, it is hard not to agree with Margaret. In one, he tries to play down their thirty-year age gap by writing:

No man can love more, or loves higher;
Old and dry wood makes the best fire,
Burns clearest, and is still the same,
Turn'd all into a living flame.[27]

No wonder Margaret felt the need to censure his efforts. She was reticent in displaying her affections, but not in asserting her literary talents. These letters – responding to poetry, commenting on court life, and describing her own emotions – are the first literary writing of Margaret's we have, given that her "baby books" have been lost. They are not just love letters, but the scribblings of an inquisitive, scholarly mind writing its way out into the world.

And she did not limit herself to discussions of their relationship or court gossip. One letter in the middle of their courtship is more illegible than the rest: Margaret writes on large paper, but – unlike other letters found in manuscripts from the period – she is rarely able to squeeze more than a handful of sentences on a side. In this particular letter, her script is so big, and so irregularly slanted as to make it appear disconcertingly childish. Words are underlined for seemingly no reason, and others are crossed out with thick black lines, or smudged as if they have got wet. Margaret writes:

> supose me now in a very mallancolly humer [melancholy humour], and that most of my contemplations are fext upon nothing but dessolutions, for I look upon this world as on a deths head for mortefication, for I see all things subject to alteration and change, and our hopes as if they had taken opium; therefore I will despis all things of this world... but I should be lost to those thoughts if I did not meet some of yours to restore me to myself again[28]

Every other word here is obscured, rewritten, or crossed out, but the meaning is still clear: Margaret was overwhelmingly depressed. She had seen her whole world "subject to alteration and change" and had been wrenched from her family, her country, and everything she held dear, only to be marooned in a court where she did not speak the language and everyone was talking about her. Her brothers were risking their lives, her childhood house had been ransacked, and the cities and towns she had known would be changed by the time she returned to London in 1651: "d[i]ssolution" was the order of the day. Her imagery – "our hopes as if they had taken opium" – is richly imagined, but her state of mind is painfully evident. The end of the letter – Margaret's plea to meet William's thoughts – is intriguing: in opening herself up and baring her melancholy, she is asking for William to rescue her and restore her to herself. Already, so early on in their relationship, Margaret relied upon William as an emotional and intellectual friend. This was not just a relationship of convenience, or the love affair of an older man who caught sight of a beautiful young woman: there were true emotions involved. And this connection did not go unnoticed. By the end of the sequence of letters, the rumour was spreading that the pair had already wed in secret.

* * *

William had been married once before. Born thirty years before Margaret in 1593 – and, at that point, without any aristocratic title – William was the son of Sir Charles Cavendish who was, in turn, the youngest son of Sir William Cavendish and his wife, Bess of Hardwick (famous for her construction of Chatsworth at the end of the sixteenth century). William's father, Charles, had served as a soldier in Queen Elizabeth's time and been knighted for his prowess. Despite his status as the youngest son, he had found wealth by marrying the heiress Katherine Ogle. William had been born into a life of luxury (the family had two large country houses at Bolsover Castle in Derbyshire and Welbeck Abbey in Nottinghamshire) and had a traditional aristocratic Renaissance education of Latin, more Latin, and a smattering of other pursuits. At the age of fifteen, he was made Knight of the Bath, and spent time with Prince Henry – King James I's son – before travelling across Europe with the diplomat Sir Henry Wotton. During a successful political career (he was an MP for the Royalist party in the House of Commons, the "King's Men", and later became a Viscount, Lord Lieutenant of Nottinghamshire, and the tutor and guardian to Charles I's son, the future Charles II), he emulated his father and married an heiress. Elizabeth Basset of Blore, the daughter of "a very honourable and ancient family in Staffordshire", was able to add "a great part to his estate".[29] In a sign of the future relationship between William and Margaret Cavendish, this first marriage was also based on love: every letter William wrote to Elizabeth started with the phrase "dearest heart".[30] The couple had ten children, but only five would survive to adulthood. By the time that Cavendish and William met, Cavendish was younger than his oldest daughter, Jane.

In comparison to his first wife Elizabeth – who had died only two years before, in 1643 – Margaret cut a sorry figure: she had no dowry, no title, and was a mute "idiot" at court. William "did approve of those bashful fears which many condemned" and rose above those who argued he could marry someone rather wealthier and better connected, but this did not mean the match was all plain sailing. Margaret, too, had her own objections to the pairing: she had a natural antipathy to marriage and "shunned men's company as much as [she] could".[31] In later years, she would return again and again to the question of whether marriage was fair on the women who entered into it – even if her own experience seems to have often been one of love, affection, and friendship.

Aside from their own qualms, the couple had to face external objections. Maids of honour were not allowed to marry without the permission of the queen – permission that was difficult to come by, as Margaret's aunt Anne Throckmorton had discovered when she had married illicitly at the court of Queen

Elizabeth. Margaret's letters to William are peppered with this fear: in the first letter that survives, she writes "I hard the qeene should tak it ell that I ded not make her acquainted befor I had resolved". This escalates to begging William to "plese ask the queen" and, by the twelfth letter, the rather sorry postscript "the queen takes noe notice of me". By the end of the courtship, she is even more plaintive: "I hop the qeene and I are frindes; she sayeth she will seme so at least, but I finde, if it had bene in her power, she would have crost us".[32] William's reticence to ask the queen – he continually suggests going through her advisors – suggests he expected not to be granted permission: either Margaret's position as a lady-in-waiting was too integral to Henrietta Maria's maintenance of an appearance of splendour and royal grandiosity, or the queen thought that one of her favoured generals deserved a better match.

But the difficulty Margaret and William experienced in marrying was, for the period, comparatively minor. They faced no overt displeasure from either side's family, and were permitted to make their own decision. As late as 1688, Lord Halifax would write in his tract *Advice to a Daughter* that "women are seldom permitted to make their own choices; their friends' care and experience are thought safer guides to them than their own fancies".[33] Margaret's direct contemporary Dorothy Osborne is clear proof of this: she had to wait until after her father's death to marry Sir William Temple. Temple was a Parliamentarian and her family were Royalists. Whilst her father lived, the match could not be contemplated.

By the time they made it to the altar at Sir Richard Browne's chapel in Paris in December – the chapel had been newly built to allow the exiled court to hear Anglican services – Margaret and William had triumphed over gossip, royal displeasure, and a pervasive atmosphere of despair. They were married on an unknown date without either of their families, and it is impossible to know who did attend. In her later poems on the subject, Margaret mixed the emotional – "hymen did join their hands, their hearts did tie" – with the imaginary: she pictured herself in a "crown of jewels" with "diamond, carbuncle, and sapphire".[34] With the state of William's debts, it is unlikely that Margaret wore anything of the sort. In a poem written a month earlier, William had described Margaret's match in comparison to the Princess Marie of Nevers:

> *The Princess Mary marries King of Poland*
> *And you my dear do marry Prince of Noland*
> *She hath a portion, I hope you have none*
> *She hath a dower, but your dower's gone*[35]

However hyperbolic William's style is ("take up your cross to follow me / Leave court, your parents, brothers, friends..."), he does succeed in expressing the truth: this wedding may have been one of love, but that would not make the ensuing years any easier. Margaret's mother, Elizabeth, wrote to congratulate the pair, but even she could not bring herself to rejoice. She ended the letter with:

> God deliver us. And send us a happy end of this troubles
> which we ought with patience to bear. Tell almighty God in
> his due time shall be pleased to deliver us, with my prayers
> for you both.[36]

The Prince of Noland, the dowerless exile, and the prayers of a mother stuck in a war-wracked country: Margaret and William had none of the normal accoutrements of a wedding feast. Margaret's ship had made it into safe harbour, but the "storms of poverty" and "showers of misery" were never far away.[37]

5

It is hard to get children with good courage

IN AN EVOCATIVELY illustrated ballad from the early seventeenth century, a sorrowful noblewoman – the song is called *The Lamenting Lady* – sings to her listeners about her unusual predicament. After she has been "barren" for many years, a poor beggar woman "with two sweet children in her arms" calls at the lady's door.[1] The noble lady turns the beggar away, grumbling about how "why should people poor" have the joys of children, and refuses to give her any money. The beggar woman curses the lady, and before she knows it she "swelled so big that [she] appeared, a strange and monstrous wight":

> *At which affright my big swelled womb*
> *Delivered forth in fear*
> *As many children at one time*
> *As days in the year*

Her 365 children were no bigger than "mice". In the ballad's illustration, they are lined up in a basket like tiny loaves of bread whilst a woman, presumably her maid, looks on in horror with her arms in the air. They were all born stillborn or, in some versions of the story, die shortly after birth. Amidst the gossip of neighbours and "strange report" of the horrifying birth, they are all buried in one grave. The lamenting lady's punishment for her cruelty and jealousy is complete, and she continues to be infertile.

It is a bizarre story, and it has its origins in the thirteenth-century legend of Margaret of Holland, Countess of Hennenberg who apparently died whilst giving birth to 365 stillborn children. She and her children were buried in a village near The Hague, Loosduinen, where, to this day, an epitaph and a memorial tablet are still visible. But the seventeenth-century fascination with her story was not just limited to the popular ballad. Pepys, in whose collection this ballad is found, went to visit the church in 1660. He appears to have not entirely disbelieved the myth, and wrote with only a hint of scepticism:

> We saw the hill where they say the house stood and sunk wherein the children were born. The basins wherein the male and female children were baptized do stand over a large table that hangs upon a wall, with the whole story of the thing in Dutch and Latin, beginning, "Margarita Herman Comitissa," &c. The thing was done about 200 years ago.[2]

Nineteen years before Pepys, the diarist John Evelyn was slightly more circumspect about the legend. In his diary, he wrote about the woman who is "pretended to have been a countess of Holland", and tells how she was "reported" to have given birth to so many children. But for all his doubt, he still found the memorial and the basins in which they were baptised "a desolate place".[3] For such a frankly unbelievable medieval myth, the story of Margaret of Holland certainly had a grip on the travellers and diarists of the seventeenth century.

The story even crops up in printed midwifery manuals, including the first of the genre to be written by a woman, Jane Sharp's 1671 *The Midwives Book*. Sharp is an uncompromising author. She begins her book with the assertion that "the art of midwifery chiefly concerns us" [i.e. women] and "even the best learned men" have to yield to women's knowledge, and she is resolutely methodical in her approach to describing conception.[4] Her description of the clitoris – "a sinewy hard body" which gives women "desire" and "delight in copulation" – is extraordinarily modern and enlightened.[5] But even she cannot resist the pull of the legend: she dismisses it as a "mere romance" but still describes how the countess gave birth to "three hundred sixty five" children as a result of a "curse" laid upon her. Sharp even adds the detail that half the babies were boys, and the other half girls. The one "odd child" left over "was divided to both sexes, an Hermaphrodite, partly male, partly female".[6]

Sharp adds the story to her otherwise non-narrative scientific advice, Pepys was intrigued by the tale, and Evelyn made a detour in his travels to see the memorial – and, of course, the ballad was popular enough to be printed and collected. Why were so many writers intrigued by this story; a story they all seem to be aware was fanciful? One clue to the answer lies in the legend's discussion of infertility. The lamenting lady is barren despite her wealth and riches; she is, in an act that hints at witchcraft, cursed to have stillborn children; and ends the tale either dead or repenting to God for her sins of presuming to question his judgement. In the seventeenth century, infertility was not a medical problem so much as a spiritual and social one – and one that could, rapidly, become all-consuming.

* * *

The nine-month romance between William and Margaret was, by all accounts, a whirlwind. They would have seen each other infrequently, either by scheming to meet when Margaret was with the queen in Paris, or by William finding excuses to visit the court in Saint-Germain. Even when they were together, they would have rarely, if ever, been alone: the ever-watchful eye of the mother of the maids would have prevented private assignations. There was evidently true affection and emotion, but, on William's part, there was also another motive for marrying a much younger woman so quickly despite her lack of money or social power. In her autobiography, Margaret would later write:

> For he, having but two sons, purposed to marry me, a young woman that might prove fruitful to him and increase his posterity by a masculine offspring. Nay, he was so desirous of male issue that I have heard him say he cared not (so God would be pleased to give him many sons) although they came to be persons of the meanest fortunes[7]

William had two sons, Charles and Henry, who were living with him in exile rather than fighting in the Civil War (Charles was eighteen and Henry fourteen; Henry suffered from regular fainting fits).[8] The realities of violence, illness, and strife undoubtedly made William fearful for his estates and title: he wanted and needed sons to ensure his name's future.

After their wedding, Margaret and William moved in together to William's Parisian lodgings, which were supported almost entirely by the loans of creditors whose good nature could only last so long. Their wartime poverty could not have made for a happy introduction to married life. On one occasion, William asked Margaret to pawn her clothes so they could buy dinner; faced with parting with her one-of-a-kind dresses of her own design, she asked her maid to pawn some of her own "small toys" instead.[9] And, aside from money worries, they had other issues: the years after their wedding were plagued by ill-health for both of them.

Sir Theodore Mayerne, the society doctor who had treated Henrietta Maria when she was pregnant in 1644, and would later minister to Oliver Cromwell, wrote to William about his ailments in 1648:

> I see that you are the same in respects of your ill health you were as first when I had the honour to know you, namely Melancholick Hypocondriak troubled with vapours[10]

Mayerne's description is more specific than it might seem. Mayerne was a pioneering physician who advanced the use of chemical treatments, but he also – as with every other doctor, scientist, and lay-person in this period – believed in humourism: the school of thought that attributed the balance of the body to the four humours of blood, black bile, yellow bile, and phlegm. William's hypochondriac melancholy is caused, Mayerne believes, by the "humour" of the spleen. After his advice – William needs to "refresh and moisten" himself at any available opportunity, to "open the obstruction of his vessels" and "rebalance his humours" – the doctor moves on to Margaret, "my Lady", of whom William must have written with concern in the same letter he relayed his own difficulties.

Given that Mayerne has just spent so much time and space in prescribing treatments for William's illness, it is almost shocking to come across the sentence: "for my lady, she doth far exceed you for matter of the hypochondry".[11] When Mayerne was writing, "hypochondry" (hypochondria) did not mean what it does now – that is, an abnormal degree of health-related anxiety – but a type of melancholy caused by too much black bile and vapours in the spleen. It had physical manifestations in the stomach but it was, more generally, a mood disorder: Mayerne writes that Margaret was far more distressed and depressed than her husband. He counsels against her rather excessive means of dealing with this illness – she had been taking "vomits" to purge herself – and prescribes, in later letters, everything from foul-sounding potions to letting leeches bleed her haemorrhoids. Margaret was comparatively lucky: another doctor told William's melancholic son to eat all his food "seasoned with the powder of frogs dried in an oven".[12]

Mayerne does, eventually, discuss an illness other than melancholy:

Touching conception, I know not if in the state she's in you ought earnestly to desire it. It is hard to get children with good courage, when one is melancholy and after they are got and come into the world, they bring a great deal of pain with them, and after that very often one loses them[13]

Here is, perhaps, the true cause of William reaching out to Mayerne: more than two years after their wedding, the couple had not had a child and Margaret showed no signs of being pregnant. But Mayerne's advice was unlikely to be comforting. He believed Margaret was in no fit state to get pregnant, and his only concession to William's wishes was to suggest she should spend some time at the mineral "baths of Bourbon". The advice made little difference. Margaret would never give birth and, by all accounts, never even became pregnant: instead, she claimed her books were her children, and writing them the closest she would get to motherly duty.

* * *

Cavendish approached her infertility with seemingly stoical acceptance. In the prefaces to many of her works, she used her childlessness and absence of normal wifely burdens as a justification for her writing. In 1653, she wrote "I have no children to employ my care and attendance on", and so replaced the chores of "housewifery" with her scribblings.[14] Her infertility is not presented as a disaster but, instead, an opportunity. Even William, who so desperately wanted more children, managed to move beyond his disappointment and called her poems her "newborn" fancies in his prefatory verse to her *Poems and Fancies*.[15] Margaret was far from the only woman to refer to her books as her "children" in this period: the American poet, Anne Bradstreet, wrote a poem in 1678 for her collected works in which she called her first book, *The Tenth Muse* (1650), her "offspring", whilst the anonymous female author of *Eliza's Babes: Or the Virgins-Offering* (1652) refers to her poems as "babes".[16] But, unlike Bradstreet – who gave birth to eight children – this was not just a metaphor for Cavendish, or an image to make women's writing more palatable: it was the truth of her situation.

Later on in her writing career, Cavendish would become bolder about her dislike of pregnancy and everything associated with it. Writing in *Sociable Letters* (1664), her (lightly) fictionalised series of letters to friends real and imagined, she writes a tirade against women who refuse to let others forget they are pregnant. She describes a pregnant woman, "Lady S.M":

> ... rasping wind out of her stomach, as childing women usually do, making sickly faces to express a sickly stomach, and fetching her breath short, and bearing out her body [...] as great bellied wives do, bearing a heavy burden in them, told me she had been with child a fortnight, though by her behaviour one would not have thought she had a week to go[17]

There's more than a hint here that Cavendish's cruel depiction is motivated by jealousy: this woman is showing off something that she, Margaret, cannot have. Margaret is her own version of the cruel lamenting lady in the old ballad, but her description of how women "take more pride in being with child, than in having a child" is insightful. As she knows all too well, it is the act of pregnancy, of bearing heirs, and fulfilling a husband's needs that is more important than the child itself.

This knowledge did not stop Cavendish from railing against women who were "melancholy... for want of children".[18] Also in *Sociable Letters*, she writes that a woman who marries a man who already has "sons to inherit his estate" and to "keep up his family" has no cause to want more children, or be sad that she cannot have any. Cavendish's outlook is harsh to the point of being almost cynical. She argues that children are no comfort to women: if they are sons, their name lives on as their husband's, and if they are daughters they will be "ingrafted into the stock of another family". "Daughters are to be accounted as movable goods or furniture", she writes in a line that would seem more fitting in a feminist tract from the nineteenth or early twentieth centuries than in a collection of fictionalised letters from the seventeenth century. For Cavendish, the only way to achieve posterity is to write; that is how her name will live on. She saw it as no "disgrace" to be "barren".

Indeed, the only clear indication of Margaret's sadness at being unable to have children is found in her biography of William. After describing how eager he was to have more sons, she writes:

> ... but God (it seems) had ordered it other-wise, and frustrated his designs by making me barren, which yet did never lessen his love and affection for me.[19]

The very fact that she felt the need to record that William's love did not "lessen" in the face of their lack of children emphasises just how important it was: despite her bravado in her other writings, other men, she believes, would have been far crueller in the same situation.

* * *

As the popularity of *The Lamenting Lady* and the legend of the 365 stillborn children shows, Margaret and William were far from the only couple to experience infertility, fertility problems, and baby loss in the seventeenth century. Medical tracts and books about childbirth abound with theories about conception – either the Hippocratic theory of two "seeds" joining in the womb, or the Aristotelian belief in the one male seed which is implanted in the womb – and all touch upon what happens when conception fails. Jane Sharp enumerates many reasons why some women are "barren that they not conceive at all".[20] One possible cause, she writes, is that "though both they themselves and their husbands are no way deficient to perform the acts of generation", the couple are too alike "in their complexions" for conception to happen, the world needing "a due disposing of contraries". Sharp dismisses this cause quite quickly – she argues it is "hard to find" a couple so alike – and moves on to "some disproportion of the organs; or some impediment not easily discerned". Another cause – and one that was used in cases to prove that a woman had not been raped if she was pregnant – was that the couple were in "want of love": conception could not take place if the pair hated each other. Her other reasons for "barrenness" are numerous: it could be caused by a woman letting blood in their arm before their period, by the "ill disposition of the body and generative parts", or by "humours" falling down into the womb. She ends with the most intriguing reason: "there is barrenness by enchantment, when a man cannot lie with his wife by reason of some charm that hath disabled him". In the seventeenth century, witchcraft could stop a man being able to have sex.

Sharp, along with other authors of midwifery books, approaches the subject from a medical perspective: she is interested in the scientific, bodily causes that might prevent pregnancy. But the experience of many women in the period was far from a neutral, scientific outlook. Mary Whitelocke, the third wife of the lawyer and parliamentarian Bulstrode Whitelocke, had been married to her first husband for fourteen years when he died, and she went on to marry Bulstrode. During these fourteen years, she had not been able to give birth to a child: in the months before her first husband's death, she had become pregnant to her "great joy", only to miscarry fourteen weeks later. Her experience of infertility – which was, we have to assume, by no means atypical for a woman of the period – is only known about because she recorded it: she wrote a memoir of her life in a manuscript she dedicated to her eldest son.[21] Intended, in part, as a book of maternal advice – the first half is full of instructions to pray and be pious – it is also a heart-breaking testament to the experience of early modern infertility.

Whitelocke was a dedicated Puritan, and the whole manuscript is written in a homiletic style, with the Bible verses her sentences correspond to noted in the margins. Her Puritan beliefs were intimately tied to her infertility: she writes, repeatedly, that she prayed "to the Lord" for a child "as Hannah did" – the biblical woman who was infertile but became pregnant after she prayed to God and told him of her sorrow.* Whitelocke was not just praying to God for help with her medical difficulties: she truly believed that it was the Lord who had chosen to "withhold" children from her. In one particularly moving image, she writes that the Lord did not want their lives to be "too happy" so that they would have "neglected" his "heavenly habitation":

> God did mingle our cup with some bitterness, least we should
> have surfeited with too much creature enjoyments which we
> are very apt to do if we have not something or other for to
> wean our hearts from this world.

Whitelocke's Puritanism meant that she saw her infertility as a reprimand from God; a reminder not to be too attached to worldly happiness. For a woman who was already distraught over her lack of a baby, the implication that this was what she deserved could not have been very comforting. She goes on to write:

> God deals with his people as a tender hearted mother does
> with her child at her breast, she puts something bitter upon
> the nipple not to hurt the child but to make the child care
> less for the breast: so the Lord dealt with me he put some
> bitter dispensation upon all my creature enjoyments

Whitelocke's insistence that her childlessness is both God-given and somehow "tender" only makes her sadness more palpable and distressing. She, like Margaret, takes comfort in the fact

---

* This biblical story meant so much to Mary Whitelocke that she too named her son "Samuel".

that her husband "did never upbraid me" for her barrenness: once again, the very fact that she feels the need to record this only reinforces the despair and sadness of the situation.

When she does eventually get pregnant with Samuel – the son to whom the manuscript is written – she also credits this to God: "God did bless me and gave me strength to conceive with child" after her marriage to Bulstrode. Her pregnancy was not only given by God, but protected by him: she had a fall and "no one could in reason think [she] could escape from miscarrying" but her baby survived. "What God will have saved nothing can hurt", she wrote.

Whitelocke's sadness at her infertility and miscarriage with her first husband is understandable, and relatable. For women in the seventeenth century, infertility and miscarriage or stillbirth were not just personal tragedies: they were also moral failings. As Whitelocke's manuscript makes clear, the belief that children were a direct blessing from God was pervasive. And, perhaps more damagingly for women who struggled to conceive, after the Reformation there was also a widespread belief that bearing children was women's primary – if not *only* – religious duty. Martin Luther preached repeatedly on the woman's role in marriage, and expounded upon the Bible verse which, in the version of the bible that English Puritans would have been using until the 1630s, read "the woman was deceived, and was in transgression... through bearing of children she shall be saved".[22] In Luther's version, this was somewhat harsher: "If women grow weary or even die bearing children, that doesn't harm anything. Let them bear children to death; they are created for that."[23] For a Puritan woman like Mary Whitelocke, bearing her husband children was, quite literally, her path to salvation.

* * *

And even for non-Puritan women, bearing children was still far from something that was morally or socially neutral. Some years after Cavendish's time, James II's daughter Princess

Anne (later Queen Anne) wrote repeatedly of her difficulties in conceiving, and the irregularity of her periods – her "courses" – in her letters to her close friend Sarah Churchill, the Duchess of Marlborough. Anne was pregnant seventeen times, but never gave birth to a child that lived for more than a few hours. Her letters are full of attempted cures, consultations with doctors, and desperation ("I being so desirous of children I would do anything to go on") – a desperation that could not have been helped by the fact that Sarah, her closest friend, had seven children.[24] She follows doctors' remedies, and even cures which come "into [her] head" – with the logic that "it can do me no harm for if the child be only weake I hope it may comfort and strengthen it".[25] But one letter is more revealing than the others: when Anne believed there was a chance she might be "with child" and was resolved to "go on with the waters", she wrote to Sarah asking her "pray don't say anything of this to anybody nor to the queen if she should ask you anything concerning me".[26] In another letter a few years later, Anne writes to "Mrs Freeman" – the pair gave each other nicknames – that she had "been on the rack this morning". The princess did not want to discuss the pain ("the violence"; "a catching in my limbs" – likely linked to her fertility problems and more general ill-health) "before my women" for fear of what "malicious people" might say.[27]* Even, or *especially*, for members of the royal family, fertility problems were something to be embarrassed about; a personal failing that she feared could become the subject of gossip. In the 2018 movie *The Favourite*, Olivia Colman's Queen Anne keeps seventeen pet rabbits: one for each of the children she miscarried. This detail is a work of fictional embellishment, but it has its origins in a rather disconcerting story: in 1726, the peasant Mary Toft managed to convince the

---

* In the same letter, Anne writes a postscript to Sarah Churchill that reads "if dear Mrs Freeman cannot come with the Doctors, pray send some chocolate by the coach, for mine is almost at an end".

medical world that she had miscarried a baby and had, instead, given birth to a litter of rabbits.

At the other end of the social scale from the royal politics of heirs and spares, children – and the ability to bear them – also ensured a degree of social power: in one brilliant story of an argument between two women, one mother responded to the accusation of being a "bitch" by saying that she was "the mother of sixteen children". Someone who was clearly so fertile could never be a bitch, the reasoning went.[28] Another argument ran that prostitutes could not have children, because their wombs were too slippery for the seed to implant: being "barren" opened women up to charges of sexual immodesty.

Samuel Pepys and his wife, Elizabeth, were married for fourteen years and never had children. In his diaries, Pepys methodically tracked and recorded Elizabeth's periods (they often confined her to her bed), and wrote about their desire for children. In one particularly odd moment, his uncle William Wight suggested to Elizabeth that he should have a child with her and would pay her in "money or jewels".[29] The implication is that it was Pepys, not Elizabeth, who was infertile: he never had a child with any of his mistresses, and had had an operation to remove bladder stones in 1657 which might have left him unable to father children. The knowledge that the infertility lay on the man's side was not unusual for the period: one of the most popular manuals for childbirth and conception, *Aristotles Masterpiece* (1684) dedicates a section to the signs of "insufficiency in men". But these medical tracts would not help Pepys: he still wrote, plaintively, that it was "a sad consideration how the Pepys decay, and nobody almost that I know in a present way of increasing them".[30]

And even when women did succeed in becoming pregnant – no easy feat in a time of poor nutrition and lack of accurate advice – the possibility of miscarriage was ever present. In the spring of 1629, the English royal family and Henrietta Maria's mother, Maria de Medici, were excited: the queen was pregnant with the long-awaited heir to the English throne. But by May of that same year, Theodore Mayerne would write "their hopes are in vain. The fruit of their desires has been cut off".[31] Henrietta Maria went into labour early, and the baby was breech. The doctor could save either the mother or the child, a son. Charles asked the doctor to save his wife. The tenderness here is undercut by what he is reported to have said: he "would rather save the mould than the cast".[32] After the boy was baptised and buried in Westminster Abbey, Henrietta Maria wrote to her close friend Cardinal Richelieu and described herself being in the midst of an "affliction". In letters to others including her mother, she alludes to it in the briefest terms as a "misfortune": she had to restrain her sadness, and keep it under wraps.[33]

The Parliamentarian and Puritan Lady Mary Carey exhibited a different kind of restraint on the occasion of her miscarriage in 1657. Her long manuscript poem "Upon the Sight of my abortive Birth" begins:

> *What birth is this? A poor despised creature?*
> *A little embryo? Void of life, & feature?*[34]

Her evident distress and sadness is modified by her piety: she writes that "God hath it done, / submits my heart" and this submission is "better than a Son". Her acceptance of God's plan in the face of such a tragedy is almost galling, but it wasn't the only time she approached such sadness in this way. She wrote poems upon the deaths of two of her sons, Robert and Peregrine, one of which ends with this couplet:

> *My dearest Lord, hast thou fulfilled thy will?*
> *Thy hand-maid's pleased, completely happy still.*[35]

To modern ears, her acceptance is almost hard to read. Out of her seven children, only five survived past their infancy. Carey's Puritanism reached beyond the personal nature of this tragedy:

she truly believed that her children had a "soul" that would be "forever blessed" in heaven.

Mary Evelyn – the wife of John Evelyn, and a contemporary of William and Margaret in exile – wrote in terms that are no less tragic. After the death of her first child, Richard, in 1658 (he had died at the age of six), she wrote to her aunt that "the great affliction it has pleased God to lay on me hath very much alienated my affections from the Kings of this world". The plural of "Kings" suggests that it is not God that Mary is writing about – this death has not laid waste to her faith, but has instead left her in a state of depressive detachment from the world. She carries on:

> I was in too happy a condition, such blessings seldom last, to have a good husband, hopefully children, and a contented mind; all which I was possessed of, when God saw it fit to take away the is-well, the joy of our lives; by so sudden and unexpected a death[36]

As with Mary Whitelocke's insistence that God made her infertile to "wean" her from the joys of life, here too is the insistence that a child's death can be a punishment or reprimand. But Mary Evelyn is not able to be as accepting of God's will as Whitelock or Carey: she writes with touching maternal pride that she has "not only lost a child, but an extraordinary child even a miracle of his age". And, rather than counting her blessings in her living children as Carey does, she ends with the tragic sentence that she looks upon her only living child "as a blossom casual and transitory as the rest of them were". It is a letter that is hard to read in its entirety without crying.

Closer to William and Margaret was the experience of Elizabeth Brackley, William's second daughter, who married John Egerton, Lord Brackley, when she was fifteen in 1641. Elizabeth would go on to have ten children (and died in childbirth in 1663), but only four lived to adulthood. In a manuscript of her prayers and poems which was "collected and transcribed" after her death – and, fascinatingly, the handwriting was made to look like print, complete with a title-page – she writes with heart-breaking frankness about the deaths and sicknesses of her children. She prays to God to "heale" her daughter from her illness, thanks him for "bless[ing]" her with conception, and asks that she may be able to "take this height of paine" – that is, labour – "patiently".[37] Her piety continues throughout the volume – she writes a prayer to God thanking him for saving her and the child when she "thought [she] should have fallen in labour" (i.e. have a miscarriage) – but it is not without sadness.[38] In a prayer "upon occasion of the death of my boy Henry", she writes with tragic poignancy:

> If God be pleased to give me a child, and to take it from me, let me not fall to wish I had never borne it, rather then to part with it.[39]

That would be, Elizabeth knows, "heathenish thought", but they were thoughts she still fell prey to in her grief.

* * *

In Theodore Mayerne's letter to William is a hint of the possible "cures" for fertility problems and miscarriage in the period: he suggests that Margaret should visit the "baths". Bathing in waters at Tunbridge Wells, Wellingborough, or – as in Margaret's case – Bourbon l'Archambault was a popular cure for all manner of reproductive problems: prior to the Reformation, it had been a place where women would ask saints to intercede on their behalf. Since the Reformation, bathing claimed a more secular, social healing power. Of course, being in France and in the entourage of the Catholic queen, Margaret need not have restrained herself to only Protestant cures. If she wanted to, she could have tried everything from wearing a girdle with an image of the Virgin Mary on it, to praying to Saint Anne, the supposed patron saint of barren women due to an apocryphal belief that she had been infertile prior to giving birth to Mary. There is no suggestion that Cavendish did employ any of these religious cures – her later writing suggests she looked dimly upon the desperation that drove women to them, and William would undoubtedly not have taken kindly to any hints of Catholic ritual.* But she did try other medical approaches: in the summer of 1649, she injected herself every morning and night for a course of days with "Doctor Farrer's Receipt for the Sterility in Women".[40] The recipe had no effect.

Mayerne was, however, more preoccupied with Margaret's other health problems. Cavendish had been suffering from "melancholy" since her earliest days at court in Oxford and, after the terrifying flight into exile, and her bout of dysentery cured with opium, she was hardly any happier or healthier, despite her marriage. In a letter a year after the one which touched upon "conception", Mayerne returns to Margaret's "indisposition". He reprimands her for purging and bleeding herself too often, and prescribes a tonic of "rhubarb, agarick, syrup of roses" to alleviate her symptoms. He ends the letter with the rather revealing sentence:

> I am aggrieved that my Lady will do nothing at all, or shall do it by peace-meal according to her customs: let not her Lady be offended with my freedom [...] do me the honour to let me know how she likes this advice of mine[41]

Just four years before she would publish *Philosophical Fancies* – a book containing many of her own medical beliefs

---

* Despite their friendliness with Henrietta Maria, there is no cause to suspect that William and Margaret harboured any interest in Catholicism: William's family were staunch Protestants for many generations, and the traces of Catholicism on Margaret's side are few and far between.

– Margaret was already practising her cures, and ignoring her doctor's advice. In an age in which women were desperate for children and writing of their willing submission to God, Margaret would not even submit to her doctor's wishes to aid her health and fertility. She was, despite her melancholy, already too busy creating her literary children.

6

A sumptuous banquet for the brain

IN SEPTEMBER 1634, a masque by John Milton – a type of courtly dramatic entertainment that took place in more exclusive and intimate spaces than a theatre – was performed at Ludlow Castle, the Shropshire residence of John Egerton, the Earl of Bridgewater and his children. The masque has a vividly peculiar plot: "the Lady" – played by one of Bridgewater's daughters – gets lost in the woods, and is almost seduced by a lecherous, devilish figure called Comus (the name by which the masque is now commonly known).[1] Comus tests the Lady's chastity, by telling her that "beauty is nature's coin" that must be spent rather than hoarded. In a scene which can be seen as an early precursor to Christina Rossetti's *Goblin Market*, he attempts to force her to drink from his magical glass of "orient liquor" that will make her want to "roll with pleasure in a sensual sty".

The Lady refuses to drink but is, nonetheless, left unable to speak and stuck on a "marbled venomed seat / smeared with gums of glutinous heat". She can only be rescued by her brothers (in the masque's first performance, played by her real brothers, Bridgewater's sons) who are desperate to safeguard her chastity, and summon the sexual, sapphic touch of the river spirit Sabrina. Sabrina appears on "printless feet" and frees the girl by delicately touching her "rubied lip".[2] This is a masque which is as preoccupied by sexual chastity as it is literary purity: it was originally unprinted, and, when it was, initially only anonymously.

If the plot of the masque seems like the product of a particularly priapic fever dream, then its critical life has been no less dramatic. Some readers have argued that the masque is a near-Freudian expression of Milton's own fears over his virginity and chastity but, most famously, *Comus* has been the subject of a dramatic debate in which some scholars have argued that it was written to "cleanse" the Egerton family of a scandal which had taken place some years before, when Bridgewater's brother-in-law the Earl of Castlehaven was executed for raping his wife and sodomising two of his servants.[3] This interpretation has been much criticised – Milton studies have a penchant for sternly worded academic quarrels – but the possibility of its veracity reveals something important about the masque genre. They were written for individual patrons, events, and grand houses – with knowledge of their landscape and family history – rather than the more open, democratic world of the playhouses. The seventeenth-century literary milieu was one of close relationships, monetary and otherwise, between writers and their audiences.

But what does a masque performed when she was only eleven – and in a castle some 200 miles away from St John's Abbey – have to do with Margaret Cavendish? And what could Milton, the Puritan Parliamentarian and undeniably rather sexist poet (Virginia Woolf called him the "first of the masculinists"), have to do with a woman who believed in her own intellectual capacities and freedom to write?[4] More generally, what does this world of masques, literary patronage, and coterie writing have to do with a woman who had only ever spent her life at home in Essex or in a war-torn court, where entertainments were rather rarer than they had been in peace time?

* * *

When Margaret married William Cavendish in December 1645, she had, to all external observers, married a broke, doting fool of a man: he was an exile whose war record was indelibly blotted, and a courtier whose political career would never truly recover under Charles II. The couple were so skint that their only currency was William's ability to charm creditors, and they had to leave the Royalist hubs of Rotterdam and The Hague in order to be able to live with fewer expenses. But for all his failings and embarrassments, William Cavendish was more than just a disgraced soldier.

Prior to the outbreak of war in 1642 and his role of "governor of the Prince of Wales" which commenced in 1638, William Cavendish had spent much of his time in his home at Welbeck Abbey, a former monastery in Nottinghamshire bought by his father, Charles, at the beginning of the century. After reading William's panting, lustful poems for Margaret ("from your lipps I will Pluck / Freshe Roses, kisses suck") it is slightly difficult to take him seriously as an intellectual figure, but this is a mistake.[5] Under his instruction, Welbeck became a centre for seventeenth-century academic and literary learning: with his brother, Charles Cavendish, he forged close friendships with leading scientific figures of the day, from Thomas Hobbes (who had been employed by another branch of the Cavendish family as a tutor since early on in the century) to the natural philosopher and scientist Robert Payne, who was Cavendish's chaplain and secretary. By many accounts, Charles Cavendish was the true intellectual of the two brothers – he kept mathematical and scientific journals, and debated ideas with the leading lights of the day, whilst William applied Hobbesian principles to horsemanship and sword fighting – but the importance of the Cavendishes as intellectual patrons during this period cannot be downplayed.[6] There is even a manuscript work, the *Short Tract on First Principles*, which embodies the importance of Welbeck as a place of intellectual exchange: it was once attributed to Hobbes, but is now thought to be by Payne writing under the influence of Hobbes whom he met through William's patronage.

William's role as a literary and scientific patron continued during the Civil War – the poet William Davenant was his

Lieutenant General of Ordinance – and during his exile. He continued to associate with Thomas while he was abroad, and, on one occasion, the traditional dynamic of patron and author was reversed: Hobbes lent William money when he wanted to join Charles II in his first campaign of the war, and demanded William's telescope as assurance for his debt.[7]

While *Comus* is now the most famous example of the genre of the masque – a genre which by its very nature involves a close relationship between the writer and their patron – it is by no means the only one during the period. Under William's ownership, Welbeck became a centre for dramatic entertainment and literary patronage.[8] William had known the poet, epigrammatist and playwright Ben Jonson since at least 1618, when William invited him to stay at Welbeck during his famous walk to Scotland (a two-month journey that saw him greeted like a celebrity wherever he appeared). Jonson wrote two masques for the family: *The King's Entertainment at Welbeck* (1633) – written for, as the title suggests, Charles I's visit – and *Love's Welcome to Bolsover* (1634), another entertainment for the king and Henrietta Maria when they stayed at William's other house, Bolsover Castle. These masques repeatedly refer to their setting, from the architecture of the two grand houses, to the landscape of Nottinghamshire. For the Cavendishes, Jonson left his much-loved literary terrain of London.[9] And the relationship between the poet and patron went further: Jonson was commissioned to write the epigraph for William's father, Charles, and William even wrote an elegy on the occasion of Jonson's death in 1637, "To Ben Jonson's Goste". Critics have often identified William as a disciple of Jonson – one of the many "Sons of Ben" – but it is perhaps rather an insult to Jonson to claim that this poem shows much similarity to his work. What it lacks in literary ability – and as one critic, Timothy Raylor, has shown, William's secretary Robert Payne had to rescue much of the text from poetic embarrassment – it makes up for in friendship and affection:

I would write of thee (Ben;), not to prove
My wit or learning, but my judgement, & love
But when I think or this, or that, to choose
I find each part of thee above my muse[10]

William's self-professed awareness of his own lack of talent – "I find each part of thee above my muse" – is rather false: he continued writing plays and poems for the next three decades without any obvious sense of embarrassment. What is clear, nonetheless, is the closeness of the relationship he had with Jonson, and other leading intellectual figures of the time: William Cavendish was one of the leading patrons of Stuart England.

And his literary and intellectual interests went beyond paying for elaborate masques or poems dedicated to his family. William also meticulously collected literature of the period, and had it copied into a manuscript by his secretary John Rolleston.[11] In this manuscript, Ben Jonson's poems for the family – a poem for William's mother, and one lauding his ability in horsemanship – sit alongside poems and texts by the physician Richard Andrewes and no fewer than ninety-eight poems by John Donne, including the great "Good Friday, 1613 Riding Westward" and "To his Mistress Going to Bed", a poem that it is tempting to imagine him reciting to Margaret on their wedding night:

Licence my roving hands, and let them go,
Before, behind, between, above, below.
O my America, my new-found-land,
My Kingdom, safeliest when with one man mann'd[12]

What he lacked in literary talent, William made up for in literary taste. In marrying William, Margaret had not just joined herself to one of the (formerly) most influential and powerful families in England, but had also entered into the well-connected upper echelons of the seventeenth-century intellectual world. She was now a member of the kind of family that masques like *Comus* were written and performed for – and was now, in fact, linked to that very family. William's daughter, Elizabeth, was the wife of John Egerton, the brother who had performed in the masque as a child. Margaret, the shy girl from St John's Abbey in Colchester, had married into the seventeenth-century literary elite.

* * *

For Margaret, however, simply marrying into this world was not enough: she needed to write herself into it. When William and Margaret were in exile, this world of intellectual connections and debate did not stop, despite the difficulties of their circumstances. After three years in lodgings in Paris, and a brief spell in Rotterdam and The Hague, the couple settled in Antwerp, where they went in search of a small house – they had let most of their servants go – that would fit with their being "much necessitated for money".[13] Never ones to rely too much on common sense, they scrapped their budget-busting ideas in favour of borrowing money, and they rented the house of the "famous picture-drawer" Rubens from his widow.[14] The house was beautiful and grand: decorated with paintings of classical figures, busts of classical scholars, and with large windows around an internal courtyard. Their new home was only a few streets away from the Platin Press – Europe's foremost printer of fine books – and was close to the wealthy and well-connected Duarte family, whom the Cavendishes met through William's distant cousin, the well-known society figure Lady Utricia Swann.

In this seclusion – "exile" seems almost the wrong word for a lifestyle so fruitful and stimulating – and without the distraction of pregnancy, children, or a growing family, William, Margaret, and William's brother Charles set up something of an academy. William continued his relationship with Hobbes, and on one occasion even brought him together with his philosophical adversary, Descartes, at a dinner party in Paris.[15] The dinner (also attended by the French priest, philosopher, and atomist Pierre Gassendi) must have been a fascinating, highly wrought occasion: Gassendi and Hobbes were friends, but both had disagreed with Descartes, and had even published their objections to his *Meditations* (1641). The dinner conversation was surely tantalising, if tense – Charles wrote that they "agree in some opinions" but "extremely differ in others" – but Margaret could not have joined in at all: she claimed she spoke no French, and Descartes no English.[16]

Also during this period, Hobbes's major work on society, man, and government, *De Cive*, was published in English complete with a dedication to one of William's relatives, who was confusingly also called William Cavendish (the Earl of Devonshire). Hobbes's *Leviathan* was published in the same year, and Charles Cavendish's notebooks and letters to the mathematician Dr John Pell reveal a continued correspondence between the family and the philosopher.[17]

The family also came to know Richard Flecknoe – later the unfortunate subject of Andrew Marvell's satire "Flecknoe, An English Priest at Rome" (he laments his "hideous verse"), and victim of Dryden's attack on fellow poet Thomas Shadwell *MacFlecknoe* (*c*.1678) – through their relationship with the Duchess of Lorraine.[18] Flecknoe wrote poems and plays in payment for staying at the Rubens house, and one of his plays would later be performed on the Restoration stage under the direction of William Davenant, another of the Cavendishes' literary hangers-on. Nor were their interests limited to plays: they also spent time with the esteemed Dutch composer and poet – and former friend of John Donne – Constantijn Huygens.

Away from this cosmopolitan literary world, the small family of Margaret, William, and Charles spent much of their time together, and William and Charles took it upon themselves to educate Margaret. In her later works, Margaret records how thankful she was for this attention:

I found the world too difficult to be understood by my tender years and weak capacity, that till the time I was married, I could only read the letters and join the words, but understood nothing of the sense of the world, until my Lord, who was learned by experience, as my master, instructed me[19]

Margaret's depiction of herself as of "weak capacity" is needlessly, consciously self-abasing – she had simply not had access to anything other than the patchiest of educations – but her description of her husband teaching her is touching: within two years, she would transform his instruction into poetry and prose that demonstrated her growing understanding of the "sense of the world".

From William, Margaret learned about politics, history, and war, and his occasionally Hobbesian theories of government and society. From his brother, Margaret learned about science: he had a particular interest in optics and mathematics, and took pains to include his new sister-in-law in his discoveries. He even bought her a model of the Copernican planetary system to allow her to see how the planets worked, and discussed with her theories about atoms, science, and mathematics that he read in Latin, and would have otherwise been inaccessible to her. She had access to the scientific experiments Charles was performing, and to his equipment: her later writings reveal a first-hand experience of experiments with mercury, and of the zoomed-in sight provided by a microscope.[20]

William and Charles's enlightened approach to educating women was not limited to Margaret. William's three daughters from his first marriage – Jane, Frances, and Elizabeth – grew up with the privilege of being at the centre of a web of Restoration intellectuals. When she was married, Jane was the recipient of a poem by William Davenant and Elizabeth, of course, married into the Egerton family who were renowned for their literary and musical patronage. Alice Spencer, Elizabeth's husband's grandmother, had even supported at various times Donne, Shakespeare, and Spenser.[21] But their intellectual exposure was not limited to patronage and marriage. William was an adoring father, and in one letter, wrote each of his children a couplet and left space beneath for them to complete their own.[22] William may not have been the best poet to learn from, but his commitment to educating his daughters is clear.

And his daughters did not squander their literary lives. In 1644, William escaped into exile with his two sons, leaving Jane, Frances, and Elizabeth behind at Welbeck, where their mother had recently died in 1643. The women were in the house when it fell to the Earl of Manchester's forces later in 1644, and, like the women discussed in Chapter 3, had lived amongst Royalist soldiers or with the threat of Parliamentary invasion for many years. Jane, the eldest – who also negotiated their finances with the Protectorate Committee for Compounding, and worked to safeguard some of the treasures at Bolsover Castle – spoke with the Earl of Manchester with "great civility", and ensured the sisters were able to continue living there with a garrison of "Notts' men". Either whilst living with the soldiers or in the later months of conflict (Welbeck was momentarily Royalist again in 1645), Jane and Elizabeth wrote a masque. Their decision to do so was evidently influenced by having seen Jonson's performances in their youth, and there is even the possibility that they still had the costumes on hand to be able to stage it despite the violence and chaos around them.[23] *The Concealed Fansyes* is found in two manuscript volumes, along with poetry by the sisters. The handsomely bound volumes in a scribal hand are proof enough that William valued his daughters' intellectual development.[24]

And he was right to do so. The plot of the sisters' masque has often been thought to be a proto-feminist rewriting of Shakespeare's *The Taming of the Shrew*: in Jane and Elizabeth's play, it is the men who have to be taught to behave properly in marriage, and end the drama chastened and altered.[25] But it is also, in part, a rewriting of Shakespeare's earlier play *Love's Labour's Lost*: just as in Shakespeare's version, the women have to keep the all-too-idiotic men at bay as they attempt to court them. The Cavendish sisters were at no loss for literary influences or inspiration, and nor were they embarrassed by their feminine authorship. The opening prologue proclaims that the "truth of our new Play... doth become a woman's wit the very way".[26] Like Shakespeare's *Love's Labour's Lost*, there is comedy: one of the sisters, Luceny, is so bored with her suitor always "speaking in a formal way" and repeating that "he loved me" that she tells him she could not "love so dull a brain as he had" and wishes he would "say he hated me, for that would be some variety".[27]

But there is also touching realism in *The Concealed Fansyes*. At the beginning of the masque, one of the unreformed men remarks "as soon as I am married I will let her know I am her husband... She shall neither look, walk, or speak, but I will be her perpetual vexation."[28] The same man remarks that his wife will not be allowed to speak to male servants, and tells of how he will torment her by keeping her locked up in the countryside whilst he "praise the Ladies in London". The masque was written some years after Elizabeth had been married to John Egerton, but before she went to live with him – she was, at that time, "too young to be bedded".[29] William may have been able to educate his daughters, and preserve and revere their literary works, but he could not protect them from the fear of men and marriage that being a woman in seventeenth-century England naturally inspired.

Across the sea in Antwerp, Margaret had taken a leaf out of the Cavendish daughters' book. As early as 1650, if not before, she had taken to writing down her thoughts about the education she was receiving from William and Charles, and testing the limits of her imagination by composing essays, discourses, and allegories. These writings would later become Margaret's third printed book, *The Worlds Olio* (1655), but their place in her publication history belies their place in her intellectual development. Here – in her essays on everything from monasticism to monarchical government; from Cleopatra to Elizabeth I – is the earliest proof of Margaret's wide-ranging, capacious mind applying itself to anything that touched her sphere. Her excitement in writing – "I have studied upon observations, and lived upon contemplation, making the World my Book" – is tempered only by her realisation that doing so calmed her.[30] Whilst previously, her "thoughts were like travellers seldom at home" and her "mind in disorder", she credits her husband, William, with teaching her how to "fortify it with patience":

> My mind is become an absolute monarch, ruling alone, my thoughts as a peaceable Commonwealth, and my life an expert Soldier, which my Lord settled, composed, and instructed[31]

Her imagery is unfailingly, unabashedly Royalist, but her sentiments are poignant: in the act of writing, and learning about the world from her husband, Margaret had finally found a cure for her melancholy – and without a potion of powdered frogs in sight.

And what Margaret wrote was as brilliantly eclectic as her education. After an opening epistle to the reader in which she apologises for the haphazard nature of the book and writes the immortal sentence "if any take a delight to read it, I will not thank them for it; for if anything please therein, they are to thank me for so much pleasure", the book then opens with essays on fame – a hallmark of her later works.[32] For Margaret "fame" is a natural response to "a doubt of an after being"; it is an alternative to the afterlife, and is "more particularly a man's own, than the child of his loins".[33] Her masculine imagery hides how sensitive a subject this notion of procreation was for Margaret. She writes brief essays on everything that comes into her mind – "the reason why old men love to tell stories..." – and challenges historical preconceptions: she wonders why Cleopatra "should be so infamous for a whore, since she was constant to those men she had taken". She wrote about Queen

Elizabeth, Henry VIII, and Richard III, alongside the classical figures of Lucretia, Caesar, Brutus, and Penelope. The breadth of her new-found education is found on every inky page. And there are hints of the Margaret that was to come later: the fiercely independent thinker. She disagrees with her husband's beliefs about the wasteful nature of monasticism – for Margaret, monks prevent the "overpopulating" of the Commonwealth, and help the Church in "nurs[ing] the quiet people" – and demonstrates her ability to write against the received opinions of the day:

> It is better, to be an Atheist, than a superstitious man; for in Atheism there is humanity, and civility, towards man to man; but superstition regards no humanity[34] *

Margaret was not just taking delight in putting pen to paper, but in stretching her capacities to confront any subject that came into her orbit.

But, unfortunately for Margaret, this delight would not last. By November 1651, she had to lock her work "up in a trunk", as if it "had been buried in a Grave", and leave it behind in Antwerp.[35] The woman who was so afraid of travel, and had recently found happiness in writing, learning, and living with her husband, had to board ship again and travel to London. She would not be reunited with William for a year and a half.

* * *

In 1651, Charles Cavendish's estates were, once again, sequestered: this was the means by which Parliament confiscated the money and land of those they deemed to be "delinquents". In order to regain possession, the delinquent had to pay a fine and, in some cases, appear in front of the Committee for Compounding. The dependents of those who had had their

---

* Margaret's atheism – or, at the very least, non-traditional theism – would later come to cause her difficulties. See Chapter 11.

estates compounded could claim for some portion to be paid to them – Jane, William's eldest daughter, had been claiming a fifth of William's estate since she appeared in front of the Committee in 1650.[36] In Charles's case, he now had to return to England to reclaim his estates, something he was loath to do. He was terrified of imprisonment and, even worse, of having to take "the Engagement" – the oath of allegiance to the Commonwealth that had been passed in 1650 as a response to the execution of Charles I in 1649. For a Royalist, it was anathema; it was akin to admitting that the conflict was completely over, and that no monarchy would ever return.

But unfortunately for Charles, the Cavendishes were even more broke than usual. William pressured his brother into returning – William himself could not return on pain of death – to try to restore some of their financial security. In November 1651, Charles packed himself up to travel to England, and began his journey with his travelling companion: Margaret.

When, in 1650, the Rump Parliament decided that an "Engagement" was necessary for the citizens to prove their loyalty, they left out a significant portion of the population: only men over the age of eighteen had to take it. Women were, naturally, thought to be so politically ignorant as to make their taking the Engagement redundant. But what started as an exclusion of women from public life ended up, paradoxically, heightening their role. As women did not have to swear against their Royalist beliefs to engage in public life – or, in Margaret's case, return to England – they could appear in front of the Committee and ask for a portion of their husband's estates without sacrificing their political integrity. It was in this capacity as William's emissary that Margaret left her new-found happiness in Antwerp, and boarded a boat to London: William's estates were being sold to fund the war in Ireland, and one-fifth of the proceeds (the proportion to which wives and dependents were entitled) would do much to alleviate their considerable financial distress.

The whole of Charles and Margaret's journey was marked by their poverty. In her biography of her husband, Margaret wrote that she only left Antwerp as a result of William's "extreme want and necessity"; her journey was funded by a "small provision of money" that could barely help them make it to London; and, upon their arrival, Charles attempted to use his credit to raise a loan but, instead, had to pawn his watch.[37] The pair settled in Covent Garden, and went about trying to glean any money possible from the Cavendish estates. In the meantime, they feared starvation, struggled to get credit and had to send what little money they did have back to Margaret's husband who was in "far greater distress". By the time their money reached William, he had managed, as ever, to charm his creditors with a great speech about his misfortunes.[38]

London in 1651 was not the London that Margaret would have known in her childhood, nor the London she saw briefly in 1644: poverty was the order of the day, entertainment was scanty, with the playhouses closed or demolished, and the Royalists who were present in town were preoccupied with petitioning Parliament for their estates. Anglican worship had been banned in favour of Puritanism, and even the pre-war pastime of riding in Hyde Park had been all but destroyed by the war. In the 1651 "Character of England" – a letter written by a French nobleman and translated for publication by John Evelyn – the depressing state of things was made clear: the park, formerly "used by the late King and Nobility for the freshness of the air" was now owned by a "publican" who made every "coach and horse which enters" pay.[39] Writing in 1653 in his own diary, Evelyn was even more damning: the park was now owned by a "sordid fellow".[40]

What they lacked in entertainment, Charles and Margaret did not make up for in financial success: Charles was only able to regain some of his estates after paying such a hefty fine that he had to sell some of his land, and Margaret had no such luck.[41] She appeared before the Committee on 10 December 1651, but she was so terrified by the prospect that her only living brother, John Lucas, spoke on her behalf. She was denied even the one-fifth proportion normally allotted to wives. In the Committee's words, William was an "excepted person" and she had married him "since he became a delinquent": she left with nothing, and would later write that she "whisperingly spoke" to her brother and asked him to "conduct [her] out of that ungentlemanly place".[42]*

Margaret's dislike of appearing in front of the Committee – she later wrote that "she did not stand as a beggar at the Parliament door" and never "haunt[ed] the committees" – was not just her natural shyness, nor her natural snobbery (at this time many poor widows of Royalist soldiers were attempting to get money from Parliament). It was also a desire to distance herself from another aspect of the Civil War conflict. While many women had been involved in the conflict, there were others whose involvement had been less physical, and more political: women had petitioned men who held power throughout the wars, intervening in the political landscape as women. They had, in the case of the dissenting Levellers, petitioned for spiritual equality; or, in the case of many Parliamentarian women, had petitioned against the king and "Popish Lords".[43] The majority of these wartime petitions were on the side of the Parliamentarians, and many of their detractors had accused the women of being little more than braying "fishwives" or "oyster wenches". Margaret's appearance in the public world of politics was, she wanted to tell her readers, something different altogether: it was reluctant, mediated by the men in her family, and personal rather than political. Her modesty is a far cry from her decision to publish her poetry a year and a half later. But, regardless of how

---

* Ann Fanshawe, Cavendish's contemporary in Civil War Oxford, also tried to regain some of her husband's estates, and wrote in her memoir to her children that it was "the first time I had taken a journey without your father".

Margaret's natural conservatism and Royalism displays itself in her account of her appearance in front of the committee, the truth is that it did not work: she and William would continue in their impoverished state until after the Restoration.

* * *

If Charles and Margaret had limited success in getting access to money, there were other benefits of their stay in London: William's two sons were in the capital (and similarly broke), as were, sporadically, his daughters. Here, Margaret had a chance to meet the rest of the family she had married into, even if the prospect of a life together after exile would have seemed so far off as to be impossible. More importantly for Margaret, she had the chance to see her own family: her brothers, Charles and Thomas, had died in the fighting, and her mother and one of her sisters had died during the war. But her beloved Catherine was still present – and lived near her lodgings in Covent Garden. This was the sister Margaret had worried about when she was sleeping, and would interrupt her prayers if she thought they had taken too long: their reunion after years of war, danger, and death must have been dramatically emotional.

Margaret did not, however, spend all her time with her family: she left her lodgings sparingly, but enough for "report" to "dress her in a hundred several fashions" (her poverty had not hindered her acquisition of glamorous outfits). She gained entry to one of the Royalist coteries at the heart of the city's intellectual life.[44]

Henry Lawes was a composer and music tutor who had written the music for Milton's *Comus* – he had, indeed, even obtained the commission from the Egerton family – and had acted in the masque as the Attendant Spirit. He was a well-connected figure in Royalist intellectual circles and, during the Commonwealth, opened his house up for music performances. His salons were collections of Royalist intellectual talent: he published volumes of their writings on three occasions in 1653, 1655, and 1658 under the name of *Ayres, and Dialogues* – the first of which even included a posthumous contribution from Margaret's brother, Sir Charles Lucas. Lawes was not just a supporter of Royalist writers and thinkers, but of women, too: he fostered the career of the poet Katherine Philips, and corresponded with her "Society of Friendship" – a group of writers who all corresponded under pseudonyms drawn from pastoral romances.

Katherine Philips was a direct contemporary of Cavendish's in the world of early modern women's writing: she was writing poetry in the 1650s and 60s which circulated in manuscript, and was often held up as the pinnacle of the "modest" female writer in comparison to her other contemporary, Aphra Behn. Her subject – neo-platonic friendship – was seen as more fitting for women than Behn's bawdy plays (despite her political undertones), and she was revered after her death by John Dryden. Philips and Lawes wrote to each other, and Philips met many of her other correspondents through him: she even appeared, identified only by her initials, in a printed volume of verses by the coterie in honour of the late Royalist William Cartwright.[45]

There is every chance that Cavendish could have met Philips at Lawes's evenings – she reports attending "three or four times" – or, even if they did not meet, she would have heard of her success.[46] In Antwerp Cavendish had, finally, received an education befitting a writer, but here in London, despite her poverty and the straitened circumstances, she saw the possibility of writing for an audience, and having her work read by her contemporaries. Philips did not publish in print until 1664 – and even then, only in a (supposedly) unauthorised edition – but she did engage in "scribal publication": that is, her works were read in manuscript by a limited circle, and were written with this form of public visibility in mind.[47]

If, as some scholars have argued, Philips offered Cavendish a model of female publication that would inspire her – and that she would later cast aside in favour of print – there is also something more crucial about her brush with Philips.[48] *The*

Worlds Olio is, with one exception at the end of the book, a volume of Margaret's prose. She does write *about* poets – "the thoughts of Poets must be quick" – but there is no sense of her own identification with them except in the book's "Epistles", which were written for the book's publication in 1655. In her writings in Antwerp – prior to her journey to London – Margaret sees poets as something separate to herself. In one of her short essays, this distinction becomes clear:

> They are not mistaken that think all Poets wits, but those are mistaken that think there is no other wit but in Poets [...] or only in words or method, or scholastical knowledge, for many may be very wise and knowing, yet have not much wit.[49]

Cavendish's short essay is a bid for her own wit to be taken seriously: earlier on in the volume, she has apologised for her lack of method and "scholastic knowledge" but here she is claiming she can have wit – the "swiftest motion of the brain" – all the same. When writing in Antwerp, she included "poets" in the world of knowledge of which she is not a part. Could Cavendish's introduction to Philips – either in person, or through the grapevine of Royalist London – have convinced her that women could, after all, write poetry? Within nine months of returning to England, Cavendish turned to verse – and, unlike Philips, she would soon commit her verses to the more public sphere of the printing press and publication.

7

The first English poet of your sex

O N THE MORNING of 1 May 1653, Dorothy Osborne –
the fiancée of the diplomat and statesman Sir William
Temple and now-renowned lady of letters – was in a tizz. Her
father was so ill that she could not "reasonably hope he should
outlive" the day, and her soon-to-be-husband, William, could
not be with her in her affliction: her family disapproved of
the match, and their relationship was limited to their letters.[1]
Dorothy had enough to worry about, but she still ended her
letter to William with the feverish question "Let me ask you if
you have seen a book of poems newly come out, made by my
Lady Newcastle?". Osborne's interest was not one of a purely
literary nature: "For God's sake if you meet with it send it
me", she demanded of William, "they say 'tis ten times more
extravagant than her dress."

Just over a month later, Osborne had come by her prize.
The obliging friend or servant who had walked up Ludgate
Hill, down the Old Bailey, through Cheapside, and stopped
in the crowded bookshop of John Martin and James Allestree
– in later years, the favoured bookseller of both Samuel Pepys
and the scientist Robert Hooke – would have found something
rather unexpected amidst the chaos of printed sermons,
religious tracts, and scientific pamphlets. The pre-Great Fire St
Paul's Cathedral, where Martin and Allestree sold their works
alongside the city's other booksellers, was crowded, riotous,

and more a hub of social activity than it was of religious devotion. Even in the midst of all these books by celebrated figures, the "Lady Newcastle's" volume of poems was still something exceptional.

Having found the bookshop (Martin and Allestree sold under the sign of the bell; other booksellers chose everything from angels to serpents to bishops' heads) Osborne's emissary would have been greeted by a book that boasted everything from rhymed couplets on the "new science" and atomism, to verses on the real existence of fairies, and elegies for those who had been killed in the Civil War.[2] And, before the reader even reached Cavendish's scandalous verses, they had something else to contend with. On the title page, Margaret's name – "WRITTEN By the Right HONOURABLE, the Lady MARGARET Countesse of NEWCASTLE"[*] – was printed almost as large as the book's title, *Poems and Fancies*: there was no mistaking who had written this book, or that the author was a woman.[3] Some editions even featured engravings of Margaret in the guise of a classical statue wearing a crown and flanked by Apollo and Athena. Cavendish was not just any poet; she was, in her eyes, the heir to the classical tradition.[†]

When Dorothy Osborne read her copy, the boldness of Cavendish's publication did not delight her. Prior to reading, she was already sceptical – "sure, the poor woman is a little distracted, she could never be so ridiculous else as to venture at writing books, and in verse too" – but by the time she had

---

[*] Margaret's noble title on the volume's first page was the subject of debate: it seems to have been reset and reprinted at least three times, occasionally with "Countess" crossed out and "Marchioness" added in. Titles during the Interregnum were a political issue: in England, William had lost the status that Charles I had conferred upon him during the war. He was now only an earl, and his wife a countess. See *Poems and Fancies: A Digital Critical Edition*, ed. Liza Blake.

[†] These title pages are thought to have been added in by Cavendish herself when she was sending out copies to leading intellectuals.

finished the book, she was not quite so kind.[4] "You need not send me my Lady Newcastle's book at all, for I have seen it, and am satisfied that there are many soberer people in Bedlam", she wrote to William.[5]

* * *

Osborne's accusation of insanity ("I'll swear her friends are much to blame to let her go abroad") is hardly fair, but it is at least somewhat understandable.[6] If Cavendish was not mad, she was certainly unorthodox. In the half-decade of her birth, only eight works by women were published – an estimated 0.5 per cent of all books printed in the period.[7] By 1651 to 1655 – the years in which Cavendish published the four volumes *Poems and Fancies*, *Philosophical Fancies*, *The Worlds Olio*, and *Philosophical and Physical Opinions* – fifty-nine new works by women appeared; an estimated 1.3 per cent of total publications. The comparatively small percentage jump belies the dramatic uptick: publication, as a whole, had also increased. But the vast majority of these works by women were religious in tone and were often, more specifically, Quaker writings.[8] In the decade 1650 to 1660, religious texts made up around 61 per cent of all published writing by women. Literature – poetry, plays, and ballads – made up only 0.016 per cent: that is, there were only two volumes by women published in these genres. And in Cavendish's other medium, prose, only 0.09 per cent of all works published were written by women: works of maternal advice, spiritual lives, and political argument dwarfed rhyme, verse, and literature. In an age when so many women could read and write and – as manuscript evidence shows – were engaged in writing poetry and creative literature, why were they so unwilling to publish? And why were they even more unwilling to publish under their own names?

The answer to these questions lies not simply in debates over gender, but in the nature of early modern print culture. Print had arrived in England with William Caxton in 1476, and was, by the seventeenth century, a substantial business. The Stationers' Company had been set up in the early fifteenth century and had become the guild for publishers and printers. Printing was confined to those men who had served as apprentices in the company, and had become "freemen".[9] By 1649, there were around forty printing houses in the city – a number which rose to fifty-nine by the time of the Restoration.[10] Why, then, is it an oft-cited fact that four of the most significant poetry books of the period – Donne's *Poems* (1633), Herbert's *The Temple* (1633), Sidney's *Astrophel and Stella* (in *Arcadia*: 1590, 1593) and the anthology *Tottells Miscellany* (1557) – were published only posthumously?[11]

Many of the great writers of English poetry of the period – Donne, Sidney, and Rochester – circulated their work only in manuscript. This form of publication did not prevent their poems from being known, and much revered, beyond their immediate circle. Indeed, William Cavendish's manuscript collection of poetry does invite the possibility that he too had access to Donne's work prior to the printed 1633 edition.[12] What manuscript publication did prevent, however, was the possibility of censorship or punishment for what was written. Throughout the sixteenth century, the government had issued proclamations which seemed to see no difference between print and scribal publication. A 1570 proclamation railed against "traitorous or lewd" books, and made it clear that this referred to both mediums: "in writing or in print".[13] Manuscript works did, frequently, make their way far beyond the original pen and hands of the author: just because these works were written by hand did not mean that they were not, in any meaningful sense, "published". But for all the proclamations that treated manuscript and print the same, one simple fact remained: it was far easier to circulate seditious material in manuscript. It did not have to go through the censorship of the Royal Court and the Star Chamber, and the smaller number of copies circulating made it much easier for works to avoid critical eyes. In the Renaissance and the seventeenth century, the fear of angering the authorities over an ill-chosen book or pamphlet was justified. In 1579, John Stubbs found this out only too late: in response to a pamphlet which suggested Elizabeth I was too old to have children and so should not marry the Duke d'Anjou, he and his publisher had their right hands cut off with a meat cleaver.

Alongside the ever-present threat of public mutilation (in the 1630s, another pamphleteer, William Prynne, had his ears cut off and his cheeks branded for his writing) there was another reason that authors may not have chosen the printing press. Back in 1951, the academic J. W. Saunders set out a case for the "stigma of print": his analysis noticed that the leading court poets in the Tudor period did not write for print, and those poets who *did* condescend to have their works touched by a printing press "liked to cover their fall through... deceptions, disclaimers and evasions" – claims that the book was printed without their knowledge, or their permission.[14] Poets wanted to see their work in print and dedicate their books to powerful, wealthy people who might then give them patronage – but they were also embarrassed by having to do so, and by the vulnerability of having to put their work on so public a stage. Passing a work through the printing press and out into the world of booksellers had something of an ungentlemanly, "mechanic, stipendiary status".[15]

As history shows, this did not, of course, stop many writers from using print – nor did it stop those who had written for the press from turning to manuscript in other cases. Mary Sidney, the Countess of Pembroke (and sister to Philip Sidney) published both his posthumous works and her own works of French translations in print in the late 1590s. But for their joint work on the Psalms, the *Sidney Psalter* (her first work of original, poetic writing – her metrical innovation and imagery go beyond "translation") she chose manuscript circulation. Once again, circulating in manuscript did not mean that the *Psalter* was unseen, or unpublished: Mary even went so far as to present a copy to Elizabeth I. The boundary between manuscript and print was far more permeable than it might seem to modern eyes, when we associate manuscript works with dusty, undigitised archives.

But however important the "stigma of print" was to Tudor and Renaissance writers, it was of dwindling relevance in the seventeenth century. Publication had increased and, especially during the years of the Interregnum and Civil War, many of the normal coteries for manuscript circulation were disbanded – along with many of the opportunities for patronage. Milton had been writing for print since his 1641 debut, *Of Reformation Touching Church-Discipline in England* – a Republican call for reform in the Church of England. But he, too, was seemingly anxious about publishing his poetry: it took until 1645, decades after he had started writing poetry, for a volume to appear in print bearing his own name. His other published works – "On Shakespeare", *Lycidas*, and *Comus* – had appeared only anonymously, or marked by his initials.

For women writers, however, the stigma was more long-lasting and less connected to notions of poetic status. Publication was, for them, not just a slightly grubby way of gaining public appreciation and an audience. It was, instead, anathema to the prized feminine virtues of chastity and modesty: it put women's words – and the women authors themselves – out into the public marketplace. In a satire of print culture written in 1604, the author Anthony Scoloker wrote:

He is a man in print, and tis enough he hath under-gone a Pressing (yet not like a Lady) though for your sakes and for Ladies, protesting for this poor Infant of his Brain, as it was the price of his Virginity born into the world in tears[16]

Scoloker is mocking the type of disavowals authors made at the beginning of their books which led to the identification of the "stigma of print", but there is also something else going on here. "A Pressing" – meaning the printing press – had another meaning in Elizabethan England. It was slang for the woman's role during sex: she was "pressed" by the man. The birth of his text ("the poor infant of his brain") is akin to the imagery women use to refer to their books, but his satire suggests something else: printing was associated with femininity and vulnerability – a vulnerability that Scoloker laughs at.[17]

If printing was itself oddly coded as female, this did not mean that it was open to women as a profession or pastime. It was not by accident that, when angrily responding to women writers, women on stage and, more specifically, a group of women's poems written on the death of John Dryden in 1700, an anonymous critic railed "What a Pox have the Women to do with Muses? [...] in that Sex they're much fitter for prostitution".[18] Forty years earlier, the Cavalier poet Richard Lovelace had made the link between publication and sexual immodesty even clearer:

> Now as herself a Poem she doth dresse,
> And curls a Line as she would do so a tresse;
> Powders a Sonnet as she does her hair,
> Then prostitutes them both to public Aire.[19]

And, in an attack on one of Aphra Behn's plays, Thomas Shadwell eschewed literary criticism in favour of arguing that she was little more than a whore who needed a "pimp to set her off".[20] Behn's profession in the theatre left her particularly vulnerable to crude sexist attacks, including one from William Wycherley in which he remarked "now men enjoy your parts for half a crown".[21] For women, publication – like acting on the Restoration stage – was akin to whoredom: both professions opened them up to abuse, criticism, and the prying eyes of all-too-lascivious critics.

* * *

By 1653, Cavendish had some forebears in the world of women's published writing. In the years of the Civil War, the number of women's political, prophetic, and spiritual texts had all increased. This was, in part, due to the increase in the population of dissenting communities, where there was a greater focus on equality, and a belief – however grudging – of the equal value of all believers recording their interactions with God.[22] Women like the Presbyterian prophetess Mary Cary printed their spiritual revelations.[*] Cary's books mixed Puritan theology with political purpose: she believed a Parliamentarian victory would bring about the creation of God's Kingdom on Earth. The Baptist Jane Turner – a direct contemporary of Cavendish as her book was also published in 1653 – wrote and printed a spiritual autobiography, *Choice Experiences*, at a time when women's life-writing was all but confined to manuscript. And Quaker women's writing alone accounts for 45 per cent of all women's printed books in the 1650s; Cavendish was not short of examples of religious sisters who had already chosen to publish. Lady Eleanor Davies – the sister of the Earl of Castlehaven, the man who was executed for rape and sodomy and may or may not have had a link to Milton's *Comus* – was unusual in being an aristocratic prophetess: her works were published throughout the 1620s, 30s, and 40s, and some were even printed in Amsterdam after she failed to get a licence to print in England.

And women also wrote in a decidedly more secular genre. The "mother's advice" book was a popular genre throughout the seventeenth century – it was a book written from a mother to her children, a particularly intimate and familiar printed text. Lady Brilliana Harley (one of the women who resisted a siege during the war) wrote a small, quarto-sized handwritten book of advice to her son, but confined her wisdom to manuscript.[23] Dorothy Leigh, on the other hand, published her book, *The Mothers Blessing*, in 1616 – complete with

---

[*] Despite the similarity in name, Mary Cary is a different author to Lady Mary Carey, who wrote about her miscarriages and children.

the recognition that she was doing something which might invite "censure".[24] But Leigh was not the first: she had been preceded by Elizabeth Grymeston, whose book *Miscelanea. Meditations. Memoratives* was published in 1604, and dedicated "to her loving son"– her only living child out of the nine she had given birth to.[25] In 1622, Elizabeth Clinton, the Countess of Lincoln, made the genre more aristocratic when she published *The Countess of Lincoln's Nursery*.

But religious experience, prophecy, and maternal advice books – however brave their authors were to publish – were not quite the same as Cavendish's poetry and philosophy. In these genres, Cavendish had far fewer non-anonymous forebears. In 1621, Lady Mary Wroth (the niece of Philip Sidney and Mary, Countess of Pembroke) followed in the family tradition and published a prose-romance akin to Sidney's *Arcadia*. Her romance – *The Countess of Montgomery's Urania* – appeared in a handsome folio (a large, expensive format) complete with engravings of the fantasy world she had described, and a none-too-subtle evocation of the author's poetic and aristocratic lineage:

> ... written by the right honourable Lady Mary Wroath. Daughter to the right Noble Robert, Earle of Leicester – And Niece to the ever famous, and renowned Sir Philip Sidney knight. And to the most excellent Lady Mary Countess of Pembroke late deceased[26]

There was no chance that *Urania* could be mistaken for a work by a man, or that any reader buying the book in John Marriot and John Grismand's bookshop in the city (marked by a sign of the gun) could mistake Mary Wroth's heritage. *Urania* was even named after a character in Sidney's *Arcadia*. Like the 1590 edition of Sidney's book, Wroth's *Urania* ends mid-sentence, and also has a sonnet-sequence appended to the volume. But, unlike Sidney's *Astrophel and Stella*, Wroth's *Pamphilia to*

Amphilanthus takes its characters and its themes from the prose-romance of the preceding pages: her created world spills over into her poetry, which is thought to be the second sonnet sequence to have been written by a woman. The first – Anne Lock's translations of Psalm 51 – was published under the initials "A.L" in 1560, and is also thought to be the first sonnet sequence by a poet of either gender.[*] Wroth's sequence is certainly the first by a woman that is secular rather than religious, and she departs from her forbears in interesting ways. A typical sonnet in *Astrophel and Stella* focuses on Stella's appearance. Sidney's Astrophel is obsessed by Stella's eyes, and hardly less enamoured with her face:

> *Queen Virtue's court, which some call Stella's face,*
> *Prepared by Nature's chiefst furniture,*
> *Hath his front built of alabaster pure;*
> *Gold is the covering of that stately place.*[27]

In comparison, Wroth's Pamphilia refuses to describe Amphilanthus's body – and, indeed, never mentions his name. A "blazon", the describing of individual bodily attributes, does not appear in Wroth's poem. This is not to say that the text is chaste – the whole sequence is sensual and passionate, as Wroth's speaker describes her love and emotional torment – but that Wroth has broken with the Sidnean tradition she has so consciously emulated and lauded elsewhere. Despite her relatives and the tradition in which she is writing, she is under no illusion as to how radical and original her work is.

But after the book was published in 1621, Wroth's readers

---

[*] Historically, Anne Lock's authorship of this sequence has been debated, but in *The Collected Works of Anne Lock*, ed. Susan Felch (New York: State University of New York, 1999), Felch makes a convincing study for her authorship – and one that is backed up by the discussion of Lock in Margaret P. Hannay's work on psalms and women's writing.

failed to see the brilliance of what she had written. One courtier, the later Earl of Norwich Sir Edward Denny, took the book to be a *roman à clef* filled with veiled topical references to other aristocratic families. He objected to being the source for one of Wroth's storylines (one sordid story, in which an unfortunate swain accuses his wife of adultery, only for her father to try to kill her, found rather spurious echoes in the life of Denny's only daughter, Honoria). In response to this perceived slight, Denny wrote an insulting poem in which he called Wroth a "Hermaphrodite in show, in deed a monster", lambasted her "witt" which "runs madd not caring who it strike", and accused her of being unchaste: "common oysters such as thine gape wide / And take in pearles or worse at every tide".[28] Not content with these insults, Denny wrapped up the poem with a verdict on women who write: "Work o th'Works leave idle books alone / For wise and worthier women have writt none."

In response to the furore, Wroth replied with her own poem in which she called him a "drunken beast" – but, despite her bravado, she was evidently shaken: she later claimed that she had not been involved with the publication of the manuscript despite evidence to the contrary.[29] And she shunned print for the second volume of *Urania*: it circulated in manuscript only amongst her friends and family.

Sir Edward Denny should not have been so shocked by the existence of women who refused to "leave idle books alone". By 1621, Wroth had one notable forebear. In 1611, the non-aristocratic, middle-class woman Aemilia Lanyer published her volume of poems *Salve Deus Rex Judaeorum*. The religious title belies the radicalism of its contents: it was the first volume of poetry to be published by an English woman, and one of the first records of a woman writer attempting to secure patronage for herself. Her opening poems are all dedicated to women she hoped might support her in her creative endeavours – from Lucy Russell, Countess of Bedford to Queen Anne, the wife of James I. The patronage she wanted was of an explicitly female nature, as was the readership she imagined for herself: she wrote poems to "all virtuous ladies in general", and, in her note to her "virtuous reader[s]" she explicitly imagines women reading her books.[30] But this wasn't the limit of her radicalism. One of her poems, "Eve's Apologie", is an argument not to blame Eve solely for the fall. "She (poor soul) by cunning was deceived", writes Lanyer, before continuing:

> But surely Adam can not be excused
> Her fault though great, yet he was most to blame;
> What Weaknesse offerd, Strength might have refused,
> Being Lord of all, the greater was his shame[31]

Lanyer's argument is that Adam's greater knowledge and power should have prevented him from acquiescing to Eve's suggestion: the fall was not Eve's fault, but "we (poor women) must endure it all". Lanyer's book was more of a "defence of woman" of the type than it was religious literature, and it received little attention during her lifetime or, indeed, for centuries afterwards.

* * *

Lady Mary Wroth and Aemilia Lanyer did write literature of the type that Margaret Cavendish was writing in the 1620s, even if her interests were rather different to sonnet sequences and defences of Eve. But the fact that the number of women who were publishing *literature* – as opposed to prayers, spiritual meditations, or prophecies – can be named on one hand proves that Cavendish's decision to publish her work in 1653 was more than unusual: it was nearly unprecedented. Unlike Wroth, she was separated from her husband and family and did not have a literary lineage to fall back on and, unlike Lanyer, she did not have the thin veneer of respectability that writing religious texts gave a woman.

Why, then, did Cavendish decide to publish in 1653? And just as importantly, how did she go about it?

When she had been in exile in Paris and Antwerp, writing had given Margaret a sense of internal calm and peace: her mind had been "settled, composed, and instructed" by her husband and the education he gave her.[32] Now without her husband in Commonwealth London – and with the Cromwellian Protectorate just about to be installed – she lacked this calm, and the outlet she had found. In the Preface to *Poems and Fancies*, she emphasised her disturbed mental state when describing the time when the poems were written:

> Since I came into England, being eight years out, and nine months in; and of these nine months, only some hours in the day, or rather in the night. For my rest being broken with discontent Thoughts, because I was from my Lord, and knowing him to be in great Wants, and my selfe in the same condition; to divert them, I wrote to turn the stream[33]

Like her works that would later become *The Worlds Olio*, Cavendish's poetry – perhaps written after she had met Katherine Philips or heard about her through the London Royalist coterie – was at least in part written as a mental exercise, to "divert" her thoughts from melancholy. This claim forms part of her "apology" to the readers: a request for them not to be "too severe" in their "censures". Her argument that it was essentially a private project, written when she couldn't sleep for fears over her husband, is an affirmation of her wifely dutifulness and modesty. In her autobiography, Cavendish similarly stresses her mental state – she "became very melancholy" as a result of being away from William, so much so that it did "break" her sleep and "distemper" her health – but does not link this distress to her writing.[34]

If writing poetry was a private project to assuage her anxiety, why did Cavendish publish her work at all? And why did she publish it with the brilliantly bold statement "all I desire is fame"? What if there was another reason for Margaret's decision to publish her poems? Could she, like the later Aphra

Behn – whom Virginia Woolf lauded as the first woman who made money by her pen – have published for money? In her preface to *Poems and Fancies* quoted above, there is certainly a hint that this was the case: she wrote not only to divert her "thoughts", but to "turn the stream" against the "great wants" of poverty that plagued both her and her husband.

In 1653, writing books was – then as now – a difficult means by which to make money: well into the eighteenth century, the "professional author" who made a fortune by his or her writing was a rare creature. And the way books were published was significantly different, too: booksellers or printers did not necessarily pay authors a percentage royalty for books sold, but instead paid a lump sum for the right to publish the copy.[35] But even this often meagre payment was not guaranteed: authors were often either paid in kind – that is, they were given copies of the book – or not paid at all. Many authors, including Margaret's husband William, paid the publishers to have their books printed.[36]

If this was the case, why and how could Margaret have had her book published? Just three years later, William wrote a letter from Antwerp which referred to the cost of printing his book on horsemanship: he had to borrow no less than £1,300, an enormous sum. While this was evidently feasible in 1656, it could not have been a possibility for Margaret and Charles in London in 1653. When William had written to his brother and wife just after they had arrived in London asking them to send him money, the most they had "at last" managed to come by on credit was £200. There is very little chance that they would have been able to fund the production of Margaret's book, which was an expensive, folio volume.[*]

---

[*] Some letters do imply that her later books were paid to be published – such as the one from Walter Charleton published in *A Collection of Letters and Poems* (London: 1678) in which he describes how "you bestow also great sums of Money in Printing Yours" – but there is no such evidence for this early volume.

Instead, there is every chance that Margaret was paid, however little, for her volume. At the end of the volume's prefatory material, and before the poetry "begins proper", is the verse "The Poetresse's Hasty Resolution". It records Cavendish's anxiety at publishing ("will you ... thus waste your time in vain / on that which in the world small praise shall gain") before going on to these lines:

> *...the printer spare,*
> *He'll lose by your ill poetry, I fear*[37]

Here is the evidence that Cavendish had not paid for this volume to be published: her printer and her booksellers, John Martin and James Allestree, stood to lose if she failed to sell enough copies. Even if she was not paid for her verse, she had certainly not paid for it to be published. A frustrating lack of material evidence for these types of arrangements exists, but there is a chance that Cavendish, like Aphra Behn, wrote for money. In her poverty-stricken years of 1651 to 1653, she would have had little choice.

In the absence of the smoking gun of evidence for Cavendish's status as a professional, paid writer, there are other clues to consider. In one of her autobiographical poems at the end of *Poems and Fancies*, she writes that she was rescued from "a storm of poverty" complete with "showers of miseries" and "thundr'ing creditors" by the "oars of honest industry".[38] Could the "honest industry" have been her writing? There would have been no form of employment possible – or conscionable – for the gentlemen in her life. And, in her preface to *Philosophical Fancies* (the book that was published later in 1653) she writes that she had "huddl'd" the book "up in haste" so as to "have it joined to my Book of Poems".[39] As it happened, her work arrived "a week too short of the press" and so was printed in a different volume. If a writer was paying to publish their works, the printers would undoubtedly be more sympathetic to a request to wait for more material. There is every chance that Cavendish was a paid, professional author. It could, also, have been the prospect of payment that persuaded her to print her material, rather than circulate it amongst family (as William's daughters did), or amongst friends (as Katherine Philips did). For a shy woman, laying her words out to everyone's eyes was a terrifying prospect – but one that Cavendish might have thought necessary if the money, however paltry a sum, would have alleviated her considerable poverty.

There is also Cavendish's choice of publishers to consider: Martin and Allestree were not a small, unimportant press. They had started working together under the sign of the bell in 1652, but both been in the business for some time. They would later rise to prominence as the official booksellers to the Royal Society, and would publish everything from Robert Hooke's *Micrographia* (1655) to John Evelyn's *Sylva* (1664).[40] By 1653, they had not yet published the big names of science, but they were still remarkably well-connected: Cavendish was certainly positioning herself as a professional woman of letters.

There is still a touching shyness to her volume. In the prefatory material, she describes how she fears she might "have proved a grief to the family I came from, and a dishonour to the family I am linked to".[41] She claims she had not told "any Friend" of her intention, for "it is easier to ask pardon than leave". She evidently had told William – he wrote a dedicatory poem for the volume in which he declared "I saw your poems, and then wished them mine" – but the only other person she had enlisted for help was her old maid, Elizabeth Topp.[42] It must have been Topp who ferried the pages to the publishers in St Paul's churchyard, and Topp who secretly carried the changes and pencil mark-ups back.

The "stigma of print" hovers over the reams and reams of prefatory material that Cavendish appended to her book. She writes, "The world may wonder at my confidence, how dare I put out a book, especially in these censorious times," before answering, "Why should I be ashamed, or afraid, where no evil is."[43] She is aware of the stigma, and denies it as she raises it: it is almost the opposite of the prefatory poems and notes found in older volumes that pretend the author had no knowledge that their work was to be published. She couches her publication in explicitly female terms – her opening note is to "all noble, and worthy ladies" asking them to "strengthen [her] side" in defending her book – and even quotes Sir Edward Denny's response to Mary Wroth's *Urania*.[44] In her characteristic combination of shyness and exhibitionism, conservatism and radicalism, Cavendish's writing career had begun.

* * *

When readers like Dorothy Osborne opened *Poems and Fancies*, they were in for a shock. Cavendish opened her volume with a dedication to her brother-in-law, Charles Cavendish, who also appears in one of the poems in the volume as a presence whilst Margaret was writing ("Sir Charles into my chamber coming in / When I was writing of my Fairy Queen").[45] Their relationship was evidently close, and the dedication is a heartfelt thanks for his compassion towards her during their stay in London together: "your kindness hath been such as you have neglected yourself".[46] But contained within such a normal dedication – complete with the expected modesty topos – is an arresting image. Cavendish writes that "studying or writing poetry" is the "spinning of the brain", and that she would have more properly spent her time "spinning with the fingers". She admits that she has not done what was expected of her sex, before abruptly performing an about-turn: she describes poetry in explicitly female terms. This spinning imagery continues – she writes of her literary "web" in terms that pre-date George Eliot's *Middlemarch*[*] by two centuries – and, in the next of her prefatory letters, she makes an even bolder claim:

---

[*] There is a chance that Eliot would have heard of Cavendish, and read her work: she would have certainly read Charles Lamb's *The Last Essays of Elia* (1833) in which he wrote of Cavendish as the most "princely woman".

> Besides, Poetry, which is built upon Fancy, Women may claime, as a *worke* belonging most properly to themselves: for I have observed that their brains work usually in a fantasticall motion, as in their several and various dresses, in their many and singular choices of cloathes and ribbons[47]

In an age in which many women were writing poetry – everyone from William's daughters, to Mary Sidney, and all the women who wrote verses on the deaths of their children or their miscarriages – to argue that poetry is a feminine medium is hardly very surprising. But to argue this in print, and to suggest that poetry is more feminine than masculine ("a work belonging most properly" to women) was radical: Cavendish was writing with the full knowledge of the manuscript tradition of women's poetry behind her, and was dragging them all into print alongside her. She was under no illusions as to how her book might be received – "I imagine I shall be censured by my own sex" – but this did not stop her from continuing.

The other prefatory verses and letters proceed along this tightrope between radicalism and conservatism, and bravery and modesty. Cavendish writes a letter to her oldest friend and servant, "Mistress" Topp, in which she recognises some might disdain her publishing career – and prints a letter from Topp back which affirms Cavendish's modesty and "honourable family".[48] Topp's compliment to Cavendish (and the title of this chapter) – "You are not only the first English Poet of your sex, but the first that ever wrote this way" – is more than just a claim for her brilliance (it echoes Jonson's verdict on Donne that he was "the first poet in the world in some things"). It is also a claim for her originality – but one that is partly mistaken: Cavendish was not the first woman to publish her poetry in print, even if she was the first to write "this way". Topp's wording is oddly specific: "the first *English* poet of your sex" leaves room for Anne Bradstreet, the American poet whose volume *The Tenth Muse* had appeared in England in 1650. Bradstreet was a Puritan and, despite some similarities to Cavendish and Topp's invocation of her, their work was very different.

Cavendish writes poems which liken her writing to her non-existent offspring – "alas it is my child" – and letters in which she argues that she wrote because she had "no children to employ [her] care" and "nothing for housewifery". But her apologies and conservative packaging of her work sit alongside a letter "To Natural Philosophers".[49] Here, again, is the modesty – "I never read, nor heard of any English Book to instruct me" – but it is incongruously followed by a statement of her intent. She is writing of her fear of the response to her books – "if it be praised... but if I am condemned, I shall be annihilated" – before she writes the sentence "my ambition is such, as I would either be a *World*, or nothing". If that statement of intent were not enough, she follows it up with this instruction:

> I desire all that are not quick in apprehending, or will not trouble themselves with such small things as *Atoms*, to skip this part of my Book... for fear these may seem tedious.

It is the typical Cavendish mix of humility and outlandish confidence: her disclaimer is not all that far from Ben Jonson's famous epigram "To the Reader", in which he asks only for readers who can "understand" his work.[50]

* * *

And Cavendish really did require readers who could "understand". After they made it through the thickets of prefatory poems and letters, readers were met with a volume that was split into five parts, with "clasps" of poems in between each section: she begins with natural philosophy, moves into moral philosophy, versifies her way through fragments of autobiography, describes a land of Queen Mab and fairies, and ends with a section focusing on the destruction of war. Even by the standards set by Lady Mary Wroth and Aemilia Lanyer, this was unprecedented in scope, and newfound territory. The volume opens with the poem entitled "Nature Calls a Counsel... to Advise about Making the World":

> When Nature first the world's foundation laid,
> She called a counsel how it might be made.
> Motion was first, who had a subtle wit,
> And then came Life, and Form, and Matter fit.
> First Nature spake: "My friends, if we agree,
> We can and may do a fine work," said she[51]

A female "Nature" who is creating the world, helped by "Life", "Form", and "Matter" – what is going on here? Cavendish has opened her book not only with a complicated description of natural philosophy, but with a possibly heretical, feminist one: in her description of the world's formation, there is no space for God at all. Instead, the world was formed by the feminine spirit of "Nature".

When she was in Paris and Antwerp, Cavendish's intellectual milieu – Hobbes; Descartes; Charles Cavendish; Pierre Gassendi – were all exponents of the "new science"; a seismic shift in scientific thinking and methodology that had grown and developed since Nicolaus Copernicus had started a revolution in 1514 with his theory that the planets moved around the sun, rather than vice versa. One of the most significant elements of the "new science" – and one that the exiled Cavendish circle was particularly interested in – was Epicurean "atomism": that is, the belief that everything in the world is either made of indivisible small atoms, or is itself an indivisible small atom.[52]

Atomism was the subject of much discussion amongst the exiles of the seventeenth century, and there was, by no means, one homogenous theory agreed by all its exponents. Pierre Gassendi (the third guest at the dinner party with Hobbes and Descartes) had recently published his work on Epicureanism, *Animadversiones* (1649), and Margaret must have been involved in discussions about it with her husband and Charles. Despite the growth of interest in atomism, even its simplest theories brought great problems for its followers. Thomas Hariot, an atomist during the sixteenth century, had published none of his theories, despite having happily published non-scientific works. And when the Epicurean philosopher (and correspondent of Margaret Cavendish) Walter Charleton published his atomist ideas, he did so almost apologetically: he touches upon them in his work *The Darkness of Atheism Dispelled by the Light of Nature* (1652).

What were all these men of science afraid of? Atomism – built upon the theories of the pagan Greek philosophers Epicurus and Lucretius – was so tainted by the accusation of atheism, that even to engage with it was thought dangerous. When Lucy Hutchinson translated Lucretius's poems (which remained unpublished during her lifetime), she even went so far as to write an apology for the undertaking – she declares she detests "all the Atheisms and impieties" within the volume, and translated it only "out of youthful curiosity, to understand things that [she] heard so much discourse of at second hand".[53] And when her fellow Puritan, John Milton, made use of atomistic theories, he wholly Christianised them. His description of "chaos" found in Book II of *Paradise Lost* – "embryon atoms" of "Hot, Cold, Moist, and Dry" – puts atomism in a wholly Christian context.[54] Even Gassendi, Cavendish's example in all things atomistic, had introduced theology into his theories when he had argued that God was the creator of all matter.

But Cavendish, right at the opening of her volume, made no such concessions. Her first poem makes no mention of God, and describes the creation of the world as a wholly scientific process – the interaction of life, form, and matter – without any divine intervention. It is difficult to overstate just how shocking this was. Cavendish had not only scandalised the world with her bold declarations of authorship and ambition, she had also invited accusations of atheism.

Cavendish's atomism went further. She uses her theory of matter – the world is made up of four types of atoms, which make earth, water, air, and fire – to explain everything from the difference between "heat" and "cold" to the existence of death, sickness, and old age, and the physics of light and motion. She was one of the first writers to bring these theories to England – even if later writers have dismissed her as having little impact on the scientific landscape of the period.

And whilst Epicurean atomism stressed the non-living nature of the atoms, her own theory gave them a degree of life and vitality: they are likened to the fairies she describes in later poems in the volume, and even have the agency to "dance" on sunbeams.[55] In the opening of her poem "The Pastime, and Recreation of the Queen of Fairies", Cavendish describes how the fairies move to music with "time and measure":

> All hand in hand, a round, a round,
> They dance upon this Fairy ground.[56]

It is no accident, or coincidence, that this description matches her vision of atoms' motion:

> Atoms *will dance, and measures keep just time;*
> *And one by one will hold round circle line,*[57]

Cavendish's fairy poems are far from mere ephemeral fancies: they are, in part, an elaborate metaphor for her scientific beliefs.

Her atomism rapidly expands to cover things beyond natural philosophy, and becomes a social theory: the relentless movement of atoms and their haphazard, ever-changing interaction provides a means of understanding the war-torn world around her. She is able to take the complicated theories of the scientists she had known in Antwerp and Paris, and render them poetically. In one of her best verses, "A World in an Earring", she takes the seemingly inconspicuous item of jewellery, and zooms in on it to the point that "an earring round may well a zodiac be":

That same which doth the earring hold, the hole,
Is that we call the North and Southern Pole;
There nipping frost may be, and winters cold,
Yet never on the lady's ear take hold.
[...]
There cities be, and stately houses built,
Their inside gay and finely may be guilt.
There churches be, wherein priests teach and sing,
And steeples too, yet hear the bells not ring.
From thence may pious tears to Heaven run,
And yet the ear not know which way they're gone.[58]

The "earring" is a chance for Cavendish to expound her knowledge of the world, from its geography to its planetary systems, and her imagined countries, cities, and people. It is, also, a chance for her to take the implications of atomism further. In Antwerp, Cavendish had had access to William and Charles's microscopes: she understood that there was a level of existence that was not accessible to unaided human sight. But here, the possibilities of invisible atoms go one step further: here, in an earring, is the possibility of unending alternative worlds, and unending alternative futures. This was no less shaky ground than her poem about creation: as one critic pithily put it, "it is difficult to understand how Christ's revelation might be preached within an earring".[59] And it is no accident that Cavendish used a piece of women's jewellery to do this: just as her opening prefatory letter likened writing to spinning, Cavendish sees no problem in describing – and containing – the world in explicitly feminine terms.

But her atomism also had other implications. If everything in the world is made of invisible atoms, it raises all sorts of epistemological questions: how can anything – from an element to an object – ever be really, truly *known*? This scepticism (she writes "all opinions are by fancy fed / And Truth under opinion lieth dead") was not just the product of her philosophical influences. It was also, in part, another defence of the type she had written in her modest prefatory material: if the impossibility of perception meant nobody could know anything, then how could her own lack of scientific knowledge hold her at a disadvantage?[60] The creations of her imagination – from the world of a fairy kingdom "in the midst and centre of the Earth", to an "Animal Parliament" formed from all the different parts of a body – could be excused, if not justified, by a sceptical philosophy that admitted it did not have all the answers.

Cavendish did not limit herself to scientific and philosophical writings in this volume – even if they were, clearly, her focus, and *Philosophical Fancies* would follow within a matter of months. The last "clasp" of poems between sections III and IV has autobiographical elements: Cavendish describes everything from her Channel-crossing into exile ("a ship of youth into the world's sea was sent"), to her marriage ("to the altar this fair bride was led"), and her second sea-journey back to England:

> *Then this same ship another voyage went;*
> *Balanced it was with spice of sweet content.*
> *[...]*
> *Fame was the land which it did traffic to.*
> *At last a storm of poverty did rise*[61]

Cavendish is clearly using the experiences of her own life as a source for her verse; she is following in the footsteps of all the women who wrote manuscript poetry about their weddings, husbands, and children. There is, however, something different about Cavendish's life-writing: the clasp opens with the declaration that "the scene is poetry" and "the stage is the brain, whereon it is acted".[62] This clasp is, in part, an early forerunner of Cavendish's later plays, which similarly had many autobiographical elements. But the insistence that "the scene is poetry" is also something else: Cavendish is writing about her life, but she does not want her readers to forget that she is a writer, rather than just the woman to whom these dramatic experiences occurred. Her status as a poet was sacrosanct.

The biographical writing continues in the fifth section of the collection, "A Register of Mournful Verses".[63] Other than the poem for her "Dear Brother, Killed in These Unhappy Wars", the inspirations of her poems are unnamed. But their subjects are still clear. "An Elegy on a Widow" is written in praise of Margaret's mother, Elizabeth, who had died in 1647 after many years of living in "her cloister" alone. Margaret's laudatory poem provides an insight into her definition of "fame":

Set altars on this hearse for memory,
And let her fame live here eternally.
Here celebrate her name, come, and do bring
Your offerings, and all her praises sing.[64]

"Fame" is less about endless acclaim within a lifetime, than it is derived from being remembered afterwards: all Cavendish wants is for her name, and her mother's, to live on. Cavendish also writes moving poems on the death of her sister – "a Mother, that Died for Grief of the Death of her Daughter" – and the daughter who had died just before her. These deaths had occurred whilst Margaret was in exile, and she could not have seen her now-deceased relations since she had left England in 1644. Whilst her verses mourning them were public, her grief was intensely private. With her poem for Charles Lucas, she did not have this luxury: his death had been reported and discussed in almost every newsbook, and there had already been a wealth of poems written about him. Margaret was writing into a public arena with this poem:

Dear Brother, Thy idea in my mind doth lie
And is intombed in my sad memory,
Where every day I to thy shrine do go,
And offer tears, which from my eyes do flow[65]

The language of shrines, tears, and memory is of the kind expected of a formal elegy, but her address to her "dear brother" reminds her reader that despite the fact Charles Lucas's death was so well known and he had become something of a martyr, he was still her family. The intimacy of private grief was denied her, but nor did she have the option, or capacity, to make this a purely formal, political poem.

The last section of the volume was something rather different. After the funereal poetry, Cavendish included a prose work of speeches and debates entitled the "Animal Parliament". This parliament was called by the "soul", and was a debate between the three parts of the "kingdom" within a human body: "soul, the body, and the thoughts".[66] As fanciful as this conceit sounds, Cavendish maps out an entire political system, where "the head is the upper house of Parliament, where at the upper end of said House sits the Soul King". If the soul is king, the "nobility" are the "spirits", and "humours and appetites" are the "commonality". This vision of the political world is clearly based upon Cavendish's knowledge – and first-hand experience – of the political debates pre-war, as the nobility and members of Parliament fought to wrest control from an autocratic king. But, rather than blindly affirming her supposedly Royalist beliefs and heritage, Cavendish envisages a world in which the "Lords" and other politicians of the "spirits" have a considerable degree of power and control – they debate the different issues of the day, and pass laws to govern the country (or, in this case, "body"). At the end, the king thanks them for their "care and industry" in "rectifying the Errors of this Kingdom": with this image of cooperation, Cavendish momentarily suggests that her own view of monarchical power could be more moderate than she proposes elsewhere.[67]

The concerns of the Civil War reverberate through nearly every aspect of the collection. Strife and fighting occur in almost every context – from warring atoms in the scientific sections, to abstract battles between everything from "Doubt and Hope" to "Honour and Dishonour" in her explorations of moral philosophy, and, more imaginatively, fights between "King Oberon and the Pygmies" in her poems about fairies. Her atomist beliefs give her a scientific basis for the world she was living in – "factious atoms" make "all go wrong" – but beneath the Epicurean theories is something far more touching.[68] War had been the reality of Margaret's life since her late teens and even now, aged thirty, she was unable to move beyond its ravages.

8

We women are miserable

A T THE END of Charlotte Brontë's novel *Villette*, published
in 1853, Lucy Snowe has spent three years away from her
beloved and betrothed, Monsieur Emmanuel. The time has
come for him to return, and Brontë describes the changing of
the seasons as she awaits his appearance: "the sun passes the
equinox; the days shorten, the leaves grow shere; but – he is
coming."[1] There is only one problem. Just as M. Emmanuel
should be safe in Lucy's embrace, a storm strikes: "It did not
cease till the Atlantic was strewn with wrecks."[2] Instead of
confirming that M. Emmanuel has perished with the rest of the
unfortunate sailors, Brontë abruptly finishes the novel with the
command to "leave sunny imaginations hope". It's a frustrating
ending: there is no hope that M. Emmanuel is alive, despite
Brontë's insistence, and there is no happy scene of reunion, or
even the catharsis of a funeral. Instead, Brontë leaves us only
with the thought of Lucy Snowe's burgeoning career: she has
established a thriving school for girls, and the reader has to
assume that she continues teaching after the novel's tantalising
closure.

Two centuries before the tale of Brontë's storm-wrecked
reunion was published, William Cavendish must have felt
somewhat like Lucy Snowe. Whilst Margaret had been in
London – meeting the remnants of Royalist society, writing and
publishing her work – William had remained in Antwerp. He

must have known about Margaret's new publishing career, but could not have been very involved given that he was in exile across the Channel. With no political position, and no money to spend on his favourite pastime of horse-riding, he had been left with little to do other than pine for his young wife. Unlike Lucy Snowe, these were hardly the "happiest years" of his life. The poems he wrote to Margaret in this period are marked with an intense longing that transcends even William's normally extravagant tone:

Beyond expression, griefe. When we did part
My blood went back, & shrunked up was my heart
My cheeks drowned in a sea of teares, so cried[3]

Margaret's penchant for a shipwreck metaphor had rubbed off on William. In another poem written in her absence, he turns the turbulent image of storm, wrack and ruin on its head. Margaret's "parting" has left the world strangely, disconcertingly calm:

... sails now stood
Like lean consumptions on the flood
No waves appeared, no tide returned
[...]
The naked masts, non tottering fall
The sinewed ropes, does slacken all[4]

Here, the scene of horror – the "wreck" – is its exact inverse: Margaret has left such a vacuum of love, passion, and vibrancy in her absence that "sailors amassed, rudder no power". Without her, William's world all but fell apart. In another poem, he writes of going to bed and dreaming of Margaret:

The Pillow in my arms I filled with Kisses
When wakt, found that they were but empty blisses[5]

Just as it begins to feel impossible not to have some sympathy for William, he returns to form with a poem that butchers the typical love-poetry conceit of turtle doves: "our love is more than turtles, when we woo / we are but one. Poor turtles, they are two".[6] William's sadness had not made him a better poet.

By February 1653 – just weeks after *Poems and Fancies* had been published – the end of the lovers' separation was in sight. Charles Cavendish had sorted out his affairs, and Margaret had been told in no uncertain terms that she was not eligible to claim any money: there was no reason for the pair to stay in England any longer. By April of the same year, the Rump Parliament – the parliament that had tried and executed Charles I – would be dismissed by Oliver Cromwell and replaced a few months later with the handpicked members of the Barebones Parliament. And by the end of the year, Cromwell would be sworn in as Lord Protector. For Royalists opposed to the growing religious fervour of the Puritans and the spectre of a Republican ruler, early 1653 was a good time be away from England.

Margaret prepared to travel, getting permission from the Council of State for her and her "four men and four maids" to cross to Flanders. She had wanted to leave with Charles, but he had fallen ill. With the assurance of doctors that he could soon follow her across the Channel, she made her final preparations. In order to leave the country, the Parliament was now requiring travellers to swear the Engagement – the same oath that had made Charles so reluctant to travel to England in the first place. Margaret, as she had done when pleading on William's behalf, used her natural defence: she was a woman, and so could *surely* not have any political opinions worth professing. Parliament agreed and on 2 March, the Council of State issued another permission: for "Lady Newcastle and servants" to go "out of England, without having the taking of the engagement pressed upon her".[7]

Now William waited anxiously for Margaret to cross the Channel. This was an age in which sea travel was notoriously dangerous, even for a relatively short journey. Margaret and her eight servants had nearly 300 miles to travel before she could settle again, and she had been away from her husband for fifteen months. How could she be certain that he would receive her as warmly as they had parted? Or that, in her absence, some other young woman had not taken her place? In their courtship, Margaret had been made aware by her worried friends of William's voracity when it came to women. His plaintive love-poetry was one assurance, but as he wrote in his poem "Of Jelosey", "doubts that putts on / falseness in love" were all but unavoidable for a couple separated for so long. William was only too aware of this possibility:

> Love, loves but one
> Let me that only one love be
> And I'll love thee.[8]

And there is even the hint of infidelity in his verse – although it is difficult to separate what William chose as subjects for his compulsive versifying from the real facts of their lives. Nonetheless, he writes how Margaret's "cheeks are fed / with anger red" and her "scornful ear / will nothing hear". This description of Margaret's anger begs the question of who has been wronged in the relationship: William writes that he will "live / not to forgive" and will "damn" Margaret for this "great sin", and ends the poem with a musing on "damnation various weave".[9] It's a pointed, angry poem – and it is, of course, difficult to read as straight autobiography. But its inclusion in the sheaf of love poems written to Margaret is incongruous, and telling.

Nor is it the only verse speaking of jealousy, fears, and changed feelings: a poem called "Loves Changeable Heart" declares that Margaret's heart is now "empty", and laments how "time... all things doth consume".[10] Could William have believed that Margaret had been unfaithful to him? Who might she have been with? By her own description, she seems to have spent little time with anyone other than William's brother, Charles, and her own family when she was in London.

William's doubts came after the reunion in Antwerp, which was neither thwarted by a storm nor marred by quarrels. William's poems are almost bursting with lust as he describes seeing Margaret again:

> Our tongues thought much
> When lips did touch
> They should not meet
> Softly[11]

In another poem he describes Margaret's "satin breasts, that are milk white" and her "plump flesh", whilst in yet another he describes how his own "lips are swelled ready to burst" and only Margaret's "dewy lips" will "quench [his] thirst".[12] In perhaps the most explicit poem of the bunch – a poem entitled "Loves Shop" about all the body parts available for purchase – William goes as far as to describe "a muff" where the "fur is Cunny".[13] He even describes how the pair would touch "belly to belly" and "make us one, of two".[14] There is little doubt what William and Margaret were doing on her first night back in Antwerp.

* * *

But Margaret was, of course, not just returning to a life of married bliss and quiet wifely seclusion. In the weeks before she had left England, she had been rapidly writing her prose work *Philosophical Fancies*: a collection of short essays. This was published in May (it arrived at the printers too late to be included with the previous volume), when Cavendish was already back in Antwerp. Some of its contents are similar to the earlier book: Cavendish reiterates her desire for fame ("to thee, great Fame, I do dedicate this piece"); continues her theologically dangerous scientific arguments ("there is no first matter, nor first motion; for matter and motion are infinite); and continues to demonstrate her insatiable curiosity about the way the world works.[15] In the new volume, she turns her back on the atomism she had so relished in exploring in her *Poems and Fancies*, and begins to develop her theory of "spirits" or "essences in nature" which are "innate matter" – that is, a type of matter that is like a "god" to other matters, and can create and form it at will.* Always ready to mix her science with political philosophy, Cavendish uses a distinctly hierarchical metaphor to explore what this division of matter meant to the world:

> Why may not every degree of Innate Matter be, as several Gods, and so a stronger motion be a God to the weaker... As we will compare motions to officers, or magistrates. The constable rules the parish, the Mayor the constable, the King the Mayor, and some Higher Power the King: thus Infinite power rules Eternity.[16]

Even in her description of the Royalist, hierarchical view of society, Cavendish still refrained from placing God as the divine body that gave the king his authority – she preferred the ambiguity of "some Higher Power". She was by no means a traditional Royalist, nor a loyal devotee of high church Anglicanism and Laudianism.

One of the most interesting aspects of *Philosophical Fancies* is found not in the body of the text, but in one of her many prefatory letters. Several of these are similar to the ones placed at the beginning of *Poems and Fancies* (she continues the weaving and sewing metaphor with an apology for "false stitches"), but there is also a letter "To Sir Charles Cavendish", Margaret's brother-in-law, intellectual helpmeet, and constant companion whilst she was in London. The letter is a proof of their closeness and of Margaret's gratitude for her education at Charles's hands:

---

* This theory of matter – now called "vitalist materialism" – is discussed more fully in Chapter 11.

"to forget to divulge your noble favours to me, in any of my works, were to murder their gratitude."[17] Contained within the conventional letter of affection and thanks is a rather striking image:

> And though I am your slave, being manacled with chains of obligation, yet my chains feel softer then silk, and my bondage is pleasanter than freedom; because I am bound to your self, who are a person so full of generosity.

In her later writing, Cavendish would use the image of being bound in chains of slavery in her debates about war and the right government of nations – in one text, a king declares that he will "bind" his subjects with "bonds of slavery" unless they "presently conform [them]selves to Peace, Law, and Government".[18] Yet she most often uses images of slavery, servitude, and dominion when referring to the place of women in society and, more specifically, in marriage:

> ... Men are made for Liberty, and Women for Slavery, and not Only Slaves to Sickness, Pains, and Troubles, in Breeding, Bearing, and Bringing up Children, But they are Slaves to Men's Humours, [...] Wherefore, those Women are most Happy that Never Marry[19]

In her *Sociable Letters* – fictionalised letters written to friends – published in 1664, Cavendish repeated this image of the "bonds of matrimony":

> But the safest way is to live a single life, for all wives, if they be not slaves, yet they are servants[20]

Marriage was, however happy the pairing might be, a relationship of obligation, and one which conjured up images of bondage and manacles in Margaret's mind. Why, then, does she describe her relationship to Charles, her husband's brother, in these terms? And why is she at pains to stress that the "bondage" is pleasant, with "chains... softer than silk"? There is something so personal and so intimate (and even erotic) about this letter that makes it seem dramatically out of place as a formal letter of thanks at the beginning of a printed book.

It is all but impossible to prove the depth or nature of the relationship between Charles and Margaret during their fifteen months in London. But, combined with William's angrily jealous verses – in another poem entitled "Loves Perjury" he lambasts Margaret for her "marble heart" and having deserted her "promises" and "oath[s]", whilst in others he rails against her being "inconstant" – it would be difficult to dismiss the possibility that Margaret *had* been unfaithful, and had betrayed William with his brother.[21] Her dedication to Charles frames their relationship as a type of marriage, but a marriage in which the "chains of obligation" felt pleasurable, rather than punitive.

Could this be the infidelity William alludes to in his poems to Margaret? The sheer number of poems which reference broken promises, inconstancy, and lack of love (out of the thirty-one poems from this period written by William, nine make explicit reference to Margaret's loss of love for William, and even more to their general incompatibility) suggests that these are not just a poetic exercise in writing about despair and infidelity. They must, surely, have an autobiographical referent: is it possible that Margaret had betrayed William, and had either told him about it after their first reunion, or had been caught by servants who were "turned eyes" and "converted spies"?[22]

But, perhaps more likely – and the way to explain the couple's rapid repair of their relationship – is the fact that William felt Margaret had betrayed him emotionally, but not physically: there are hints throughout the poems that he finds her cold, or unresponsive to his lust. And it is more likely that poems about his wife's changeable temperament would be included in a bound manuscript volume, rather than overt admissions of his status as a cuckold. But in the absence of reliable documentary evidence, the ambiguity persists. Either way, the fairy-tale marriage had encountered its first moment of visible tension.

* * *

In Antwerp, Margaret was reunited with her earlier writing: the short essays and salon-pieces of *The Worlds Olio* that she had locked up and left behind in a trunk all those months ago. If she had begun her printing career in London, it was in Europe where it was consolidated.

Using money that Charles had secured for the Cavendish family in London, Margaret commissioned the Dutch artist Abraham van Diepenbeeck to create two engraved, ornate frontispieces as visual proof of her status as an author. These illustrations (perhaps included in copies sent to Cavendish's friends, or at the front of more expensive editions of her books) are uncompromising demonstrations of how Margaret saw herself, and wanted others to see her. In one, the so-called "classical frontispiece", she stands as if she were a marble Greek statue, with Athena and Apollo on either side. She is the natural heir to the poets of antiquity, Ovid and Homer, but she is also the epitome of English aristocracy: her classical-style dress is accessorised with an ermine-lined gown and a marchioness's coronet. She stands confidently, wearing her status and her ambitions proudly. In the other illustration, the "melancholic frontispiece", she again wears her coronet, and sits in front of an opulent background in keeping with her noble status. Instead of classical allusions there are nods to her own, contemporary, learning: a paper and pen are in front of her, and a clock on the desk that suggests the *tempus fugit* motif of other portraits from the period. The verse beneath stresses the solitary nature of her study:

> *Studious she is and all Alone*
> *Most visitants, when she has none*

Margaret's self-proclaimed status as an author and scholar gave her a convincing excuse for the shyness and introversion that had plagued her younger years.

With William's help – proof of the short-lived nature of their disagreement – Margaret sent out copies of *Poems and Fancies* and her new book, *Philosophical Fancies*, to leading figures in court and intellectual life. For a woman who, like every member of her sex, was barred from university education, it was quite a coup to know that the Bodleian Librarian Thomas Barlow had received copies of her books and had distributed them amongst the colleges with "an Inscription as Posterity might know who was their Benefactor".[23] Constantijn Huygens – a friend of the Cavendish circle in Antwerp – also received a copy, as did the Royalist scholar and (former) king's chaplain Robert Creighton. Margaret must have adored the letter he sent in response, even if she was too clever not to see through the insincerity of the flattery:

> Were those Ancients now alive, who first discoursed of Atoms, Matter, Form, and other Ingredients of the Worlds Fabric, they would hang their Heads, confounded to see a Lady of most Honourable Extraction, in Prime of youth, amidst a thousand fasheries of greatness, say more of their own Mysteries, than they with all their worldly contempts, long Lives, Cells, and Solitary Retirements.[24]

He even reiterated the idea that Margaret's books were her children, and ended the letter with the command, "Go on then (most Honourable Madam) to bless the world with these noble infants of your brain."

Given the extent of the praise – Mildmay Fane, the Earl of Westmoreland, had even composed a poem in honour of Margaret's literary achievement – the letter that the couple received from Sir Edward Hyde (better known by his later title, the Earl of Clarendon, he was an advisor to Charles I, now a part of Charles II's court, and the author of *The History of the*

Rebellion) must have come as something as a shock. Whereas the other correspondents had been rather (over) flattering, Hyde added a barb to his praise. He suggested that Margaret, a woman "unskilled in any but our mother tongue" and devoid of a formal education, could not have written a book with "so many terms of art, and such expressions proper to all sciences".[25] The book was, for Hyde, far too good to have been written by a woman.

Hyde's comment does, of course, amount to a back-handed compliment to Margaret, a woman who, by her own admission, had suffered from her lack of formal schooling. But, given her obsession with fame, posterity, and the afterlife of her books, the chance that people would not believe that they had been written by her – that her children were not her own – was not to be countenanced. *Philosophical Fancies* appeared with an epilogue which tackled and refuted the accusation: "I hear that my first book was thought to be none of mine own", wrote Margaret. She told her readers she was too "honest. As not to steal another's work... nor so vain-glorious as to strain to build up a Fame upon the ground of another man's wit."[26] Cavendish wanted fame, yes, but only fame she had earned. And she was not going to wait to achieve it: after arriving back in Antwerp, it wasn't long before she published yet another book – *The Worlds Olio* – which was sold in London despite its author still being on the continent. Cavendish had gone from an ingenue educated by her husband and his brother, to a debut author, and now a thrice-published *international* author, all in the space of three years.

Both *Philosophical Fancies* and *The Worlds Olio* (its title refers to a stew of diverse ingredients that was popular in the seventeenth century) have an almost overwhelming focus on mortality. In *Philosophical Fancies*, Cavendish expounds her theory about the totality of death:

Death is an annihilation... Like as a house that is ruined by time, or spoiled by accident; the several materials are employed to other uses; sometimes to the building of a house again. But a house is no longer a building then a pulling down, by reason of the cutting, carving, laying, carrying, placing, and fitting every part to make them join together; so all the works of Nature are sooner dissolved then created.[27]

There is more than a slight premonition of Edmund Burke in Cavendish's use of the house as a metaphor for change – hints of another revolution over a century later – but this is an important image in its own right: Cavendish appears not to believe in an afterlife. Her theological heterodoxy increased in her later writings, but here is an early indication of her beliefs: death is annihilation, and the reuse of matter and materials does not, in her view, allow for any sense of continuity. It is this description of complete obliteration that gives context to her other statements in the volume: she writes with great anxiety how she "write[s], and write[s], and't may never be read; My books, and I, all in a grave lie dead" and, in another poem, she declares:

> *Body, when thou art gone, then I die to*
> *Unless some great Act in thy life thy do*[28]

The first essay of *The Worlds Olio* opens with the unflinching statement that the "desire for fame" stems from the "doubt of an after being".[29] By her second and third books, Cavendish's obsession with posthumous fame was not shocking – even if the same cannot be said for her theological musings – but given what would happen just before the publication of the third book, it is certainly poignant.

As Cavendish was pondering her own mortality and preparing *The Worlds Olio* for publication, Charles Cavendish was still in London. He had remained in England when he was too ill to travel with Margaret but, nearly a year later in February 1654, he had still not rejoined the couple. Then, just as the situation in Antwerp was beginning to improve – the money that Charles had secured from his estates at the committee had alleviated their debts and even made quite lavish spending possible – the couple received devastating news. Charles had died of an "ague".[30] This news was an "extreme affliction" to both William and Margaret: they had lost a brother and a friend, and an integral part of their little Antwerp family. William felt beholden to his brother: he had returned to England at his behest to secure the funds that went to finance his expensive way of life. Margaret felt the loss of her intellectual friend – or perhaps, something more – intensely. In her autobiography, she wrote that she would "lament the loss so long as I live":

> I will build his monument of truth, though I cannot of marble, and hang my tears and scutcheons on his tomb. He was nobly generous, wisely valiant, naturally civil, honestly kind, truly loving, virtuously temperate[31]

Regardless of the precise nature of the relationship between them, it is clear that Charles's death shook Margaret badly. She had already lost her mother, a sister, a niece, and two brothers and now, just as she was beginning to publish and find joy in her work, she was stalked by loss once more.

* * *

There is more than one reason for starting this chapter with Charlotte Brontë's *Villette*. In histories of English feminism, the Brontë sisters tend to feature heavily. What are *Jane Eyre* (1847), *Wuthering Heights* (1847), and *The Tenant of Wildfell Hall* (1848) other than feminist expressions of women's power and independence, and their current subjection in Victorian patriarchal society?[32] Charlotte, Emily, and Anne even wrote under the names Currer, Ellis, and Acton Bell to avoid being condemned as writing, in George Eliot's words, "silly novels by lady novelists".[33]

But histories of feminist writing often fail to go back much further than the nineteenth-century debates over women's rights, or the early twentieth-century battles of the suffragettes. And it is only with Mary Wollstonecraft's 1792 tract, *A Vindication of the Rights of Women*, that many see the beginning of the history of feminist thought and philosophy. For some, the period prior to Wollstonecraft's famously wry comments ("My own sex, I hope, will excuse me, if I treat them like rational creatures") is intellectually barren of feminist philosophy.[34] And, if there is any feminist thought in the period, it can only be thought of as "proto-feminist", coming as it did some centuries before that word was widely used.

This is surely a mistake. The 1640s and 50s were a period of hugely radical political and religious thought in England, from the democratic desires of the Levellers to the near-communist beliefs of the Diggers (also known as the "True Levellers"). Amidst theories of equal rights, broad suffrage, common use of land, and even sexual freedom and free love (the Ranters and other groups can be linked to a Puritan "sexual revolution"), why would there not have been serious consideration of women's rights, or the place of women in society?[35] It is, of course, certainly true that a growth in sexual freedom – many of the dissenting groups made divorce significantly easier – was not real freedom or liberation for women given the absence of birth control.[36] But the shift went beyond sexual pleasure: everyone, from the Baptist preacher Elizabeth Attaway to John Milton (with his tracts on divorce), was discussing the relationship between the sexes. The (occasionally) radical theoretical equality of dissenting sects – "the soul knows no difference of sex" – was rarely put into practice, and nor did much of the spirit of change survive the Restoration. But if this intense moment of radicalism was short-lived, there was a growth of feminist thought – a raising of consciousness – throughout the century that should not be ignored.

With her bold statement of herself as a female author in 1653 – and her continued position as a "Princess" of poetry, philosophy, and science throughout the latter half of the seventeenth century – Margaret Cavendish is one of the earliest, and most significant figures in this development of feminist thought. Every aspect of her work is aware of the difference between sexes, from her description of poetry as something "proper" to her "sex" to her call upon the sisterhood to defend her work:

> But if they do throw scorn, I shall intreat you... Therefore pray strengthen my side, in defending my book, for I know women's tongues are as sharp as two-edged swords.[37]

Margaret's call to the sisterhood is not simple: she attacks women just as she asks for their help. But her feminism persists throughout her work, from her plays revelling in the power of women (and even triumphing over men), to her most famous work, *The Blazing World* (1666) in which she satirises the male-dominated Royal Society and posits a utopia run by an empress.

Some of Cavendish's most trenchant and overt expressions of feminism are found in two works from the early 1660s: *Orations of Divers Sorts* (1662) and *Sociable Letters* (1664). In *Orations*, she even included a section of "Female Orations" focusing exclusively on the concerns of "ladies, gentlewomen, and other inferiors" who she insisted were "not less worthy".[38] The first speech would not be out of place in the debates over women's powers in nineteenth-century England, or in the heat of second-wave feminism in 1960s America:

> ... now we Live and dye, as if we were produced from Beast rather than from Men; for Men are Happy, and we women are miserable, they possess all the ease, rest, pleasure, wealth, power, and Fame, whereas Women are restless with Labour, easeless with Pain, Melancholy for Want of Pleasures, Helpless for want of Power, and die in oblivion for want of fame

Here is an unfairly neglected root of feminist thought and writing in the English-speaking world. Margaret is one of the earliest amongst a group of seventeenth-century writers – including Bathsua Makin, Mary Astell, Mary More, and Jane Sharp – who wrote with a female audience in mind, and about issues of sex-based inequality.[39]

Some of Margaret's most effective and consistent feminist writing can be found in her discussions and asides on marriage. She would influence Mary Astell, the author of *Some Reflections Upon Marriage* (1700); a woman who would find it easier than Cavendish to be taken seriously as an "intellectual", perhaps because of her chaste, pious life. Astell, most famous for her *A Serious Proposal to the Ladies* (1694) which proposed that women should live in spiritually and morally pure seclusion, wrote this in 1700:

> If all Men are born free, how is it that all Women are born slaves? As they must being subjected to the inconstant, uncertain, unknown, arbitrary Will of Men, be the perfect Condition of Slavery?[40]

In her assertion that only *men* are "born free", Astell was turning the philosophy of the seventeenth-century thinker John Locke on its head. But she was not just writing against a male philosophical tradition; she was writing within a female one. Four decades earlier, in *Orations of Divers Sorts*, Cavendish was uncompromising about what the "noose" of marriage meant for women.[41] In one of her many "funeral orations", she writes of a recently dead "new-married wife" who has "made an unequal change from a lively hot husband, to a deadly cold lover":

> .... yet will she be more happy with her dull, dumb, deaf, blind, numb lover, than with her lively, talking, listening, tying, active husband, were he the best husband that could be; for death is far the happier condition than marriage.[42]

Cavendish was adept at adopting different voices and viewpoints, but could there be a hint here of her displeasure with her married fate? In another poem, she writes a homage to a widow who had wasted her later years in an excess of grief for her husband ("she sat not on the knees of amorous lovers, but kneeled on her knees to God"), and in another poem she praises an "old lady" who had remained single without being "tempted with courtship".[43] Cavendish certainly wouldn't have been able to express any displeasure with her own marriage in the prefaces to the books which her husband had helped to be published, but the sheer profusion of her critical remarks about marriage could hint at growing disagreements and struggles behind the façade of the doting husband and loyal wife.

But why did Cavendish believe that "death is far the happier condition than marriage"? As discussed earlier in the chapter, Cavendish frequently uses images of bondage and slavery when describing relations between a husband and wife, but she makes clear that this slavery is biological, if not innate:

> ... Nature seems both unjust and cruel to her female creatures, especially women, making them to indure all the pain and sickness in breeding and bringing forth of their young children[44]

Given her infertility, did Margaret believe she had escaped the biological slavery – in Germaine Greer's words, "the wicked womb" – by not being able to give birth?[45] In her *Sociable Letters*, she certainly makes it clear that childbirth is all that men – and many women – think wives are fit for. She savagely mocks women who "take pleasure" in the performance of being pregnant: "rasping wind out of her stomach... making sickly faces to express a sickly stomach" and choosing bed-linen and baby clothes. She writes:

For like as Women take a greater Pride in their Beauty, than Pleasure or Content in their Virtue, so they take more Pride in Being with Child, than in Having a Child, for when they are brought to Bed, and up from their Lying in, they seem nothing so well Pleased, nor so Proud, as when they were great with Child[46]

The whole letter is a scathing satire on the men and women who measure a woman's whole worth by her ability to have children. But contained within her witty mockery is real anger – Cavendish thought, and knew, that women could do more – and true radicalism. The twentieth-century radical feminist Shulamith Firestone had, probably, not read any of Cavendish's work prior to writing *The Dialectic of Sex* (1970). But Cavendish's despair over the biological inequality of sex differences finds an echo in Firestone's call for a "new population biology" and the possibility of "artificial reproduction".[47]

If Cavendish was so radically ground-breaking in expressing and publishing these feminist sentiments – and, indeed, was more radical in many ways than most of the women who wrote in the decades and centuries after her – why has she not been praised or noticed more?

As is often the way with Cavendish, the answer lies in how contradictory she was. It has been hard for historians and philosophers to take her seriously as a "feminist thinker" when she also wrote so many prefaces to her books apologising for her lack of knowledge, or the feminine nature of her writing. And, of course, much of her work has a distinctly "anti-feminist" bent too: her call to the sisterhood of female readers is combined with a recognition that women can be cruel and bitchy, and her attack on motherhood and pregnancy is as much an attack on the women themselves as it is an attack on the society that has put child-bearing on such a pedestal. She repeatedly admits her dependence on her husband, and her subservience to his wishes and his intellect. And she herself accompanies her most radical attacks on marriage and sex inequality in *Orations of Divers Sorts* with anti-feminist replies. Just as some women argue that men are "our Tyrants" and "devils" who "keep us in the Hell of Subjection", others respond with the argument that men are "our Protectors, Defenders, and Maintainers".[48]

The importance of these ripostes – the whole set of "orations" is an imagined debate, in the conventional seventeenth-century style – can be overstated: Cavendish writes from the feminist position with the most passion, and gives it the most space on the page. The replies are simply to give the text a feeling of conflict, and a sense of being engaged within a broader debate. The confusion over whether Cavendish believes in the speeches that affirm men and women's positions has arisen from the fact that, in her prefatory material, she often pays homage to her husband as her "protector". But it is clear that she does not see such a role as fixed, or necessary for all women: in almost every single one of her texts, she suggests that women can "act masculine parts".[49]

These contradictions offer fascinating insights into Cavendish's life, but they should not prevent us from regarding her as a serious, feminist thinker – and from treating this as a more significant, original aspect of her work than even her science, philosophy, or poetry. If her *apologia* for her feminine writing are a sort of verbal tic – something she had to write to clear her throat and begin the rest of the work – and her attacks on women part of a natural anger from a writer who had been scorned and marginalised, then we are left with a body of thought and work that predates the other feminist thinkers of the period, and rivals them in scope and power.

But there is another apparent contradiction in Cavendish's feminism. Unlike the Quakers, Ranters, Diggers, and Levellers who were discussing the equality of souls, and the possibility of free love, Margaret was, quite decidedly, *not* on the radical side of the civil wars and the subsequent Revolution. She was evidently in favour of some ideas of equality and social change – and, in *Orations of Divers Sorts*, even appears to support the position of the peasants, the "most / unhappy people in the world" – but the bulk of her writing makes her Royalist and anti-democratic beliefs clear.[50] As her theological inconsistencies reveal, she was by no means a "traditional Royalist", but she did believe in hierarchy, order, and established power.[51] She differed from the "Cavendish circle" in some aspects of her Royalism – and was, if her extended metaphor of parts of the body debating with each other in "The Animal Parliament" can be trusted, perhaps even inclined towards a more moderate, constitutional form of monarchy – but she was far from being a Republican, or a part of the radical world of the dissenters.[52]

How, then, did she marry her belief in the potential power and creativity of women with her hierarchical opinions, which seem to deny the very possibility of those lower down in the social scale than her? Or her belief that marriage was an oppressive form of bondage, with her lack of interest in the existence of people who were kept in true slavery and servitude? The answer is two-fold, and both parts seem, at first, to contradict the other.

First, Cavendish's feminism is surprisingly broad in its reach. Whilst she was the wealthy daughter of a wealthy family who had married into the aristocracy and would later become a duchess, her writings about women cut across conventional social divides. Her female orations open with the repeated line "Ladies, Gentlewomen, and other Inferiors": inferiority is the thing that links all women across the social spectrum. And while her comments on childbearing and pregnancy focus on aristocratic and wealthy women (peasants and servants were not buying new linen for each child, or spending the whole of their pregnancy in bed), she is not completely blind to social differences. In her poems about marriage, one of the few that is not *wholly* negative about the impacts upon women is "A Marriage-Oration of two Poor Servants". Cavendish's speaker asks the guests to give to the couple "For it may make them Rich, and your selves not Poor".[53] In suggesting that a match between two "poor servants" will be more favourable to the woman than an aristocratic marriage, Cavendish draws attention to a salient point: here, both the husband and wife "may nevertheless by their Industry thrive". Unlike herself, or the women she associated with, this imagined "poor servant" bride had a job – and was on an equal footing with her husband. It would be too much to over-stress Cavendish's social radicalism but she was, by no means, a wholly traditional Royalist.

And, second, there is the fact that much of the influential feminist thought and writing that came out of the seventeenth century – Bathsua Makin's writing on education; Mary Astell's writing on women's retreat; and the feminist poetry of Anne Finch, Countess of Winchelsea and Mary, Lady Chudleigh – was written by Anglican, Royalist women. While the dissenters had all the radical ideas about society and religion, it was, more often than not, the Royalists who wrote feminist works that had an impact beyond the heady years of the 1640s and 50s. (Although, of course, the fact that the Royalists eventually won the war in 1660 may have helped their longevity.) Margaret Fell Fox, one of the founders of Quakerism, advocated for women to be able to preach and be treated as equals in the meeting house, but it was Makin, Astell, Finch, and Chudleigh who took a consideration of women's place within society beyond single issues, and would write some of the earliest feminist work after Cavendish. Take Anne Finch's poem "The Unequal Fetters" as an example. Her privileged aristocratic position did not stop her, in the late seventeenth century or early eighteenth century, from writing:

> Marriage does but slightly tie Men
> While's close prisoners we remain
> They the larger slaves of hymen
> Still are begging love again
> At the full length of all their chain.[54]

For a woman whose intellectual importance has been denied and mocked, it is fascinating to trace Cavendish's influence on this poem – and others of Finch's and Chudleigh's.

But just because so many of the early feminists were Royalist aristocrats does not mean that the contradiction between their social status and political beliefs is negligible, or easily ignored. If anything, the contradiction is more widespread. Like Cavendish, Astell's writing is marked by the contradiction between her Anglican, "Tory" attitudes and her opposition to the status of married women.[55] She makes use of revolutionary rhetoric to further her cause – "if Absolute Sovereignty be not necessary in a State, how comes it to be so in a Family" – but, at other points in her writing, expresses an intense horror of opposition or disobedience to the state.[56] Of course, none of these women lived through the contradiction in quite the same way as Cavendish: as the earliest, she was the only one to be writing at a time when new ideas about social order and possible equality were not just abstract ideals but subjected to the test of war and revolutions.

In her writing there is, perhaps, a sense that women could unite beyond these political differences and the wars that were fought over them. In her *Sociable Letters*, Cavendish wrote:

> But howsoever, Madam, the disturbance in this Country hath made no breach of Friendship betwixt us, for though there hath been a Civil War in the Kingdom, and a general War amongst the Men, yet there hath been none amongst the Women.[57]

The women who fought in the wars, or suffered at the hands of enemy soldiers in battle, would disagree with this – as would Cavendish, if she were to meet the wives of the men who had executed her brother, or the women who had joined in the mob violence which had desecrated her mother's grave. It's simultaneously a statement of utopian feminist sisterhood, *and* a statement of the exclusion of women from political life. As ever with Cavendish, just as one contradiction seems to resolve itself, another one takes its place.

9

I have been asleep sixteen years

ON 23 APRIL 1661, Katherine Philips was ecstatic. In a brief burst of clear weather "snatch'd from storms", the "Star King" Charles II was finally crowned:

> ... *we knew not which look'd most content,*
> *The King, the people, or the firmament*[1]

Her poems describing the coronation are almost overwrought with happiness – "heaven delights to see what man performs" – but also, undeniably, shocked: Charles's return is the product of "miracles".[2] And Philips was far from being alone in her surprise. Writing in his diary on 29 May 1660 – the day that Charles II re-entered London after his exile – John Evelyn wrote that he "stood in the Strand and beheld it, and blessed God":

> ... all this was done without one drop of blood shed, and by that very army which rebelled against him: but it was the Lord's doing, for such a restoration was never mentioned in any history, ancient or modern...[3]

The Republican Puritan Lucy Hutchinson was no less surprised, even if she had adopted an anti-Cromwell stance in the later days of the Protectorate. In her *Memoirs*, she noted the king's "own amazement" at his return: "he saw all the nobility and gentry of the land flowing in to him" and "asked where were his enemies". Hutchinson was shocked less by the reappearance of the king than by the public's fickle change of mood: "it was a wonder... to see the mutability of some and the hypocrisy of others, and the servile flattery of all".[4] In Philips's poem, even the weather capitulated to the importance of the day. The storm stopped to allow the king his moment in the sun, and then "returned with impetuous haste".[5]

Every witness to these extraordinary events had good reason to be stunned into momentary silence or inaction. The king who had entered London in 1660 and processed with a "magnificent train on horseback" through the city on the eve of his coronation was the boy prince who had fought in the Civil Wars, and had been resoundingly defeated by Cromwell's army at the ill-fated Battle of Worcester in 1651. His flight into exile – and the day he spent hiding from Roundhead soldiers in "the branches of the Loyal [oak] tree" – was already the stuff of legend: he was the defeated son of a beheaded, treasonous, monarch, and the heir to a throne that no longer existed. England, in 1659, was a Republic.

How, then, was he able to return? On 3 September 1658, "his most serene and renowned highness Oliver Lord Protector" died mid-afternoon, probably from malaria and after a long period of ill-health. He died in an atmosphere of religious fervour (declaring "Truly God is good, indeed he is") and having named his successor only the day before.[6] The question of a successor – that is, dynastic rule – was difficult for Cromwell. It was the only way to secure the future of the Republic and, indeed, his legacy, but it was all too close to traditional monarchical hereditary rule. (Hutchinson, ever the staunch Republican, wrote that Cromwell's "wife and children were setting up for principality".)[7] His son, Richard, was only named after his council of ministers proposed his name to Cromwell and, on the second repetition, he was able to make some sign of agreement: hardly the ringing endorsement that any man wanting to take control over the four unruly kingdoms needed.

Unfortunately for the thirty-one-year-old Richard Cromwell, he lacked the force, support, and authority of his father. Within nine months of becoming Lord Protector, he had written a letter resigning the post (and acquired the unflattering nickname of "Tumbledown Dick"). The pressure on him came from two sides: a newly recalled Parliament which contained only a minority of Republicans, and his father's New Model Army, which resented Richard's lack of military experience. The same army that had ensured Cromwell's rise to power brought down his son. They insisted that Parliament be dissolved (the MPs had been in the process of impeaching Major-General William Boteler for his alleged cruelty to a Royalist prisoner), and surrounded Richard in his residence at St James's Palace.

Even after Richard had been removed from power, the return of the monarchy was by no means certain. The Republican – "Commonwealthsmen" – New Model Army had, after all, brought about this change of regime. It took George Monck, an English soldier who had fought, at different times, on both sides during the Civil Wars, to engineer the Restoration: he brought his army down from Scotland to the English border to meet the troops of the radical Republican John Lambert, and then marched on London. A "Convention Parliament" was elected – which, after Charles II issued the Declaration of Breda promising to forgive all the crimes of the Revolution (except that of regicide), then proclaimed that Charles II had been the lawful monarch since the death of his father. Yet even George Monck, who would later be made Duke of Albemarle as a reward for turning his coat, might have been surprised by the eventual outcome: as late as April 1660, Monck still "continued his sollemne protestations that he would be true to the interest of the Commonwealth, against a King and Howse of Lords".[8] Samuel Pepys wryly noted in his diary the growing rift between the Parliament and the army, and remarked "things seem very doubtful what will be the end of all".[9]

It is hard to overstate just how chaotic the months after Oliver Cromwell's death had been. After Richard had resigned, both the Army Republicans and Monck's troops tried to fill a power vacuum. There was a Royalist uprising, rule by a Committee of Safety and Council of State, and general confusion and fear of "new design[s] hatching".[10] For a generation that had lived through the wars and the unending sequence of Parliaments prior to the Protectorate, this uncertainty must have felt like the beginning of a new war, or a continuation of the old chaos. Even under Cromwell in the last months of his rule, the cracks had begun to show. Republicans like Lucy Hutchinson and her husband, the regicide John Hutchinson, had turned against the leader, writing that "Cromwell and his army grew wanton with their power" and that, under Richard, "true religion was now lost, even among the religious party".[11] In an unpublished manuscript poem directed at Edmund Waller, the author of "A Panegyrick to My Lord Protector", Hutchinson went further. She turned Waller's language on its head, and wrote an angry, bitter poem about the state of the Protectorate:

> *Our soft remorse made Civil Wars to cease*
> *And we are healed now with the Axe of Peace,*
> *Which doth our quiet spirits disengage*
> *Turns our affections and revives our rage*[12]

"The Axe of Peace"; reviving rage; disengaged spirits – Hutchinson was not happy with the changes brought about by the Protectorate. This did not mean she was content with the Restoration: in the book published in 1679 and now attributed to her, *Order and Disorder: or, the world made and undone*, she rails against the princes and courtiers of the restored monarchy. But her displeasure, and the widespread fear and uncertainty left by the brief reign of Richard Cromwell ("not a spirit... to manage such a perplexed government"), goes some way to explaining why the people of England embraced the return of

Charles II so readily. They were not just welcoming the return of monarchy, they were welcoming the return of stability.*

And welcome it they did: the announcement of Charles II's Restoration on 8 May 1660 was met with a carnival-like outburst of joy and relief. The bells of city churches were rung, people drank beer and wine in celebration, and bonfires were lit. The king had travelled to Brussels from Breda, and was met with a stream of well-wishers and exiles, which was only trumped by the welcome he received when he landed in Dover, on 25 May. Crowds lined the roads all the way from the coast to London, and his entry into the capital was described in contemporary literature as on a par with Jesus's entry into Jerusalem. "The ways strewed with flowers, the bells ringing, the streets hung with tapestry, fountains running with wine," wrote John Evelyn.[13]

* * *

Where were the Cavendishes in this moment of Royalist triumph; the moment that should have marked the end of their exile, their money troubles, and separation from their families? William had good cause to hope that the Restoration of Charles II would be particularly beneficial to him: he had been tutor to Charles when he was the Prince of Wales, and had overseen his early life and education. In 1659, when the hope of a restored Stuart monarchy began to seem plausible, William resumed his role: he wrote a long letter to his former pupil about how to govern "when you are enthroned".[14]

William's link to Charles II was so strong that his son, Henry – Charles Cavendish had died in 1659 – even went to Dover to meet the king's ship, expecting to be reunited with his father "with all joy and duty".[15] William was not with the king's party,

---

* This is, of course, not true of everyone: even in February 1660, Milton still published his Republican tract *The Ready and Easy Way to Establish a Free Commonwealth*.

but only because his desire to return to England was so great that he had left The Hague before the royal entourage, and in a "boat" (in her version of the story, Margaret claims that it was not worthy of the designation "ship") that was little more than "an old rotten frigate". It sank on its next journey, and might well have done on this crossing had William not been "becalmed" for "six days and six nights upon the water". Even this hiccup (there are, seemingly, very few sea-journeys in this period that went smoothly) could do little to dampen William's spirits at the prospects of a restored monarchy: he "pleased himself with mirth". His description of re-entering London for the first time in sixteen years – recorded verbatim in Margaret's biography of him – deserves quoting:

> At last, being come so far that he was able to discern the smoke of London, which he had not seen in a long time, he merrily was pleased to desire one that was near him, to jog and awake him out of his dream, for surely, said he, I have been sixteen years asleep, and am not thoroughly awake yet.[16]

Her description of William's reunion with Henry is no less moving: "with what joy they embraced and saluted each other, my pen is too weak to express", she wrote.

But why do Cavendish's descriptions of these moments rely on William's reports? Why was she not in the becalmed ship that sailed into the brave new world of Restoration London? She, like William, was an ardent Royalist. And, like William, she had family she was anxious to see again. Margaret did follow William, but after a delay of at least three months: when William left Antwerp, he flew to the king in such a rush that he had to leave Margaret behind as a security for his debts.

This is another classic Cavendish contradiction. Her position in Antwerp was one of both curious independence – she was in charge of packing up and ensuring the transport of their belongings, and taking leave of Antwerp society – and weakness:

she was "command[ed]" by William to remain as a "pawn for his debts".[17] She had to do a great deal of administrative work – she wrote letters trying to ensure that their "30 trunks" would be able to pass through all the required ports – and was of significant ceremonial importance: she had to apologise to the magistrates of Antwerp for William's hurried departure, and had to express thanks for their treatment in exile.[18] She had come a long way from the shy girl who had first come to Europe as a part of Henrietta Maria's retinue, or even the young bride who was dependent on her older husband.

When Cavendish was, eventually, all packed up – and after she had secured another loan to pay off their bills – she made her way to the port-town of Flushing in search of a sea-worthy ship to take her to England. She wanted to travel in an English "man-of-war" – a sturdy Navy ship – but, finding none there, and being "loath to trust [her]self with a lesser vessel", she boarded a Dutch warship which took her all the way to London.

* * *

Margaret's journey – the last sea-voyage she would make – was safe: she made it to England without any trouble. But she had reason to be scared. After *The Worlds Olio* in 1655, she had published two further works whilst in Antwerp: *The Philosophical and Physical Opinions* (1655) and *Natures Pictures* (1656). It was *Natures Pictures* which contained an outlandish number of disastrous shipwrecks, and even a story whose express "endeavour" was to "show young women the danger of travelling without their parents, husbands, or particular friends to guard them".[19]

Natures Pictures contains a mix of poetry and prose, and a mix of autobiographical stories and imagined flights of fancy (it was also the volume to which, initially, Margaret's autobiography *A True Relation of My Birth, Breeding, and Life* was appended). Cavendish writes of her own experience – women who travel overseas "in banishment", leaving their husbands in an attempt to escape poverty – alongside aspects of contemporary life she would have noticed (one story is about a "preaching lady", a phenomenon in Puritan England she would have heard about, or even seen).[20] These more factual stories are set alongside her romances: one of her best, "The Contract", is the winding story of an orphan who manages, eventually, to win the affections of the husband she was married to when she was but a child through a combination of her beauty, modesty, and knowledge of moral philosophy.

Philosophical and Physical Opinions, published within months of both *The Worlds Olio* and *Natures Pictures*, is, in many ways, a continuation of her scientific speculations in *Philosophical Fancies*. It opens with a condemnation from William of those who don't believe that the work was her own ("envious supposition"), continues with a refutation of those who argue that her ideas are stolen from "Descartes or Master Hobbes" (in a rather amusing aside, she writes that she "never understood" what Descartes said, as he "spoke no English", and that when she met Hobbes in London, he refused to have dinner with her), and even has a dedication to the "wise school-men" of Oxford and Cambridge.[21] Like her previous two works, this is a bid to be taken seriously in the learned world.

This is emphatically not a book of atomist theory. In the midst of the profusion of prefatory materials (they take up the first twenty-four pages of the volume), she writes "A Condemning Treatise of Atoms". Just two years after she can be given credit for bringing European theories of atomism to England, and for her boldness in expressing atheist Epicurean philosophy, she now backtracked:

I cannot think that the substance of infinite matter is only a body of dust, such as small atoms, and that there is no solidity [...] as only by fleeing about as dust and ashes, that are blown about with wind, which me thinks should make such uncertainties, such disproportioned figures, and confused creations, as there would be an infinite and eternal disorder[22]

Her opinion is couched in scientific terms – "infinite"; "solidity"; "atoms" – but her conclusion is fundamentally political: the ramifications of atomism mean the "infinite and eternal disorder" of a world without structure, without a ruler, or without an absolute monarch. Cavendish was writing after the Protectorate had been established – that is, England had a single ruler again – but the disorder of the fighting, the Interregnum, and the continuing conflict in Ireland and Scotland left her unable to contemplate, even in her science, a world without structure and order.

Margaret expanded the focus of her science from her first two volumes: in this book, she writes of psychology – "some... passions are made in the head; others... are made in the heart" – alongside illness and "maladies".[23] This is not entirely new (in *Poems and Fancies*, she explored why atoms caused illness), but the nature of her writing on sickness and psychology, and the fact that these subjects are treated at some length in the book, suggest a new-found interest. Margaret was no longer content being the patient of medical men; she wanted, at least partially, to join their ranks. In both her theoretical works and in her prose and poetry – which combined her empirical observations with autobiography – Cavendish's writing had developed and deepened.

Why, then, is there a gap in her publishing career between 1656 and her return to England? After *Natures Pictures*, Cavendish would not publish again until her *Plays* in 1662. As her first cluster of publications show, Cavendish enjoyed writing and publishing her work without pause. The issue wasn't money – in 1657, William paid for his treatise on horsemanship to be published, and the couple were sufficiently in funds (or credit) for him to establish a stables at Antwerp, and to be able to pay for new engravings and frontispieces (there is a family scene at the front of *Natures Pictures* and, in 1658, an engraving was made of the pair on horseback together).[24] Margaret had even bought herself a set of pearls.[25]

Could the cause have had a link to Margaret's developing medical interests? Whilst she was no longer being treated for infertility, she was far from well. William frequently castigated her for neglecting her health with her intense focus on writing, and her taking of exercise – in contrast to her husband, who was riding horses well into his sixties – was limited to "walking a slow pace in [her] chamber" whilst her "thoughts run apace in [her brain]". Cavendish's description of why she could not take more exercise than this is so wonderful that it bears quoting:

> ... the motions of my mind hinders the active exercises of my body; for should I dance or run, or walk apace I should dance my thoughts out of measure, run my fancies out of breath, and tread out the feet of my numbers[26]

The scene is almost a reverse of *The Red Shoes* – the Hans Christian Andersen fairy-tale (and later, the inspiration for the film by Powell and Pressburger and an album by Kate Bush), about a dancer whose shoes control her. Cavendish is controlled by her art, but rather than it forcing her to dance herself to death, it stops her from moving altogether. Her physical, bodily conception of her writing shows her descriptive powers at their best, but it is also linked to other aspects of her work. It has often been speculated that Cavendish had dyslexia, or some other form of learning difficulty: her spelling is erratic even by seventeenth-century standards, and her handwriting is by far the worst to be found in any archive of letters from the period. She not only struggled at the level of the single word, but with her sentences: lines often stop before they should, or with their ideas only half-expressed, having "out-run [her] pen".[27] Her printed works are riddled with errors: it would, of course, be unfair to blame these entirely on her, and her anger about them (in *The Worlds Olio*, she argues that her printers should have corrected her spelling, for "it is against nature for a woman to spell right", and rails against them for adding typos through "false printing") proves that she was aware of the problem, even if she was powerless to solve it. But the combination of printing errors and Cavendish's own inconsistencies leaves a body of texts which are often fiendishly difficult to read in the original editions.

But it couldn't have been dyslexia which made her stop publishing for six years, and nor was William corresponding with Theodore Mayerne solely about his wife's writing habits (although the doctor did believe that Margaret's "occupation in writing of books... is absolutely bad for health"; one wonders if he ever said the same to a male author).[28] As early as 1654, Margaret had been plagued by fears of diabetes and had been treated with tonics and potions. Her more worrying health concern was her continuing "melancholy": the sickness that had plagued her at court and in the earliest days of her marriage. Even writing "sad feigned stories... or melancholy passions" overpowered her brain with "oppression".[29] In her most recent medical tract, she had been unafraid of expounding the benefits of melancholy (that is, the humour, rather than the disease): "Those that be naturally melancholy, have the soundest judgement, the clearest understanding, the subtlest observation, and curioust inventions... the fancies, and the readiest wit."[30] For all her praise of the humour, it had been an excess of "melancholy", and her self-described melancholic temperament, which had plagued her while she was in London and left her unable to sleep. Charles Cavendish's death may well have caused a relapse.

However, melancholy had not stopped her writing in London – if anything, her poetry had been a respite – and nor did it again in Antwerp. Many of the plays she published after the Restoration in 1662 were written in these years, when "England doth not permit" the theatres to be open.[31] In her 1664 *Sociable Letters*, a fictionalised version of Cavendish complains that the plays she had written had "drown'd" on their way to printing in England. But any argument that attributes the gap in publishing to this marine accident is flawed: even within this perhaps fictionalised story, Cavendish stresses the fact that she still had the "original" copies of the plays with her, and the "twenty lives" of her "twenty plays" were not yet lost.[32]

There is, however, another possible cause for the hiatus in her career as a published writer. In 1655, just after the publication of *The Worlds Olio*, she received a letter from her correspondent and fellow atomist philosopher Walter Charleton. Charleton begins in terms of typical praise when writing to a noble woman – "Excellent Madam" – and thanks her for the gift of the book and expresses, perhaps disingenuously, his intellectual debt to her.[33] But midway through the letter is a change: he proclaims to be reporting the conversation of "infidels" who have read her volume, and describes how they refuse to believe that she was "so free from the contagion of books and book-men". His reasons are, in short, that her language was too sophisticated for her professed lack of education; the implication is that either the work was not her own, or she was far better schooled than she let on. Scholars now think that Charleton was expressing his own opinions, rather than malicious conversations he had heard, but the result was the same: Cavendish was incredibly upset, and William's preface to *The Philosophical and Physical Opinions* is a point-by-point refutation of Charleton's argument.[34]

Cavendish had to publish in order to refute the arguments made against her *Worlds Olio. Natures Pictures*, too, had a prefatory note from William attacking readers who lay "aspersions with a jeering brand".[35] Had the pressures of fame and the cruelty of her readers become too much for Margaret? All the volumes from this period bear the notes of pre-emptive attack, and it could have been this fear which caused her to leave off publishing for years, despite continuing to write.

*

When Margaret left Antwerp to join her husband, she was not retreating from these braying critics but rather going to enter their poisonous milieu. As unpleasant as that thought was, she had other reasons to hope for a better reception. The London she had left in 1653 had been that of the radical, turbulent Commonwealth, and the intervening years of the Protectorate would not have been any more enjoyable for her. The contemporary vision of the fun-hating Puritan is, at least partially, historically accurate: the celebration of Christmas, Easter, and Whitsun had been banned since 1647, and, under the rule of the Major-Generals, there had been even greater emphasis on preventing "drunkenness, blaspheming", adultery, fornication, and all "such like wickedness and abominations".[36] No plays were performed, no dances, and there was, of course, no decadent court life.

Returning in late 1660, or even early 1661, Cavendish could look forward to a city, and country, where such Puritan morality had been abandoned: the king's procession upon his arrival and the splendour of his coronation were so theatrical and spectacular as to be a complete refutation of all that had come before him. In a perverse inversion of Charles's coronation, Cromwell's body was exhumed, dragged through the streets of London, and hung in chains, before his head was impaled on a metal spike above Westminster Hall, where it remained until 1684. In a rather less gruesome act which proved the country's determination to rid itself of the Puritan past, the delighted inhabitants of London even re-erected their maypole in April 1661; a symbol of the festivals which had been banned under Cromwell's reign.

And the repressive political regime was also a thing of the past: under Cromwell's rule of the Major-Generals, former Royalists – all those who had fought against the Parliament in any way since 1642 – had to pay a tax which provided for their own oppression. Twelve Major-Generals controlled separate regions of all four nations. The Royalists under their watch were not

Margaret, painted by Peter Lely in 1665 – the year she
became a Duchess. She is wearing a masculine, feathered hat
instead of the expected coronet.

A military portrait of
William Cavendish
wearing armour,
made before he went
into exile and met
Margaret.

Queen Henrietta
Maria painted by
Anthony van Dyck in
the years prior to the
outbreak of war.

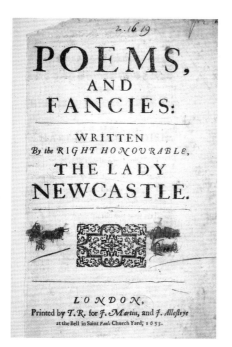

The title page for Cavendish's first published work: *Poems and Fancies* (1653).

One of the frontispieces Cavendish had printed for her books in the 1650s by the engraver Abraham van Diepenbeeck. Note the paper and ink ready on the table.

Rubens House in Antwerp, where the Cavendishes spent much of their years in exile.

A portrait of Charles I, Henrietta Maria, and their two eldest children.

An engraving of William Cavendish as a young man.

In this frontispeice (also by Abraham van Diepenbeeck), Cavendish is depicted as being surrounded by her husband and his children and grandchildren — an image of wifely respectability and domestic happiness that was far from the reality of their fertility problems and life in exile.

Thus, in this Semy-Circle, wher they Sitt, Telling of Tales of pleasure & of witt. Heer, you may read without a Sinn or Crime, And how more innocently pass your tyme.

A recontruction of how the entrance hall at Bolsover Castle would have looked in the seventeenth century.

A nineteenth-century engraving of Welbeck Abbey.

A detail from Christine de Pizan's *Le Livre de la Cité des Dames* in the British Library MS Harley 4431.

Another of the frontispieces Cavendish had made by Abraham van Diepenbeeck. Here, she is flanked by Apollo and Athena, and dressed to look like a figure from antiquity.

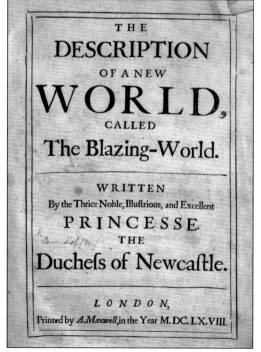

THE
DESCRIPTION
OF A NEW
WORLD,
CALLED
The Blazing-World.

WRITTEN
By the Thrice Noble, Illustrious, and Excellent
PRINCESSE,
THE
Duchess of Newcastle.

LONDON,
Printed by *A. Maxwell*, in the Year M.DC.LX.VIII.

The title page for Cavendish's 1666 *The Blazing World*, in which she affirmed her status as a "Princesse".

Newcastle House in Clerkenwell prior to its
eighteenth-century redevelopment.

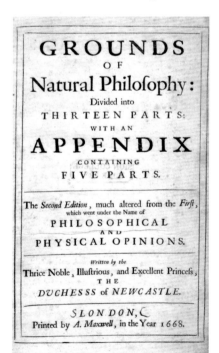

The title page to Cavendish's
1668 *Grounds of Natural
Philosophy*.

Margaret and William Cavendish's final
resting place in Westminster Abbey.

allowed to bear arms, and a central registry attempted to keep a track of their movements. One of the few conditions placed on Charles II's Restoration was, as the Declaration of Breda put it, a "free and general pardon" for those who had worked with the Protectorate or against the king. The final agreement – the Indemnity and Oblivion Act – did exempt some thirty men who had been directly involved in the regicide of Charles I, but the premise of the Act remained: there would not be the same level of political repression as there had been under Cromwell.

William and Margaret had more personal reasons to be hopeful for the political changes under Charles: as his former tutor and governor, William was surely in line for a well-paid, prestigious court appointment. His first hope was to become "master of the horse" – a well-remunerated, prominent position in which he would be responsible for the royal stables – but when he met Charles at The Hague, he was told that the position had already been awarded to Monck who had, it must be said, done rather more to ensure the Restoration. And back in London, William was no luckier: though he was able to reclaim much of his estates and possessions, no position at court, either ceremonial or powerful, was forthcoming. The new king was too busy trying to navigate a new political landscape to reward his former tutor, who had neither a sparkling war record nor great political nous.

Margaret returned to this rather anti-climactic scene of qualified joy. William's London house at Clerkenwell was still not open to him, and the couple had to remain in lodgings which were, in Margaret's words, "not fit for a person of his capacity".[37] William "gently reproved" Margaret for her displeasure, but the couple nonetheless moved to Dorset House, on the site of what is now Salisbury Square, not far from Fleet Street.[38] This was a little better, but, given that the couple only had a part of the house, and William still had no political position, Margaret thought the situation "not altogether to [her] satisfaction". She was soon to discover something else that was not very satisfying:

having been denied access to their Clerkenwell townhouse, the Cavendishes were about to have an even ruder shock when they visited William's estates in Nottingham. And Margaret was about to experience a situation that was normally the fate of wives much earlier in their marriage: for the first time, she had to meet William's family, as their new step-mother.

10

Women's kisses are unnatural

IN EARLY 1661, Samuel Pepys went to a play at Salisbury Court, a pre-Civil War theatre which was only a few metres away from Dorset House, the more sumptuous lodgings William and Margaret had moved to after her arrival in the city. The theatre – the last to be built before the conflict, and the only one to be constructed under Charles I's reign – had, quite literally, been through the wars.[1] It had been used for illicit performances during the conflict (on one particularly bold occasion, they had staged a Beaumont and Fletcher play called *A King and No King*); had seen its actors arrested still in their costumes during a raid in 1649; and had had its interiors "pulled down" to make it unusable as a playhouse during the early months of the Interregnum.[2]

When Pepys visited the theatre on 29 January 1661, it was not the first play he had attended since Charles II had made theatre legal again in November 1660. That honour had fallen to Thomas Killigrew's company, and their performance of *The Beggars Bush* in the makeshift theatre at Gibbon's Tennis Court in Lincoln's Inn. Pepys was so overjoyed that he called the small space the "finest play-house... that ever was in England". The rather less glorious Salisbury Court was one of the first residences of William Davenant's company – who had, along with Killigrew, been given a royal patent by the king – before they moved into the better-appointed playhouse at Lisle's Tennis Court, also in Lincoln's Inn Fields.

Reinstating theatre had been one of Charles II's first acts as king, and it set the tone for the rest of his reign: fun, games, and drunkenness; actress-mistresses; elaborate costumes; and scandal. But by January 1661, the sheer delight of being able to visit plays once more had become commonplace for Pepys and the other courtiers and aristocrats who could afford the expensive ticket prices that dwarfed the cost of pre-war plays at the likes of The Globe. Pepys, with Sir Edward Montagu (a Cromwellian who had recently switched his allegiance to Charles II), waited with "great patience and little expectation" after a "poor beginning", and settled in for three acts of John Fletcher and William Rowley's *The Maid in the Mill*.[3] The play – with its plot of squabbling nobles, the mistreatment of women by men, and the difficulty or inequality of marriage – was "well acted", and pleased Pepys. It would also have interested Margaret, even if she might have been compelled to shout from the audience about one particular plot-line: a young woman called Florimel manages to stop her would-be rapist's advances by pretending she is no longer a virgin, but nevertheless ends up marrying him after he discovers that she is not of as low birth as he originally thought.

* * *

William and Margaret were both keen playwrights and would have, undoubtedly, explored the new theatrical scene of London in the brief period they were in the capital together. But they could not have seen this particular play: by the time it was staged, William had "begged leave" from the king to depart from the court, and to retire to his "confused, entangled, and almost ruined estate".[4] This decision to leave the court he had fought so long to re-establish and to rejoin was not an easy choice, and nor was it the result of Margaret's continued pleas (she had a "great desire for a country life", and had found London living difficult). William left, in part, because he had not been awarded the titles or funds he believed his loyalty merited. In comparison to his first few months back at court in which he had received absolutely no preferment, he had been made a gentleman of the bedchamber in September 1660 – a prestigious court appointment but one with no real power. A month later, he was made the Lord Lieutenant of Nottingham: a more significant position, and one that gave him another excuse for his exit from London. William's worries were not just about status: he had expended much of his own money on the war and throughout his exile, and had made a sizeable loan to Charles I, and he struggled to recoup these costs.[5] His letter to the king is at pains to stress that he does not "retire through discontent" and he is "in no kind or ways displeased", but he goes on to write:

> I am so joyed at your Majesty's happy restoration, that I cannot be sad or troubled for any concern to my own particular[6]

Embedded in this letter of flattery and apology is the tacit admission that he *is* "sad or troubled", and knows he shouldn't admit it.

Retiring to their country estates was by no means as peaceful or easy as it sounds: Margaret and William had to pack up all their worldly belongings, and undertake a week-long journey with carriages and horses on rough, dangerous roads. But the Cavendishes also faced a more existential problem. They were travelling north to William's family homeland of the Midlands (Margaret's family home in Essex would not recover from the attacks and riots of the Civil Wars; she never returned to St John's Abbey) but they could not have been sure what awaited them when they arrived. Welbeck Abbey, the grand country house and former monastery in Sherwood Forest, had been bought by William's father, Sir Charles Cavendish, in 1599 and since then had been the family's primary residence. It was at Welbeck that William had left his daughters and his first wife

Elizabeth when he went off to fight and later when he went into exile, and it was Welbeck in which garrisons of troops on both sides of the war had made themselves at home.

But Welbeck was not William's favourite house: he much preferred Bolsover Castle, the fanciful hill-top structure ten miles to the west. It had been initially built by William's father on the site of the old medieval castle with the assistance of the famous designer Robert Smythson (responsible for Hardwick Hall, Longleat and Wollaton Hall), and had then been finished by William and Charles in a style influenced by Inigo Jones.[7] It had long, galleried staterooms, a wonderful view down into the countryside below, and a purpose-built riding school for all of William's horses: it was a house fashioned for pleasure and peace, rather than the rigours of wartime.

And wartime had not been kind to it: in 1649, long after William had retreated into exile and just after Charles I had been executed, the Council of State issued orders for the castle to be made uninhabitable. They ordered the "outworks... garden walls... the turrets and walls of the frontier court that are of strength" to be demolished, in order to prevent a Royalist garrison from sheltering there, and then went even further, ordering "all the doors of the house be taken away".[8] Even the woods – Robin Hood's woods, no less – had suffered: a "Mr. Clark", who had bought the land through the "Committee for Sale of Traitors' Estates" and decimated them by cutting far too many trees. "He has felled 1000 trees, and daily fells more. He fells in the heart of the forest, where the deer have their greatest relief", complained the verderers.[9]

Bolsover was a sorry sight: it was an uninhabitable scene of destruction, and the only objects saved – tapestries and paintings by Van Dyck – were those that William's eldest daughter, Jane, had managed to negotiate or bribe past local officials. When William had built the house after his father's death, it had been a symbol of his political and court ambitions: it was a house that could host kings, entertain other aristocrats, and demonstrate his mastery of intellectual pursuits and horsemanship alike. It must have felt tragically fitting to see its ruined walls after having left Charles II's court, with no hope of further political reward or favour.

In many ways, Welbeck was in no better state. The house had been managed during William's exile by his younger son, Henry, and his wife Frances, but the fact that it had been lived in did not mean that it was any closer to its former glories.* In the place of expensive silverware, luxurious table linen bought to entertain the king and queen, and glorious wall hangings and tapestries, nothing was left "but some few old feather-beds, and all those spoiled, and fit for no use". For a couple whose life in Antwerp had been predicated upon appearing wealthy, even if they could not always afford their excesses, this downturn in fortune – and a reminder of how William's family had been living during his absence – must have been shocking. Luckily, the Cavendishes didn't have to sleep on the "spoiled" mattresses: before moving out of the Abbey, Frances kindly left some furniture and linens behind for the couple, a fact that Margaret neglects to mention in her writing about the period.[10]

* * *

Margaret's role as step-mother to William's family would haunt the pair's first few years back in England. Whilst in exile William and Margaret had been joined sporadically by William's sons, or his brother Charles. These relationships may well have been fractious in their way, but the difficulties were broadly personal, rather than to do with the family's status, wealth, or inheritance. Now, back in England, William was the owner of an estate that was "very great before the wars", and Margaret's relationship to it was far from simple.

---

* Henry and Frances's eldest daughter, Elizabeth, went on to marry Christopher Monck – the son of George Monck, the man who made the Restoration possible.

In June 1659, Margaret's childlessness once again became an issue: Charles, William's oldest son, died of a stroke aged only thirty-two (despite his brother being the one who struggled with "convulsive trembling").[11] His title – and the prospect of all the land after his father's death – passed to Henry, by all accounts the less charming and well-loved of the sons. For the rest of the family, the tenuous nature of having only one heir was intolerable: his sister, Elizabeth, wrote that even "a girl of his would have been some comfort".[12] It wasn't until 1663 that Henry would have a son (also called Henry), but he would be unable to carry on either the Cavendish name, or the Newcastle dukedom: when he married the heiress Lady Elizabeth Percy in 1679, he had to agree to take her name.

After Charles's death, these difficulties only became more pronounced: Henry was afraid that William was trying to short-change him, and William was desperately begging Henry to save whatever he could from the estates without selling them to finance their debts. This was a moment of financial disagreement between father and son, made worse by the fact that, prior to his return to England, William lived on money his children had sent him. But Margaret's name is often mentioned. In one pleading letter, William writes, "I protest that is all the design my wife and I have in that business, for believe me she is as kind to you as she was to your brother, and so good a wife as she all for my family".[13] The invocation of Margaret is not accidental: Henry evidently thought that it was she who was influencing William, and she who threatened his financial stability.

And this early moment of familial discord, with Margaret as the "evil step-mother", was far from the only example. When the couple had married, they had both been penniless (in William's verse, the "Prince of Noland" married a woman whose "dower's gone").[14] But now, back in Nottinghamshire and with Henry and his wife Frances displaced from Welbeck, they could make the arrangements that should have been finalised at the time of their wedding: William had to settle a "jointure" on Margaret

– a portion of his estate that would be hers in the event that he died before her; a possibility that seemed more than likely, given the significant age gap. In October 1662, this settlement was finalised: Cavendish was to have an annuity of £1,125, and the manors of Chesterfield, Woodthorpe, and William's favourite, Bolsover Castle. This was a generous settlement, especially given that a jointure was normally matched by a dowry; something Margaret's scattered, much-diminished family were still unable to provide.* And it also altered the normal succession of the estates: William had had to break the entail (with Henry's permission), and there was no guarantee that these properties and lands would return to the male line after her death.[15]

In later years, the scope of her jointure would be increased – she would secure for herself Newcastle House at Clerkenwell, and more land in Sherwood Forest and Sibthorpe and Clipstone Park – but before this would happen, there would already be some disagreement.[16] Henry feared that, especially given the amount of land William had sold to fund his renovations, there would be no land left for his own children, or for the continuation of the family name and the dukedom. Both he and his wife wrote panicked letters to William, and William's telling response included the line "though I am very old, I do not yet dote, thank God".†[17] Once again, the implication is that Henry believed the sale of lands and the management of the Cavendish estate were controlled by Margaret.

Henry did have some cause to believe that his father's management of the estates was far from perfect, or was influenced by Margaret. The whole process, from the initial bill in the House of Commons to restore the estate which had

---

* At the time, they were more concerned with exhuming and re-burying their brother, Charles Lucas, after his execution at Colchester.
† Dote here does not have its contemporary meaning of affection and kindness, but rather means folly and madness brought on by old age; the implication is still that Margaret could not have been taking advantage of him.

resulted in a public quarrel between William and two other dukes who were also trying to recoup their wealth and an order from the king "not to stir out of their lodgings", had been marked by disagreements and drama.[18] And Margaret was not a woman who would have accepted anything other than a good settlement from her husband: much of her writing is driven by women who are cheated in marriage, or "forced... with threats" to "yield up" their "jointure".[19] Her own mother had managed her family's sizeable lands and mercantile concerns in Essex after her husband's death: Margaret was not brought up to believe that this was an area of life that a wife, or any woman, should be excluded from.

But there was a more pressing reason for Henry's concerns. Margaret was not the only young woman who had returned from Europe with a new husband on her arm: her life-long friend and maid since her days at St John's Abbey, Elizabeth Chaplain, had married Francis Topp, a businessman from Antwerp, and the pair had returned to England with the Cavendishes. William evidently trusted Topp, and by the mid-1660s he had a prominent role in the management of Welbeck. He had even replaced William's long-term steward, Andrew Clayton. Topp, who with William's help later became a baronet, Sir Francis, took over the day-to-day management of the estate, from drawing up important contracts and indentures, to dealing with tenants, paying servants, and controlling Henry's allowance. If you wanted anything doing at Welbeck, Topp was the person to have on side. And as the husband of her childhood friend, Margaret naturally had his ear, and his influence.

This uneasy situation continued throughout the 1660s. Henry evidently knew that Topp held the reins of power: in 1666, when he wanted William to sign a document agreeing not to sell any more of the lands so as to preserve them for future generations, he used Topp to draw up the document. But the simmering tension reached a head in 1670. Andrew Clayton (the now usurped steward, who still had a position at Welbeck) had promised one of William's tenants, Francis Liddell, that he could lower his rent, and get William to pay Liddell a bond that he owed him. Clayton soon realised that this would be impossible because "the Duchess did so narrowly... inspect his graces affairs". He detested Margaret's influence, and even accused her of wanting to remarry, "break up the family", and "go to rant at London".[20] Clayton and Liddell – along with their fellow conspirator, John Booth – decided the only way to lessen William's affection for Margaret (in order to better cheat him by lowering rents), was "to give her grace a dead blow and to divert his graces affections from her".[21] Accordingly, they wrote a letter "in an unknown hand and without a name", in which they blamed all recent diminishing respect for William upon his wife. In case the force of their rhetoric wasn't enough, they added an accusation: they claimed that Margaret was cheating on William, and with none other than Sir Francis Topp.

William did not believe the allegation for a second – he declared that someone "had abused Peg", his nickname for Margaret – but the elaborate conspiracy deserves some consideration. Why did the three men feel such a need to get rid of Margaret? They evidently believed, like Henry, that she was much too involved in the management of the estate. But why did they immediately turn to the possibility of Margaret cheating on William – and with a close member of the household? It is possible they thought this might work because knowledge of Margaret's closeness with William's brother, Charles, had spread. Some scholars have even suggested that the conspirators could have been paid by other family members to sow discord between the married pair, although the evidence for this is scanty.[22]

Even aside from monetary matters, family life was still not harmonious. Lady Jane Cavendish – William's oldest daughter: the woman who had written with her sister the play *The Concealed Fansyes* during the war, and had secured some of the house's riches against besieging Parliamentarian forces – had married Charles Cheyne, Viscount Newhaven, at some point during the Interregnum. Jane was not a fan of Margaret, and railed against the man she insisted upon calling "Mr Topp" in letters to her sister-in-law. But both Margaret and Jane were writers: could there not have been some common ground between them? Apparently not. Jane's funeral sermon, preached by Adam Littleton in 1669, is a call for women's equality, education, and engagement in public affairs:

> [Woman] is no less fitted in her natural Ingeny for all kind of *studies* and *employments:* though a *Salique Law*, hath excluded them from public offices and professions; and confined them mostly to the narrow territories of Home.[23]

To imagine hearing this preached inside a late-seventeenth-century church is to remind us that feminist history starts far earlier than we might otherwise imagine. But surely Margaret Cavendish – the poster girl for women's education and role in "public offices and professions" – should have been mentioned in such a eulogy? She is not mentioned by name, and, if there is an allusion to her, it is a cruel one. Littleton tells how Jane practised "economical government" and "play[ed] the purchaser and the merchant", but only "wherein her husband's cares are not concerned". Margaret, the implication is, had taken equality a step too far.

* * *

During these years of family disharmony, and squabbles over entails, indentures, and jointures, Margaret published two collections of plays: *Plays Written by the Thrice Noble, Illustrious and Excellent Princess* (1662), and *Plays, Never Before Printed* (1668). The eighteen plays in the two collections (plus a fragment called "a piece of a play") are the works that Margaret had written in Antwerp, and which she claims in *Sociable Letters* had "drowned" on their journey over to England to be printed the first time.[24] Her claim that their watery demise hindered their printing is somewhat disingenuous, given that she stresses her luck in still having "copies of them safely with me". Why, then, did she choose to print them now?

Intriguingly, they are the first of her books to be printed by a woman: Thomas Warren's widow, Alice, took over his printing business in 1661, and it is possible that the book's publication was delayed by his illness.[25] Women working in printing – and, indeed, many other guilds – were far from unusual during this period: by marrying a man who had "the freedom" to practise his trade, his wife or widow also had the same liberty.[26] From 1666 onwards, almost all of Margaret's works were published by an "A. Maxwell" – Anne Maxwell, the widow of David Maxwell, who managed a large printing business by herself.

The moment Cavendish chose to publish her plays was a dramatic time for the theatre, with both the King's Company (Killigrew) and the Duke's Company (Davenant) scrabbling for texts to perform, and actors and actresses to perform them. But Cavendish's works were radically different from the pre-war plays that were the staple of the companies in the early 1660s, or the world of Restoration drama that would soon come (think William Wycherley's infamous "china scene" from *The Country Wife,* and endless bawdy comedies). Instead of writing for two hours of traffic upon a stage, Cavendish's plays – written under the influence of her playwright husband, and when theatres were closed with no reopening in sight – were hardly designed for performance. Many of them were in two parts, with each part five acts long; a length that would make performance an interminable ordeal for the audience. Nor were their plots intended for the stage: Cavendish wrote texts more akin to a cacophonous episodic TV series, with subplots and simultaneous narrative arcs which seem to have nothing to do with each other. Cavendish was aware of the faults – or unique qualities – of her works, and in her typically numerous prefaces to the reader, addressed them:

... most of my Plays would seem tedious upon the Stage, by reason they are somewhat long, although most are divided into first and second Parts; for having much variety in them, I could not possibly make them shorter [...] yet, I believe none of my Plays are so long as Ben Jonson's Fox, or Alchymist, which in truth, are somewhat too long[27]

She goes on to say that, having been printed, they could now never be performed, since "what men are acquainted with, is despised".

Cavendish was certainly not publishing for performance, or even to join in with the burgeoning Restoration theatre culture – if anything, she seems to shun it, and all the conventions it requires. She despairs of plays which require "all the actors to meet at the latter end upon the stage in a flock together", and rejects the assumption that all her characters should be "of an acquaintance", or that there should be a reason for them all to be in the same play together. It is no surprise that very few of her plays have ever been performed, despite the strength of Margaret's ideas, and the fact that her husband's dramas were a feature of the Restoration stage.*

Cavendish saw her plays less as texts for performance than as vehicles for her ideas – ideas more radical, and more difficult to couch in philosophical and scientific terms, than in many of her other texts. There is a hint of this in one of her prefatory notes:

I Know there are many Scholastical and Pedantical persons that will condemn my writings, because I do not keep strictly

---

* There is, however, a chance that one of Cavendish's plays was performed on stage during the period: James Fitzmaurice argues that *The Lottery* – a manuscript play found in Nottingham University's Portland Collection – was written by Margaret rather than William, and was performed at some point in the early 1660s. See James Fitzmaurice, "'The Lotterie': A Transcription of a Manuscript Play Probably by Margaret Cavendish", *Huntington Library Quarterly*, 66 (2003), 155–67.

to the Masculine and Feminine Genders, as they call them
as for example, a Lock and a Key, the one is the Masculine
Gender, the other the Feminine Gender...

She goes on to rail against the fact that "the seven deadly sins
are shees" and claims she "know[s] no reason but that I may
as well make them Hees". In the tradition of Jacobean theatre,
cross-dressing and gender-swapping were commonplace and
accepted; and, on the Restoration stage, it reached new heights
with the possibilities of women actresses playing the "breeches
parts" and titillating all the men who came to see their shapely
calves (and more). Given that Cavendish has just made it clear
that her plays are not for performance, her point is rather more
radical: she is not just writing about changed costumes and
disguises, but rather the supposed "natural" characteristics of
each gender.

And her first collection of plays does, indeed, not "keep
strictly to the Masculine and Feminine Genders": there are
plays about cross-dressing, battle-hardened heroines (*Love's
Adventures*), women who take on martial roles (*Bell in Campo*),
and women who disagree with the fate of their sex in marriage
(*Wit's Cabal*).

It is this last subject that provides a clue to why Margaret
chose to publish these two collections of plays in 1662 and
1668 – just when the family she had married into in 1644
began to make her life difficult. Almost every single one of
her plays depicts women who are unhappy with marriage, or
who feel they have been swindled into a life that is less than
they deserved. In the 1662 collection, *The Several Wits* (the
women are the wits, rather than the men who come to pay them
homage) tells the story of three young women who find their
suitors rather lacking: one "sting[s]" them with her tongue; the
second tricks all the men into believing she is "in love with
them"; and the third – the most Cavendish-like – extols the
benefits of a solitary life:

Few doth live as they should, that is, to live within themselves; for the soul, which is the supreme part of life, is never at home, but goeth wandering about, from place to place, from person to person...[28]

It is intellectual pursuits, rather than marital delights, that get Lady Solid hot under the collar. The other plays in the collection are no less damning of all the pleasures that marriage can provide. The plays are replete with women who are only married for their money; women (and men) who only marry on their parents' wishes; and women who are left in poverty by their husband's poor financial decisions. In *Youths Glory, and Deaths Banquet*, the clever philosopher-child eschews the delights of marriage and society in favour of her books, and utters the immortal sentence, "For Heaven knows, it is the only curse I fear, a husband."[29] In *The Matrimonial Trouble*, there are no fewer than nine unhappy couples – and the play ends with so much divorce, murder, and general unhappiness that even the repaired relationships begin to look rather shaky. And when the four "Sociable Virgins" in *The Unnatural Tragedy* sit down for a moment of light chatter, the dialogue opens thus:

MATRON: Come Ladies, what discourse shall we have to day?
1 VIRGIN: Let us sit and rail against men.[30]

At the end of the last play in the collection, *The Female Academy*, the young men who have been plaguing the women who live in a secluded school finally learn that the women there are not "cloister[ed]" but are instead being "taught how to be good wives when they are married".[31] After reading some six hundred pages of feminist anger about marriage and the state of women's role in it, it is hard not to read that line as ironic.

If Cavendish was obviously not an admirer of the institution of marriage – and, by 1662, had begun to see its flaws all too clearly – her relationship with William still had its perks: as the more experienced playwright, he wrote a handful of the scenes in the 1662 volume, and wrote all of the songs that appeared within the plays. These volumes, like the part of *Natures Pictures* that includes William's texts, are material proof of the couple's intellectual collaboration.

Her much smaller 1668 volume contains some of her most autobiographical plays. After a prefatory note in which she once again apologises for not conforming to "ancient Rules", that is, the Aristotelian unities, she prints *The Presence* (about her time at court), and *The Bridals* – a play with three brides, one of whom is called "Lady Vertue" who is married to "Sir William Sage".

If "Lady Vertue" is meant to be a portrait of Cavendish – as some scholars have suggested – then her predicament paints an interesting picture.[32] After a stoic, sensible approach to marriage, and the supposed sensible decision not to feign the modesty and skittishness usual to other brides ("if marriage had been an act that deserves a blush, I would not have been married"), she nonetheless does not find married life as simple as her name might suggest. In a bold speech, she declares:

Women are the unhappiest creatures which nature ever made; not only that they are the most shiftless creatures, but the most abused of any other creatures, and only by men; who do not only continually assault them, and endeavour to corrupt and betray them, but they have enslaved them[33]

She goes on, and even announces "Men are like devils to women." Nor does the play end with a happy reconciliation: after Sir William asks his wife to "dress your self fine" for some dinner guests, she argues that she "cares not" how the guests like her. His response is to "keep [her] in [her] chamber".[34] If this is a moment of comedy, its humour is rather lessened by the vitriol of Lady Vertue's speech.

Despite the clear autobiographical referents in some of her plays, it is impossible, and mistaken, to read Cavendish's plays as little more than fictionalised fact. Whilst the strength and variety of the anti-marriage sentiment clearly reveals her beliefs, she would have been unlikely to publish something that could, so clearly, be interpreted as a polemic against her husband. These plays are less the autobiography of one woman than they are a collective autobiography of "women" as a whole.

* * *

In one 1668 play, this ambition and scope beyond biography becomes clear. *The Convent of Pleasure* is the last full-length play in the 1668 volume, and it is also the shortest: it is comprised of five short acts, with one act containing just one scene. But its brevity belies its radicalism, and its bravery: it is one of the earliest plays that stages lesbian, homosexual desire, and certainly the first to be written by a woman.*

In the late seventeenth century, the idea that women could love other women and want to have sex with them was not entirely new. In medical texts from the period – including Jane Sharp's *The Midwives Book* – there was much discussion of "women *Hermaphrodites*": women whose "clitoris" was "greater, and hanging out more than others have, and so shows like a man's yard [penis]".[35] These women, with "a thing like a Yard", were supposed to be sexually attracted to women: their enlarged clitoris "will swell and stand stiff if it be provoked, and some lewd women have endeavoured to use it as men do theirs".[36] The quasi-anatomical discussion here belies an interesting truth: doctors, writers, and scientists had noticed that women were interested in other women – and even wanted to have sex with them – but attributed this to an anatomical abnormality, rather than a difference in sexuality.[37] To modern ears it sounds

---

* "Stages" is a difficult word for Cavendish's unperformed plays, but I use it for comparison's sake.

reductive and insulting, but it does, at least, demonstrate an engagement with the idea of female homosexuality; an engagement that was not limited to medical books.

Throughout the period, classical texts that discussed lesbianism were available in translation: from the poems of Sappho to the cruder writings of the second-century Greek writer Lucian, who in his *Dialogues of the Courtesans*, wrote of a conversation between two women, Leana and Clonarium, in which one of the women admits to a moment of sapphic pleasure:

> Then I threw my arms around her as though she were a man, and she went to work, kissing me, and panting, and apparently enjoying herself immensely[38]

In a translation from 1684, Leana is seemingly afraid of elaborating on what this moment of pleasure was like: "Paw, paw! Enquire no further; for it's neither handsome for me to say, nor you to hear it", she says to her companion.[39]

In the hugely popular pastoral tragicomedy *Il Pastor Fido*, which had been translated into English as *The Faithful Shepherd* in 1647, the shepherd Mirtillo is in love with a nymph, Amarillis, but cannot marry her. To get around this pesky difficulty, he dresses as a woman, and is in disguise when the other nymphs then suggest they "wage a kissing war".[40] The ensuing scene of (pretend) homosexual embraces was inordinately popular: it was painted by everyone from the Dutch painter Jacob van Loo, to the court painter Van Dyck (who also painted William's portrait). Even though the romance ends with the triumph of heterosexuality (and the paintings, too, often show Mirtillo as conspicuously masculine), the popularity of the story is still interesting: as the literary critic Valerie Straub asks, "What are we to make of an all-female kissing war? Is this standard sport among female rustics?"[41]

In 1633, John Donne (perhaps – the attribution of the poem is dubious) contributed to the debate, with his "Sappho to Philaenis". Here, Sappho lusts after her female lover:

Thy body is a natural paradise,
In whose self, unmanured, all pleasure lies,
Nor needs perfection; why shouldst thou then
Admit the tillage of a harsh rough man?[42]

And a century earlier, Pietro Aretino's rather more pornographic *The Ragionamenti* was published in London (in Italian, a language accessible to many of the scholars of the day). Aretino portrayed a frank discussion about the benefits of being either a nun or a whore, before he described a midwife watching another woman have sex:

> My God, her neck! And her breasts, Nurse, those two tits would have corrupted virgins and made martyrs unfrock themselves. I lost my wits when I saw that lovely body [...] I put my hand on my you-know-what and rubbed it just the way a man does when he hasn't a place to put it.[43]

Evidently, scandalous lesbian literature had a long history before the infamous trial over Radclyffe Hall's *The Well of Loneliness* in 1928.

But other than Sharp's *Midwives Book*, all of these depictions of lesbianism are fictional, fanciful, and were written by men – and bear the sticky, lecherous hallmarks of their over-excited authors. What about lesbian literature written by women?

Women in the period were not afraid of writing poems that made the strength of their feelings for other women clear. Katherine Philips wrote poems to her friends that have the hint of more than friendship, such as "To Mrs Mary Awbrey":

Soul of my Soul, my Joy, my Crown, my Friend,
A name which all the rest doth comprehend;
How happy are we now, whose Souls are grown,
By an incomparable mixture, one:[44]

The very invocation of the word "friend" being "a name" which others might "comprehend" suggests that the pair must be more than friends. This is far from the only poem of intense love for a woman that Philips wrote, and a similar preoccupation can be found in Aphra Behn's verse from the period. In one poem, "To the Fair Clarinda, who made Love to me, imagin'd more than Woman", she pokes fun at men, and a society, which did not quite believe that women could have sex with each other:

> In pity to our Sex sure thou wert sent,
> That we might Love, and yet be Innocent:
> For sure no Crime with thee we can commit;[45]

Either sex with a woman – the "crime" – is either impossible (which Behn's poem rather disproves) or it is nothing illegal, and is instead a joy sent to the "pit[iful]" sex, Behn's poem seems to laughingly suggest.

But women did not just *write* about lesbian desire and close relationships between women: some of them even lived it. Some Quaker women who toured the country and preached together in pairs during the wars and the Interregnum were, it has been suggested, in romantic relationships.[46] And, years later, in the late eighteenth century, Lady Eleanor Butler and The Hon. Sarah Ponsonby ran away from their intended marriages and moved to a gothic cottage in North Wales, where they lived out the rest of their days together and referred to each other as "my Heart's darling" and "my sweet love". They dedicated their lives to each other, had a succession of dogs called Sappho, and entertained a long stream of esteemed literary guests: as one scholar has put it, "they were the Gertrude Stein and Alice B. Toklas of their age".[47]

But, back in the seventeenth century, why are Aphra Behn and Katherine Philips now not heralded as early lesbians, or at least, early modern women who wrote about homosexual desire? This is a subject of some debate – a debate which spilled over into the battlegrounds of second-wave feminism. In Renaissance England, there was a cult of "Romantic Friendship": a type of friendship influenced by Platonism, that made little difference between deep friendship and erotic love. In the Renaissance period, it was male friendship that received the most attention but, by the seventeenth century, women had taken over, and some scholars see Katherine Philips's writing as the "best literary record" of this type of relationship.[48] For them, she was writing about a Platonic ideal of a friendship which was no less than an erotic relationship – and was, indeed, superior to it – but was not itself sexual. In this argument, even the relationship between the Ladies of Llangollen was a "romantic friendship" and nothing more.

This view was picked up by Germaine Greer and other editors in their collection *Kissing the Rod: An Anthology of Seventeenth-Century Women's Verse*, in which they write that "some of [Katherine Philips's] champions choose to ignore her own stipulation that such friendship be free from carnal interest".[49] Elaine Hobby, writing just three years after the anthology was published in 1988, did not accept this argument, instead positing that Philips was a "closet lesbian", and that the "asexual reading" of her verse was "more comfortable to these heterosexual feminists".[50] Hobby was writing in the period after second-wave feminism had often excluded lesbianism for fear "the Lavender Menace" would discredit the movement. Her argument is bold, but it loses some of its force towards the end: she attacks Philips's Royalism as something "that not all lesbians today would celebrate", as if all gay women must, necessarily, be Puritans or Republicans.

The debate here is heated on both sides – and, perhaps, both are missing the point. As Aphra Behn's poem about the "crime" of sex between women shows, so-called "romantic friendship" evidently did function as a cover for homosexual activity in some cases, but in others, it also must have been the truth. The sheer number of intensely romantic poems Philips wrote to her female correspondents suggests that, unless she was something of a female Lothario, at least some of them must have just been friends.

* * *

But in Cavendish's *The Convent of Pleasure*, there is rather less ambiguity about romantic friendship. The plot follows the premise of many of her other plays: after Lady Happy is left a wealthy orphan, she is much courted by men who want to marry her. In response, she and a band of other women retreat into female-only seclusion in "The Convent of Pleasure". Their "incloister[ing]" is along the lines of what Mary Astell would suggest two decades later in her *A Serious Proposal to the Ladies*: it is a life "retired from the World", but "not from pleasures".[51] The women will still read, educate, and entertain each other – all in a countryside retreat, an ideal that would continue long after Cavendish's death.[52]

The women proceed happily to their convent, where they make do without any of the male sex – Lady Happy has "Women-Physicians, Surgeons, and Apocatheries" – which greatly angers the men who had intended to woo her.[53] Lady Happy's opening address to her women about their new style of life is so idyllic that it bears quoting:

> In the Spring, our chambers are hung with silk-damask, and all other things suitable to it; and a great looking-glass in each chamber, that we may view ourselves and take pleasure in our own beauties, whilst they are fresh and young [...] in the Summer I have all our Chambers hung with Taffety [...] To invite repose in the Autum, all our Chambers are hung with Gilt Leather, or Franchipane...[54]

This is no austere nunnery: it is a house of relaxation, delight, and material pleasure (a subject on which Cavendish differs from Astell). It recalls something of the opening of bell hooks's essay "Women Artists: The Creative Process":

I am a girl who dreams of leisure. Reverie has always been
necessary to my existence. I have needed long hours where I
am stretched out, wearing silks, satins, and cashmeres, just
alone with myself, embraced by the beauty around me.[55]

It would be too much to argue that hooks had read Cavendish
– or that an essay collection about Black American artists in
the twentieth century has much *need* for Cavendish – but the
same principle of female relaxation and delight in seclusion can
be found in the two texts, despite the centuries that separate
them. This is a world where solitude is necessary to think and
create, and where women, in the absence of men, can "explore
intimately and deeply all aspects of female experience".[56] It is
no surprise that, once safely inside the Convent of Pleasure,
Cavendish's women act, sing, and dance – and rail against the
men and marriages that exist outside their walls.

Into this hooksian world of reverie and relaxation enters a
distraction and, unlike what distracts hooks, it is not a pen or
the desire to write. One day, when the women are rehearsing a
play (which is, naturally, about marriage), a messenger comes
in to tell Lady Happy that a "foreign Princess" has arrived,
who wants to join the convent and become one of "nature's
devotees". This princess had heard of the convent and had
heard that some of the ladies within "do accoustre themselves
in masculine habits, and act lovers-parts".[57] She adopts
this role, and soon becomes a close friend of Lady Happy.
After a scene in which the women perform a play about the
deficiencies of marriage (one woman even rails against her
"jointure" being taken off her), Lady Happy appears on stage
alone, and speaks:

LADY HAPPY: My Name is Happy, and so was my
Condition, before I saw this Princess; but now I am like to
be the most unhappy Maid alive: But why may not I love a
Woman with the same affection I could a Man?[58]

This is not mere romantic friendship: Lady Happy has told the audience she wants to love a woman as she would "a Man". After the Princess appears on stage, the pair debate about whether or not they should kiss. Lady Happy knows that a kiss would be beyond the bounds of romantic friendship; she declares "innocent lovers do not use to kiss". But, nevertheless, they do "embrace and kiss, and hold each other in their arms". Afterwards, the Princess speaks:

These my Embraces though of a female kind,
May be as fervent as a masculine mind.[59]

Cavendish was exploring and writing lesbianism in ways that transcended the romantic friendship of Aphra Behn and Katherine Philips, and in a different way to the titillating desires of the men who were writing about same-sex love in the period. And she was also writing outside the stage conventions of the time. Women had been actresses on the stage since the Restoration, and many plays gave them parts that required cross-dressing in order to show off their form in male clothes, and invite the possibility of homosexual desire when another actress falls in love with a woman who is disguised as a man. But in writing a play that was not meant to be staged, and without any hint of titillation or erotic thrill for the audience, Cavendish was not exploring lesbianism as a site of lustful, voyeuristic desire. Her interest was far less base, and far more ground-breaking. She was truly exploring the idea of women loving each other as if one were "a Man".

But a problem irrupts into this pastoral, lesbian idyll (the women play at being shepherdesses, dance round a maypole, and act out a tableau with water-nymphs and sea-goddesses). In Act V – and in a conspicuous echo of *The Faithful Shepherd* – a woman runs on stage and shouts, "O Ladies, Ladies! You're all betrayed, undone, undone; for there is a man disguised in the Convent, search and you'll find it."[60] It is not too far-fetched to think that the "it" is the man's penis, and they do find it: the "foreign Princess" is, in fact, a foreign prince, and has tricked Lady Happy. From this point onwards, the previously verbose Lady Happy falls silent, and only speaks two lines when asking the fool Mimick to accompany her in her marriage. The Prince has no problem speaking: he decides the fate of her convent (half for "virgins" and half for "widows": women are now defined by their marital status), and even directs the remaining action of the play.[61] Critics have argued that Cavendish is restoring the natural order of the world; she "reimposes marital alliance as the necessary outcome of female affectivity".[62] But given Lady Happy's sorry state – and the play's unrelenting focus on the horrors of men and marriage – can we really read this ending without a disquieting, foreboding sense of what is to come?

From her enviable place as the lady and mistress of all, Lady Happy has fallen far, and fallen silent. The culprit? Marriage to a man, of course.

11

The thrice noble, illustrious, and excellent Princess of Philosophy

IN 1666, CAVENDISH published her now most-famous and most-anthologised work. *The Blazing World* is a full-length work of fiction that encapsulates so many of Cavendish's fears and ambitions: it is the story of a young woman who is wrenched from her home by a marauding sailor and an inevitable storm, before she passes into "another world" which is joined to her own "pole to pole". In this other world, she becomes the Empress, and sets about learning as much philosophy as she can, all whilst displaying her regal brilliance and beauty and, in a moment of extreme meta-narrative, she even meets the Duchess of Newcastle. It's a brilliant work – quixotic; ambitious; at times hilariously comic, at other points wonderfully sensual – and will be discussed fully in the next chapter. But there's a moment when the Empress and the fictional Cavendish are in conversation that bears quoting now. Cavendish is telling the Empress "the reason of her melancholic humour":

> The Duchess answered... my present desire is that I would be a great Princess. The Empress replied, so you are; for you are a Princess of the fourth or fifth degree; for a Duke or Duchess is the highest title or honour that a subject can arrive to, as being the next to a Kings Title; and as for the name of a Prince or Princess, it belongs to all that are adopted to the Crown[1]

Fittingly enough, the book was published with a title-page which proclaimed that Cavendish was the "Thrice Noble, Illustrious, and Excellent PRINCESS, the Duchess of Newcastle".[2] Margaret had come a long way since 1653, when there had been such debate about her noble title in the years of the Interregnum that the frontispiece to *Poems and Fancies* had had to be reprinted. (The debate was due to the fact that William's title in 1653 – "Marquess of Newcastle-upon-Tyne" – had been awarded during the wars, and so was not valid in the Interregnum.)

But how had Margaret become a duchess (or, as she was so keen to point out, technically a "princess")?* After the rather ungrateful response to William's loyalty in the early years of the Restoration – as Cavendish would later calculate in her biography of her husband, he had lost nearly a million pounds as a result of his support for the king during the Civil War – things began to improve in 1664. William was still owed money by the Crown, and was not about to return to the centre of political affairs (where his rival, Edward Hyde, Earl of Clarendon, was now Lord High Chancellor). But the new king did not forget his former tutor entirely. On 7 June, William must have been ecstatic to open this letter:

> I have received yours by your son, and am resolved to grant your request. Send me therefore word what title you desire to have, or whether you will choose to keep your old and leave the rest to me. [...] I am glad you enjoy your health for I love you very well.[3]

William was to have his ultimate prize: he was to be made a duke, the highest level of nobility, just one notch below the monarchy. Such an honour required William to leave the countryside and travel to London for the ceremony at court – something he had

---

* There seem to be no other non-royal duchesses who insisted upon this honorific title in the period.

not done for either the king's coronation in April 1661, or for the ceremony in the same year that formally inducted him into the Order of the Garter (the order of chivalry he had been appointed to in 1650). On both occasions, it was his son, Henry, who had been present instead.

This occasion was far too splendid for William to rely on a deputy. Nearly a year after the king had promised to grant the request (in his letter, Charles had written that "you must leave the time to me, to accommodate it to some other ends of mine"), William and Margaret made the journey down from Welbeck to London. As in the early days of the Restoration, they could not stay in Newcastle House in Clerkenwell, which was still the subject of an on-going court dispute. This did not prevent the Cavendishes from revelling in their splendour and status: the couple entered the restored capital "with a princely train" and were greeted by "many of the nobility". William went to court "in great state", and accompanied by his "good duchess".[4] The countless iniquities and disappointments of the exile and Restoration could not have been erased by this moment of grand ceremony, but it certainly pleased both Margaret and William: in works published after this date, Cavendish is always at pains to stress her noble lineage, and in her biography of William, she includes a translation of the letters patent that made him a duke.

Cavendish's ambitions were always of a literary, rather than a social nature – when she had been around the other noble women at Henrietta Maria's court, she had parodied their fripperies and seemingly nonsensical concerns in her writing. Nevertheless, given her desire for fame – and a part of her to live on after her death – she must have delighted in the sense of history and status that came with becoming a duchess. It was probably during this brief stay in London that she was painted by Peter Lely, the preeminent portrait painter of the period, and the "Principal Painter in Ordinary" to the king. By 1665, Lely was in high demand, and had a whole studio of assistant painters who would often complete a canvas after he had finished working on the face. It was long thought that this was how the portrait of Cavendish was executed, but specialists at Christie's recently updated the attribution to Lely himself. This would have been an expensive painting. Lely was busy: he had recently completed his series "Windsor Beauties" of paintings of court women (many of whom were Charles's mistresses), and was in mid-commission for his "Flagmen of Lowestoft" series – a group of portraits of naval leaders who had fought in a great battle with the Dutch off the Suffolk coast in 1665. Whilst his portraits of the men show them standing in commanding positions, holding swords or gesturing at naval scenes, his depictions of women were rather more gentle. His ladies were normally painted seated, either dressed in the height of court fashion, or in loose robes meant to suggest the togas and dresses of antiquity. His women all have the idealised, small oval face of the seventeenth century, and are shown with much of their bust on display, as was the fashion at the time. For portraits of mistresses, Lely went even further and often depicted them with one breast entirely bared.

There was precedent for this type of hyper-feminine portrait in the Lucas family. Margaret's sister, Mary, had been painted in 1636 by Adriaen Hanneman: the canvas is awash with expanses of pink and white silk, and this colouring is echoed in his rendering of her skin. Mary looks like a Stuart beauty, but an ultimately unremarkable – and unmemorable – woman. Indeed, the painting's sitter has been misidentified many times.[5]

In Cavendish's portrait, however, there is no doubt about the identity of the woman at the centre of the composition. The painting is full-length, and Cavendish stands with her head and body turned just towards the viewer: hers is no demure, coy gaze, but instead a haughty, regal stare. Her positioning is more akin to Van Dyck's portrait of Henrietta Maria – or even the forceful, standing portraits of the military men Lely was working on in the same period. Like them, Margaret stands with one hand resting on an object in the background, and one hand raised in the foreground. It is a pose that suggests strength and action, rather than delicacy and passivity. Cavendish is dressed in extraordinarily ornate clothes (when the couple stayed in London, they managed to spend £700 at one silk merchant alone), and the background seems to be the opulent setting of a grand house or country seat.[6] She is even wearing the red formal robes of a duchess which were normally reserved for coronations – there is no mistaking the status, or the power, of the woman in this portrait. The only thing that *does* clash with her newfound role is her headwear: instead of the expected ducal coronet, Cavendish is adorned with a black velvet feathered hat – a masculine, unexpected touch to her outfit. If Cavendish was now a duchess, she was by no means a typical one.

* * *

Cavendish's sojourn in London in 1665 was, by all accounts, not as spectacular or glamorous as the visit she would make in 1667. The Newcastle dukedom or their appearance at court is not mentioned in either Pepys's or Evelyn's diary, and it seems the couple left London within a few months of the ceremony. The early delight of Restoration London had waned as the city was in the grip of the worst outbreak of plague since the Black Death in 1348. By July, Charles II and his followers relocated to Hampton Court, before eventually settling (as in the Civil War days) in Oxford. That same month, Evelyn would write that "there died of the plague in London this week 1,100; and in the week following, above 2,000".[7] Even by autumn, things had not returned to normal, as both Parliament and the law courts were relocated out of the capital.

Regardless of the brevity of her stay in the city, this period marks a new stage in Cavendish's life: a stage in which she, finally, achieved the fame and renown she had craved all her life, and, more importantly, the intellectual reputation she had been continually seeking.

When Cavendish published her plays in 1662 and 1668, she was publishing work that she had written and refined while in Antwerp. After her return to England, and the comparative calm of Welbeck, she began to write new pieces. In the years between 1662 and 1668, she published – excluding the plays – no fewer than seven original works, including her *Orations of Divers Sorts* (1662), her *Philosophical Letters* (1664), and her biography of William in 1667. In this period, she also radically altered and developed her thoughts on scientific natural philosophy, and published *Observations Upon Experimental Philosophy* (with *The Blazing World* appended) in 1666, and *Grounds of Natural Philosophy* in 1668.

The country retreat of the couple at Welbeck was far from isolated: they were close to Nottingham – one of the major cities in the North – and could send for books and other objects from London, which they often did. Now with a secretary to transcribe her writing and assist with the printing process of her work, Cavendish also began an ambitious programme of further self-education and of reading other authors. One bill for books Margaret ordered from London suggests that she bought one or two hundred volumes at a time.[8]

The product of this voracious reading is felt throughout her writing in the period, but the scale of its effect can be seen by comparing the two books she published in 1664: *Sociable Letters* (which was written in Antwerp) and *Philosophical Letters*.[9] The epistolary form was not entirely new, given that "real" (as opposed to fictional or written-for-publication) letters had been a feature of the literary scene for some years; in 1645, *The Kings Cabinet Opened* – a collection of letters taken from the king's "cabinet" at Naseby – had been published as a form of Parliamentarian propaganda. Mothers' and fathers' "advice" letters to their children were a mainstay of the publishing world. And a decade later, Aphra Behn's *Love-Letters Between a Noble-Man and his Sister* (1684-7) would – with all its attendant incestuous scandal and raunchy lasciviousness – pave the way for the more famous epistolary novels of the eighteenth century: Samuel Richardson's *Pamela* (1740), and Frances Burney's *Evalina* (1778).

Cavendish's books were subtly different to earlier work of this kind, or the epistolary novels that would come later. Whilst many of her epistles in *Sociable Letters* do relate to the events of her life – and, from the initials she uses, the identity of some of the people she discusses can be discerned – she was not simply publishing her verbatim correspondence. In this in-between genre – not entirely fact, nor entirely fiction – she creates an explicitly female readership, akin to those imagined in books about midwifery or childbirth. Each and every letter is addressed to "Madam", and the intimacy implied – gossip about marriages, other women, and husbands being "persecuted by another man's whore" – conjures a sense of closeness, the illusion that the letters really *were* written to the reader.[10]

Within this community of female readers, Cavendish's concerns go well beyond the expected discussion of "women's subjects". One letter describes how Cavendish, "being not in the humour of writing", took up a book: "Plutarch's Lives, or as some call them, Plutarch's lies". Her discussion of the classical writer is not overly reverent, but tempered with humour. After reading "the Life of Pericles", she writes:

> ... this Pericles I did much Admire all the time I read of him, until I did read where it was mentioned of his marrying Aspasia, a famous courtesan, and then I did not think him so Wise a man as I did before, in that he could not rule his Passion better, but to marry a whore[11]

This combination of censorious prudishness and educated commentary is typical of Cavendish, with her many interests and contradictions. But her engagement with literature and the writing of other authors is present throughout *Sociable Letters*. In what is the first recorded instance of a woman writing literary criticism on Shakespeare (and, regardless of gender, among the earliest published critiques of the playwright), she defends his comedies against an unnamed person who claimed they "were made up only with clowns, fools, watchmen, and the like":

> Tis harder, and requires more wit to express nonsense than sense, and ordinary conversations, than that which is unusual; and 'tis harder, and requires more wit to express a jester, than a grave statesman [...] and so well he hath express'd in his plays all sorts of persons, as one would think he had been transformed into every one of those persons he hath described[12]

Cavendish's defence of Shakespeare's comedy was not just an indication of her wide reading and intellectual interest, but also her originality. In the mid-seventeenth century, Shakespeare's reputation was far from the near-deified status he enjoys now. Cavendish was writing a decade before John Dryden's *Essay of Dramatic Poesie* (1668) would argue for the bard's supremacy, and even he rails against Shakespeare's comedy: "he is many times flat, insipid; his comic wit degenerating into clenches".[13] Dryden's commentary on Shakespeare's successes – "he was the man... who had the largest and most comprehensive soul [...] when he describes any thing, you more than see it, you feel it too" – echoes Cavendish's affirmation of his tangible, transformative powers. In a work which appeared six years before Dryden's essay, she wrote:

> [Shakespeare] presents passions so naturally, and misfortunes so probably, as he pierces the souls of his readers with such a true sense and feeling thereof, that it forces tears through their eyes, and almost persuades them, they are really actors, or at least present at those tragedies.[14]

Is there a chance that Dryden – the premier male poet of the Restoration, and the first Poet Laureate – had read Cavendish, and been influenced by her? The two writers undoubtedly share a certain sensibility: an ability to see the *spirit* of Shakespeare's work, rather than be wholly distracted by his supposed "oddities" and differences from popular plays of the age. This was, after all, the period in which Shakespeare's plays were being edited, and supposedly "improved upon", with rampant abandon – a fashion Dryden would join in with, but not quite to the extent of some other authors (in 1681, Nahum Tate even gave *King Lear* a happy ending).

In her writing after her return from exile, Cavendish's engagement with the works of other authors increased. Her *Philosophical Letters* is rooted in the texts she critiques, and is peppered with quotations. The book is split into four sections, each with multiple parts, and is prefaced by an apologetic letter to her husband ("by reason it is a book of controversies") and a letter to "the most famous University of Cambridge".[15] The apology and the over-effusive letter to Cambridge ("I pray God your University may flourish to the end of the World") make more sense when the reader reaches the third prefatory letter:

> I took the liberty to declare my own opinions as other philosophers do, and to that purpose I have here set down several famous and learned authors opinions, and my answers to them in the form of letters[16]

Here is the reason for the apology and the sycophantic dedication to the University: Cavendish was aware that what she was now offering was potentially inflammatory. The book is a critique of different philosophers' beliefs: she goes head-to-head with Hobbes, Descartes, Henry More (a philosopher from the Cambridge Platonist school), and the alchemist Jan Baptist van Helmont. If Cavendish's previous works could be criticised for philosophical speculation that bears little relation to the common use of terms and definitions in the period, no such critique could be made of this new work: now was the moment for her to engage directly with other "scientists" of the period.

Her discussion of the work of these thinkers is more important – and more successful – than scholars have sometimes suggested (one of her earlier biographers remarked that many of the theories she engaged with "were simply beyond her comprehension").[17] Cavendish recognised that some of her earlier works had not been rooted in a knowledge of contemporary philosophy ("I began to write so early, that I had not lived so long as to be able to read many authors"), but does not believe this should prevent her, now she has read these "many authors", from disagreeing with them.[18] Nor does she understand why men will not engage with her own writings: "no man dare or will set his name to the contradiction of a Lady", she complains.[19]

Indeed, by 1664, the only public disagreement with her had been written – supposedly – by a woman, and was a critique of her beliefs on monasticism in *The Worlds Olio*.[20] Cavendish believed that the woman's name was a pseudonym – despite the fact that the woman, Susan du Verger, had published translations of French literature under her own name, one of which was even dedicated to Henrietta Maria – and declined to answer a "hermaphroditical book".[21]

In *Philosophical Letters*, Cavendish does not shy away from robust argument. Once again within a constructed community of female readers and writers – each letter is addressed to "Madam", supposedly an unknown woman who has been sending Cavendish these works of philosophy and encouraging her to read them – Cavendish fervently expresses her opinions on the matters of the day: from how the world was formed to where man stood in relation to the universe. She disagrees with Hobbes's views on motion – "when a thing lies still, unless somewhat else stir it, it will lie still for ever" – and, instead, advances her own belief in self-moving matter: "If matter moveth itself, as it certainly doth, then the least part of matter, were it so small as to seem indivisible, will move itself."[22] She takes issue with Hobbes's theory of sense perception, and quotes from his *Leviathan* before expressing her own theory: "perception is but the effect of sensitive and rational motions" rather than, as she quotes from Hobbes, "the external body or object, which presses the organ proper to each sense".[23] She disagrees with his judgement that "man doth excel all other animals", and responds with a visceral defence of animal sentiency:

> For what man knows, whether Fish do not Know more of the nature of Water, and ebbing and flowing, and the saltness of the sea? Or whether birds do not know more of the nature and degrees of air, or the cause of tempests? [...] For, though they have not the speech of man, yet thence doth not follow, that they have no intelligence at all[24]

With Descartes, her disagreements were more piecemeal – "I intend to pick out only those discourses which I like best, and not to examine his opinions... from beginning to end" – but the quotations from his work, and explanations offered by Cavendish, conjure an imagined community of women philosophers corresponding and debating with each other.[25] "Madam", she writes, "I am reading now the works of that famous and most renowned author, Descartes."[26] The erudite gentility of this statement belies the force of her thought: in just one of many disagreements, she "does not assent to his opinion" on motion, because he abstracts "motion" from the "body" that moves.[27]

With More, she was not quite so courteous. She begins with a scathing attack on his book *Antidote* (written "to convert atheists"), and questions why it was written at all: "considering, he says himself, that *there is no man under the cope of Heaven but believes a God*".[28] She then returns to one of her favourite subjects – the supposed, false, primacy of man amongst animals – and affirms that "elemental creatures are as excellent as man, and as able to be a friend or foe to man, as man to them".[29]

More was a Neoplatonist, and his theories on the nature of the soul enraged Cavendish, who believed in a division between the material "natural soul" and the supernatural "divine soul" – the former, a corporeal soul on earth and a fit subject for natural philosophy; the latter an immaterial concept, fit only for theology.[30] More, however, did not believe in this dichotomy, and described an immaterial soul existing in space. For Cavendish, this was too much, and she turned the full force of her scathing rhetoric on him:

> The soul is not like a traveller, going out of one body into another, neither is air her lodging; for certainly if the natural human soul should travel through the airy regions, she would at last grow wearing, except she did meet the soul of a horse, and so ease herself with riding on horseback...[31]

Here is Cavendish's wit, familiar from her fiction and her plays, applied to philosophy and theology; despite the hefty intellectual weight of her subject, she is still able to have fun with the genre. More was not best pleased with Cavendish's attacks, and wrote a letter to his friend and correspondent Lady Anne Conway (a fellow female philosopher, whose *The Principles of the Most Ancient and Modern Philosophy* would be published in Latin translation in 1677) about the "great Philosopher" who deigned to disagree with "sundry passages in my writings".[32] More's letter drips with sarcasm and irony – he believes Cavendish will be "secure from any one giving her the trouble of a reply" – but perhaps he should have engaged with her critique. Conway herself, in her later book, also disagrees with More's vision of a travelling soul.

Cavendish chose not to address Van Helmont's chemical ideas but instead focused on his philosophical treatises. In what is perhaps the most brilliant letter in the collection, she responds to Van Helmont's views on witchcraft with a nuanced open-mindedness that sets her apart from other philosophers in the period. Van Helmont was far from the only philosopher of the time to hold forth on witchcraft. In his *Leviathan*, Hobbes had declared that there is no "real power" in witches, but had still seen fit to mention them.[33] And More, unlike Hobbes, affirmed the power of demonic spirits (he would later aid Joseph Glanvill with his 1666 *Philosophical Considerations about Witchcraft*). Cavendish takes a different position to that of her male predecessors. She admits that some form of magical witchcraft might well exist:

> My sense and reason doth inform me, that there is natural witchcraft, as I may call it, which is sympathy, antipathy, magnetism, and the like [...] but that there should be any such devilish witchcraft, which is made by a covenant and agreement with the devil, by whose power men do enchant or bewitch other creatures, I cannot readily believe[34]

Cavendish's level-headed approach to the issue is more radical than it sounds. Just two decades previously, the country had been swept up in one of the largest witch-hunts in its history when the "witchfinder general", Matthew Hopkins, was responsible for nearly 100 executions. By the 1660s, scepticism had broadly replaced this fanatical misogyny, but Cavendish was still bold to declare that "many a good, old honest woman hath been condemned innocently, and suffered death wrongfully".[35] This was in sharp contrast to Hobbes who, despite proclaiming not to believe in witchcraft, suggested that the women were "justly punished" for their "false belief".[36]

* * *

Philosophical Letters demonstrated Cavendish's growing confidence as a commentator on contemporary philosophy (and despite what More wrote to Conway, it would elicit some replies – including one from Glanville about witchcraft). But it is also important as a document of her own philosophical theories and their development since her earliest days of writing and publishing.

In 1653, Cavendish had posited – in verse – a non-mechanistic atomist view of the world: that is, everything in the world was made up of small atoms of different forms, whose behaviour and nature can be explained in terms *other* than their motion and relationship to the motions of other objects (the "mechanist" school of thought proposed by, amongst others, Hobbes). In Cavendish's partly Epicurean view, these atoms have a degree of innate life. Later in 1653 – and in a move which has led some scholars to suggest she was less attached to atomism as a scientific school of thought than she was to the idea as a poetic metaphor – she changed her outlook: *Philosophical Fancies* is a description of a world made up of "matter", rather than atoms.[37] This new philosophy (which has been dubbed "vitalist materialism") is the school of thought that would, with some changes, dominate all of Cavendish's thinking until her death.

* * *

But what exactly *is* vitalist materialism? And how did it shape the rest of Cavendish's thoughts and writings?

The starting point for understanding Cavendish's philosophy is her theory of matter. As she first stated in 1653 and then developed in the 1655 edition of *Philosophical and Physical Opinions* and the works of the 1660s, she believed that the world was made of eternal "matter" and "motion" – eternal because they are "infinite". This matter is, on one level, made of "one kind", but is also split into three types of matter: "dull matter" (later called "inanimate"), "innate matter" (later called "sensitive"), and "rational" matter. These types of matter form a hierarchy: rational matter and innate matter have the capacity to move themselves without an external force, and so therefore control the "dull" matter. The "innate matter is a kind of god or gods to the dull part of matter, having power to form it, as it please".[38] As ever with Cavendish, there is a strong element of social order here, and she goes on to use the following metaphor:

As we will compare motions to officers or magistrates. The constable rules the Parish, the Mayor, [rules] the constable, the King the mayor, and some Higher power the King[39]

Cavendish's theory may sound unorthodox to modern ears but, to her contemporary readers, it was no more unusual (and possibly less radical) than her poems on atomism. It was certainly no stranger than many other theories circulating at the time – from Hobbes's strict materialism (that is, everything in the world is tangible, rather than incorporeal) to Descartes's mechanical Corpuscularianism (that is, everything in the world is composed of "corpuscles" of matter).

In Cavendish's view of the world, these three types of matter are present in everything and mingle to form a "commixture". Not only do rational and sensitive matter have the power to *move* themselves, they also have the power to *think*: they are intelligent. This had radical implications. Cavendish fiercely opposed the dualism of Descartes which proposed a difference between a physical body and an incorporeal mind. Her materialism means that everything in the world, from a human brain, to a table, to an apple, to a book, is composed of the same three types of matter, mixed and mingled together. And if at least some of the parts of matter were capable of thought, this means that every seemingly inanimate thing has a capacity for thought and feeling. In Cavendish's words,

> ... who knows, but *Vegetables and Minerals* may have some of those *rational spirits,* which is a *minde* or *soul* in them, as well as man?[40]

(In *Philosophical Letters*, Cavendish explained her decision to stop using the word "spirit" to refer to matter to avoid "misapprehensions and misinterpretations" given that "spirit" had incorporeal associations.)[41] Cavendish's entertainment of the possibility of thought, consciousness, and a "soul" in inanimate objects is essential – it is a moment in which she deviates from her social belief in the "Great Chain of Being", and explains her vitriol against Hobbes's comments on animals in *Philosophical Letters*. If a table or a stone could have rational thoughts and feelings, animals certainly could.

If, then, on the zoomed-in level of individual objects and animals, Cavendish's natural philosophy had radical implications, what about the universe as a whole? Alongside her description of the world being composed of three different types of matter, she also advocated a description of "infinite matter": the totality of nature. Nature (with a capital "N") was, for her, indivisible ("in Nature there is no such thing as number or quantity"), eternal, and the composite of the other types of matter – their divisions and differences vanish in the presence of this near-deified force. This "Nature" is not necessarily above the matter she is composed of but she does have the power to direct it. She is the world's housewife:

> Being a wise and provident Lady, governs her parts very wisely, methodically and orderly; also she is very industrious, and hates to be idle, which makes her imploy her time as a good Huswife doth[42]

The use of such a gendered image is not accidental. As the scholar Lisa Sarasohn has noted, a female vision of nature was normal in pre-modern Europe but, by the sixteenth and seventeenth centuries, it had been "disenchanted" – to borrow the historian and sociologist Max Weber's famous phrase – by a worldview that rejected such "spiritual and animistic forces".[43] Cavendish re-enchanted the world, and rejected the mechanistic view of matter: the world was shaped by a female life-force, rather than dull, inert laws. Even her way of describing how matter moved was a part of this re-enchantment: instead of echoing the popular images of clocks and machines that were in vogue at the time, she described how matter moved itself as if in a "dance".[44]

The world that this "Nature" shaped is minutely described: in Cavendish's view, it is a "plenum" – that is, a world in which there is no empty space. The idea of a "vacuum" in the universe was one which was much discussed in the period, and something that Cavendish would alter her opinions on throughout her life as she tried, through axioms and reason, to work out if such a thing could exist. In her 1655 text, she turned to verse to express her thoughts:

> *In Nature if Degrees may equal be,*
> *All may be full, and no Vacuity.*
> *As Boxes small, and smaller may contain,*
> *So bigger, and bigger must there be again.*
> *Infinite may run contracting, and dilating,*
> *Still, still, by degrees without a separating.*[45]

For Cavendish, writing something in verse was less of an overt commitment than writing in prose – a way of hiding her "fancies" in an imaginative setting. But this idea of a Russian doll type of universe where there is no space between individuals and objects – and there are more porous boundaries between them than we might expect – is one that will have significant ramifications on her ideas, and will reappear, in different forms, in her later work. It already has one dramatic implication: if there is no empty space in the universe, it means that "nothing in nature can be annihilated".[46] What sounds like a rather abstract principle – and, perhaps, an early indication of the "conservation of energy" principle which would be developed in the early eighteenth century – has a particularly important result: Cavendish believes that, on a fundamental level, everything in the universe is infinite. For her, death is but a "separation" of the "motions and figures" that made an object or being and, inversely, life is a "contraction".[47] This is subtly different to her earlier statement in *The Worlds*

Olio that death is an "annihilation" with no afterlife – even if the individual does not live on, their matter does – but there is no way of hiding the fact that here, too, Cavendish is far from the conventional Christian theology of the period.

* * *

And where, exactly, *does* God fit into a universe that has rational, thinking matter which can move and direct itself? And a female, enchanting spirit of Nature that watches over it? Cavendish often had difficulties reconciling her philosophy with theology. One of the opening epistles to her 1655 *Philosophical and Physical Opinions* approaches this problem frankly. She asks her readers to "pray account me not an Atheist, but believe as I do in God Almighty".[48] This is a rather defensive statement of her theology, and her philosophy often tells a different story. Her belief that matter is infinite and eternal – and that Nature, as matter's entirety, also has these properties – infringes on what is normally believed about God. She resolves this difficulty by arguing that there are two different types of eternity: that God is infinite and divine, and nature is infinite and material. In her last work of philosophy, *Grounds of Natural Philosophy*, she sets out this difference clearly:

> God is an eternal creator; Nature, his eternal creature. God, an eternal master: Nature, God's eternal servant. God is an infinite and eternal immaterial being: nature, an infinite corporeal being.[49]

Cavendish's use of such hierarchical language is hardly a surprise. In her view, God is entirely separate from the realm of nature, and matter. Whilst these are material, corporeal beings, he is utterly *in*corporeal. It is this division, too, which led to Cavendish's disagreement with More over the possibility of an incorporeal soul: only God, the divine, could have such a thing.

But Cavendish's theology is not as reverent as her hierarchical language might suggest. While she proclaims the higher power of God, most of her writing is marked by his notable absence: it is Nature that is present in the matter of the world. She explains this through a form of extreme fideism – that is the belief that God cannot be known, and his existence cannot be reasoned – that sees her proclaim in her 1662 work, *Orations*, that God is "something that cannot be Described or Conceived; not prescribed or bound".[50] There's an interesting abnegation here: a refusal to speak of God, the being who is, supposedly, at the pinnacle of her philosophy. It was also a theologically unusual position. Such fideism was condemned and distrusted by both Catholics and Protestants alike.[51] Whilst theological arguments do recur throughout her philosophy, they are never her most strongly set-out beliefs, or her most well-reasoned concepts. God exists, yes, but he has delegated his "authority to a female deity": Nature.[52]

Where do humans fit into this material world? Like every other being, Cavendish believes, they are made from a mixture of all three types of matter. But her description of how they perceive this matter is interesting. As the scholar David Cunning has noted, Cavendish's epistemology – her theory of knowledge – sets out that ideas can only be known through their images: every thought we have is "pictorial images that have figure and dimension".[53] It is *this* that makes God so impossible for us to think about: we can have no picture of him. In Cavendish's words, "unfigurative thought" is impossible.[54] This theory of human knowledge puts Cavendish in direct contention with Descartes, who had stated that an image cannot capture the nature of an idea, *or* an object.[55]

How did these images of ideas come about for Cavendish? She believed that these images entered the brain through sense perception, but that this perception was more complicated than just looking at an object, or touching it:

... there is a double perception in the infinite parts of Nature, sensitive and rational: the perception and information of the rational parts is more general, than of the sensitive[56]

Rational perception might create an idea – a pictorial image – that is different to the original object ("more general"), but it always has its origins in the senses.

And, importantly, the brains that these ideas were perceived in were material: they were, like bodies and objects, made of the same three types of matter that made all the rest of the universe. Cavendish fiercely opposed Descartes's dualism of body and soul. In her view, everything in the world was matter.

How can Cavendish's theory of free will be reconciled with self-moving matter, the world as a "plenum", and material, sentient Nature? This was a thorny issue at the time, and one of which Cavendish could not have been unaware: in 1645, her husband William had invited Thomas Hobbes and the theologian John Bramhall to debate the concept.[57] In a division that has its descendant in Isaiah Berlin's famous 1958 essay, *Two Concepts of Liberty*, Bramhall advocated for a type of "libertarian" freedom – the freedom to do something without it being caused – whilst Hobbes advocated for a more limited sense: the freedom to do something unimpeded by constraints.[58] In discussions of Cavendish's concept of free will, it has generally been understood that she meant this in the former sense: the libertarian capacity to initiate something without it being caused. There is certainly a libertarian strain in her discussion of the movement of matter – the rational matter is "free" to move as it may wish, and the world adapts as a result of this – but, as will become clear, she may well have had the more Hobbesian theory of freedom in mind.

* * *

There is no shame in admitting that some of Cavendish's philosophy and theology may well sound simply incomprehensible to modern readers. But it's important to remember that, in this sphere at least, she was no odder than the other thinkers of the time. The "scientific revolution" was well underway by the seventeenth century, but theories of knowledge and ways of puzzling out the universe were still very much the domain of non-specialists who produced a combination of shrewd observations and seemingly bizarre ideas. When read in its entirety, Cavendish's corpus is no more confusing, or more self-contradictory, than many male thinkers from the period. As one scholar notes when trying to establish why Cavendish's philosophy has not been appreciated, perhaps the only true reason – alongside sexism – was that it simply "has not been picked up and read and interpreted".[59] Another academic has even made the case that, when her work is actually read, Cavendish appears as "one of the most prolific and philosophically informed English writers of the seventeenth century".[60]

In recent years, there has been a recognition that all philosophy from the period can seem fanciful or plain "wrong-headed" to modern thinkers (one scholar, Cunning, draws attention to holes in Descartes's thinking that have not prevented later thinkers from revering him, and reminds us that Cicero quipped that "there is no position so absurd that some philosopher has not defended it").[61] Cavendish's autodidactism and patchy education from her husband and brother-in-law may well have resulted in a philosophy more idiosyncratic than modern readers generally expect when opening a book of science or philosophy, but she was hardly more unsystematic than other writers of the period – from the wide-ranging writings of the polymath Thomas Browne, to the unusual religious ideas of her contemporary Nicolas Malebranche, who worked in the same period of post-Cartesian thought. (Amongst his most confusing ideas is his belief that human, finite minds are directly connected to God's infinite mind.)[62]

If Cavendish's idiosyncrasies and unusual beliefs need not preclude an academic interest in her, what about the charge that she did not produce a complete, internally coherent body of thought? It is, of course, true that her beliefs changed over time, as she moved from atomism to vitalism, and altered the language she used to describe this vitalism. Her beliefs in freedom, God, and the nature of the universe also change and, of course, she often posited many different opinions on the same subject in the style of her debates or "orations". Recently, there has been a move away from insisting upon Cavendish's contradictory nature (in the scholar Deborah Boyle's words, "reading Cavendish as so deeply inconsistent and confused should be a last resort").[63] But there is still a debate over what Cavendish's corpus reveals in its entirety. Is it an original early modern theory of freedom and free will?[64] Or a fully thought-out feminist contribution to the scientific revolution?[65] Or is it a statement of a teleological need for order and structure in the universe?[66] All of these interpretations are possible, but only if Cavendish's work is read with care and interest, rather than relegated to a philosophical oddity or curio.

* * *

1664's *Philosophical Letters* showed how much Cavendish enjoyed disagreeing with other scholars and courting controversy. And in the winter after it was published, she began work on a new volume of polemics, *Observations Upon Experimental Philosophy*. This volume – published with *The Blazing World* appended – is not Cavendish's last work of philosophy (this was *Grounds of Natural Philosophy*, published in 1668), but it is the work which provoked the most vigorous responses, and brought her the most fame (or infamy).

In November 1660, in the first flush of the Restoration, a founding group of twelve natural philosophers started a society for the "promotion of physico-mathematical experimental learning".[67] By December of the same year, the king had approved of the meetings, and the Royal Society was born.

The Royal Society was the home of (male) scientific and philosophical endeavour, and at its heart were the principles of experimental research: that is, the use of new techniques of research and observation to understand the workings of the world, rather than speculation and abstract thought. This emphasis on empirical science ("the plainness and soundness of observations") may not sound radical or worrying to modern ears.[68] But for those who had been so recently horrified by the bold, over-arching claims of the utopian Puritan reformers, to hear arguments, once again, about how "there is nothing that lies within the power of... human industry, which we might not yet compass", was more than just a scientific provocation.[69]

These statements of empirical belief came from Robert Hooke's *Micrographia* (1665) – published, rather ironically, by Cavendish's first booksellers Martin and Allestree. Hooke was the Royal Society's "curator of experiments" and he, along with the scientist and fellow Society-member Robert Boyle, expounded an approach to scholarship that posited physical experiments as the only way of reaching any "truth". *Micrographia* is, as its name suggests, a record of the investigations Hooke undertook with a microscope: he proudly declared "there is nothing so small, as to escape our inquiry".[70]

This hubristic approach to life and science was too much for Margaret. Despite the fact that whilst in Antwerp and Paris both her husband and brother-in-law had been intrigued by optical glasses, her 1666 *Observations* is a methodical take-down of Hooke's and Boyle's beliefs. She quotes Hooke's belief that "art" – that is, his method of science – may repair the errors "made of the mischief and imperfections" that "mankind has drawn upon itself", and forcefully disagrees. She resents the claim that experimental science will bring perfection, and instead argues that no creature has an "infinite perception", and as a result, cannot know infallibly, how "nature" functions.[71] She moves on from this wide-ranging opposition to Hooke's claims about the perfectibility of his new, experimental science, to more specific disagreements. As her other philosophy shows, she does trust sense perceptions – they are what form the images of ideas in the brain, after all – but she resents the involvement of the new optical machines. She believes that all their parts don't reveal the object, but distort it:

> Art makes cylinders, concave and convex-glasses, and the like, which represent the figure of an object in no part exactly and truly, but very deformed and misshaped: also a glass that is flaw'd, crack'd, or broke, or cut into the figure of lozenges, triangles, squares, or the like, will present numerous pictures of one object.[72]

This tirade is not anti-empiricist – she believes in the importance of a mixture of "rational" and sense perception – but it is anti-utopian: she resents the idea that these new machines could bring about perfection. In her words, "experimental and mechanical philosophy cannot be above the speculative part".[73]

Cavendish was far from the only philosopher to be unsettled by the Royal Society: she was following in the footsteps of Hobbes, whose *Dialogus Physicus* (1661) had attacked Robert Boyle's famous air pump experiments. Both Hobbes and Cavendish would be upstaged by the sheer vitriol of Henry Stubbes's attacks on the Society in 1670: in one volume he railed against the "deceitfulness of telescopes", and then published another in which he argued that the Royal Society was engaged with "reducing England unto Popery".[74] Stubbes's hysterical claims were not as outlandish as they might seem: his fear about Catholicism at the highest level of British society was rooted in the growing concerns about Charles II's successor, James, and his religion.

Observations Upon Experimental Philosophy is typical of Cavendish in more ways than one. Having criticised the beliefs and theories of classical philosophers in her earlier works, here she defends them, simply because the men of the Royal Society had been so scathing about them. Her contrariness and her natural defence of the underdog or the outsider are on full display. And she lambasts the men of the Society for not turning their skills towards more profitable uses of their talents:

> But, as boys that play with watery bubbles, or fling dust into each others' eyes, or make a hobby-horse of snow, are worthy of reproof rather than praise, for wasting their time with useful sports, so those that addict themselves to unprofitable arts spend more time than they reap benefit thereby.[75]

To Cavendish, the esteemed savants of the Royal Society were little more than naughty boys who needed telling off.

12

The Duchess of Newcastle is all the subject now discoursed on

IN HER TIRADE against Cavendish in *A Room of One's Own*, Woolf wrote that Margaret "frittered her time away scribbling nonsense and plunging ever deeper into obscurity and folly".[1] In Woolf's analysis, the fame Cavendish achieved in her lifetime was far from the considered intellectual appreciation she would have wanted – and which Woolf suggests she does not merit.

It is, of course, true that Cavendish was hardly lauded as the pinnacle of scientific or literary endeavour in her time. Unlike Ada Lovelace, who lived and worked some two centuries later, she was never part of a respectful scientific circle. Nor did she have an extended group of female intellectual companions like the Bluestockings of the eighteenth century, or the Chelsea circle around Mary Astell at the end of the seventeenth century. And indeed, the most profuse and numerous accounts of her contemporary acclaim can hardly be trusted as unbiased critical comment. The hyperbolic praise she received from the universities – they declare that she is "an ornament to learning, and a patroness to the learned" – can be explained by the formal deference required when writing to a person of her status, and the hope of some form of donation or bequest from her and her husband.[2] In Woolf's words, "No one checked on her. No one taught her. The professors fawned on her."

While most of her works had been published when she was

either sequestered in Antwerp or at Welbeck, and she had no recognisable circle of supporters or collaborators, she had still been taken more seriously than Woolf's assessment suggests. After the harsh criticisms of 1653 (in Dorothy Osborne's words, "there are soberer people in Bedlam"), she had continued to circulate her works, sending them to leading thinkers and academics throughout Europe. Some of the replies collected in the posthumous volume *A Collection of Letters and Poems* (1678) are evidently still constrained by the formalities of writing to a woman of such high status and privilege – and are laden down with their expressions of gratitude for "such rich volumes".[3] But there are others that reveal a genuine engagement with, and appreciation of, her ideas. The Epicurean philosopher Walter Charleton was one of Cavendish's most prolific correspondents. In 1667, he wrote to her about her most recent publications. He was careful to state that this letter was not "a Panegyric of your worth", but instead a "short scheme" of his own "grateful sentiments". On the subject of her recent works in natural philosophy, he wrote:

> It is ingenious and free, and may be, for ought I know, Excellent: but give me leave, *Madam*, to confess, I have not yet been so happy as to discover much therein that's *Apodictical*, or wherein I think myself much obliged to acquiesce[4]

It is far from the only time Charleton criticised Cavendish (William refuted one of his earlier letters which claimed Cavendish was obscuring the amount of philosophical knowledge she really had). Here – in claiming that there is nothing "apodictical" (that is, demonstrably accurate) – he was siding with the Royal Society and all their claims of empirical truth. His criticism extends to her moral philosophy, in which he rather patronisingly suggests that Cavendish "has not, indeed, tied up [her] pen to the laborious rules of method, or the formality of a new system in ethics".[5] It is worth noting that, despite his criticisms of Cavendish, Charleton did not publish his atomistic theories fully until after Cavendish's efforts. However patronising his criticisms, they are worth far more than the blind praise of the universities and librarians: here was a philosopher, scientist, and thinker – and an elected Fellow of the Royal Society – who took the time to read Cavendish's science and philosophy, and engage with it seriously. And Charleton was far from alone: Cavendish received letters from the philosopher and clergyman Joseph Glanvill, the natural philosopher and astrologer Kenelm Digby, and the royal chaplain Robert Creighton. Glanvill's letters, in particular, reveal a real engagement with Cavendish's ideas. He disagrees with her anti-empiricism:

> I humbly desire that your Grace would consider, that there are two sorts of reasoning, *viz*. Those that the mind advanceth from its own imbred Ideas and native store, such are all metaphysical contemplations. And those natural researches which are railed from experiment, and the objects of sense.[6]

Other scientists and philosophers read her works closely without being her correspondents: the pioneering plant anatomist and subsequent secretary of the Royal Society Nehemiah Grew wrote an eight-page summary of her 1655 *Philosophical and Physical Opinions*.[7] Cavendish was, clearly, not writing in *complete* "obscurity".

* * *

In September 1666 – after a year of plague and all the disorder that wrought – London was hit by yet another disaster: after a fire started in a bakery in Pudding Lane, much of the City was burned down whilst the flames raged for four days. St Paul's Cathedral was destroyed (and would later be rebuilt by Christopher Wren), and many of the booksellers and printers who had their premises there were financially ruined as all their stock and material turned to ash. Pepys famously buried his diary and his parmesan cheese to keep both his prized possessions safe. Later that same year in October, he recounted a conversation with a bookseller who was "utterly undone" by the destruction. He could have hardly been alone: Pepys described how the men tried to safeguard their goods in St Faith's church near St Paul's, but the fire made it "through the windows" and "burned all the books and the pillars of the church". Pepys's acquaintance estimated that £50,000 worth of books had been burned, and Pepys predicted "a great want" of books throughout the city.[8]

In the summer of 1667, a year after the fire, and whilst fierce debate was raging about how to rebuild, London would be greeted by something nearly as dramatic (if far less destructive).* Cavendish returned to the capital for the first time since the splendour of 1665. The restrained, cerebral epistolary engagement she had enjoyed previously was about to be replaced by something far more theatrical, and far outstripping the public notoriety any other philosopher or scientist enjoyed during the period.

Newcastle House stood on Clerkenwell Close, just north of the City of London. Whilst it was the Cavendishes' "town house" (William had bought it in the late 1620s, and had lived in it throughout the 1630s), it was far from a small pied-à-terre. Modelled in the style of a miniature country house with its classical features, it sprawled over much of the land of the old, dissolved nunnery which used to stand on the site. It had a formal parterre garden, and a larger open space that made use of the former nunnery's cloisters. It was a magnificent house, but, by 1660, its name of "Newcastle" House was a mockery:

---

* Everyone, from John Evelyn to Robert Hooke, put forward their own plans about how the City should be redesigned. In the end, it was largely rebuilt along the same lines as the medieval road plan.

it had been sold in 1654 to pay off some of William's debts, and had not been included in the estates restored to him since the Restoration. William had attempted to reclaim the house through the Chancery courts, but all his attempts failed: he had to sell another of his country estates to buy the London house back in 1666.

The house – which stood opposite "Cromwell House", so named for the spurious claim that Oliver Cromwell had lived there – was the ideal space for the duke and duchess: it was close enough to court, and in what was still an aristocratic, well-heeled area. In the summer of 1666, the couple sent their servants and Francis Topp to prepare the house. They arrived the next year after the week-long journey from the Midlands, and plunged straight into a world of gossip, court intrigue, and high-profile visits. The king was among the first to see the couple; this occasion was soon followed by a visit to court to meet his queen, Catherine of Braganza. They met aristocratic acquaintances, and intellectual correspondents including those Margaret had only ever met through their letters. Margaret met many of the guests by herself, in her capacity as a philosopher, rather than a duchess, and "sat discoursing" with them "in her bedchamber after dinner".[9]

John Evelyn, the Cavendishes' contemporary in exile, visited Margaret no fewer than four times in three weeks, and never failed to remark on her "extravagant humour and dress" or "extraordinary fanciful habit, garb, and discourse".[10] It is no surprise that his wife, Mary Evelyn – who he had married in the same church as the Cavendishes when she was only twelve years old – did not quite feel the same about her husband's repeated visits to Cavendish. She wrote a letter to the clergyman and tutor Ralph Bohun in which she railed against Cavendish's appearance ("her curls and patches"); attacks her manner ("her gracious bows, seasonable nods... twinkling of her eyes"); and mocks her achievements: "Never did I see a woman so full of herself, so amazingly vain and ambitious."[11] She even mocked the men who took her "airy, empty, whimsical, and rambling" books seriously, and wrote:

> This lady and Mrs. Philips! The one transported with the shadow of reason, the other possessed of the substance and insensible of her treasure; and yet men who are esteemed wise and learned, not only put them in equal balance, but suffer the greatness of the one to weigh down the certain real worth of the other.[12]

The allusion to Katherine Philips was apposite: the posthumous authorised edition of her poems had appeared in the same year. Philips and Cavendish were evidently the two women intellectuals on the tip of everyone's tongue, but Mary Evelyn could not abide any suggestion of their equivalence. It is tempting to imagine what she made of her husband's assertion, published in 1697, that both Philips and Cavendish were examples of the "fair sex" who deserved to have a medal minted in their honour – alongside Boudicca, Mary, Countess of Pembroke, and Saint Elfreda.[13]

Mary Evelyn's criticisms are biting – she mockingly describes Cavendish telling Walter Charleton that the universities should "banish Aristotle and read Margaret, Duchess of Newcastle" – but they do reveal something about how Margaret portrayed herself during this period. She was desperate to be taken seriously as a philosopher (despite Mary claiming that her books "aim[ed]" at science and "high notions" but "terminat[ed] commonly in nonsense, oaths, and obscenity"), and would talk to anyone who listened about her theories:

> Sometimes, to give her breath, came in a fresh admirer; then she took occasion to [...] cite her own pieces line and page in such a book, and to tell the adventures of some of her nymphs

Evelyn's mocking tone obscures the truth of the situation: Cavendish was trying to present herself as an author, and to put to bed any of the lingering accusations that she was not responsible for her own work. If she could cite the books by line and page (no mean feat given their irregular pagination) how could they possibly be written by anyone else?

And the oddness of her behaviour – she was "more than necessarily submissive", and her humility was paired with an insistence on discussing her or her husband's successes – can be explained by her extreme shyness. After years in exile on the continent, and then retreat in the English countryside, the appearance of so many court figures and renowned gossips could not have been easy for her to manage.

The effect of this strange combination of talkative philosopher, and shy, humble social butterfly – complete with her outrageous clothes – certainly didn't go unnoticed in the summer of 1667: the Cavendishes, and Margaret in particular, appear in many diaries and letters from the period. Many, like Mary Evelyn (and Dorothy Osborne back in 1653) simply accused her of insanity: how could a woman who had the temerity to express her ideas publicly, seemingly unafraid of conflict or controversy, be anything but? Katherine Jones, the sister of the Royal Society member Robert Boyle, wrote in a letter to her brother that Cavendish had "escaped Bedlam only by being too rich to be sent thither", and that she was nevertheless "mad enough to convey the title to her place of residence".[14] Others, like Pepys, sidestepped the charge of insanity, and instead insisted that she was something fantastical or not quite human; one of the fairies or heroines she described in her poems and stories. "The whole story of this lady is a romance, and all she do is romantic", he wrote.[15] It is hardly an accident that this kind of prurient interest resulted in praise from men, and disapproval from women. Cavendish was, despite her reported eccentricities, still an attractive woman – something many men preferred to focus on over her writings and ideas.

Pepys had first spotted Cavendish at the performance of her husband's play *The Humorous Lovers* (although he believed it was written by her), and then described the courtiers anxiously expecting her appearance at Whitehall as if she were "the Queen of Sweden". His rather scathing description of other "many people" who wanted to see her was rather disingenuous: he was also desperate to catch a glimpse. Later the same month, he described his chance encounter with typical attention to detail: she was "naked-necked", and "seemed to [him] a very comely woman". He attempted to see more of her on May Day, but failed as she was "being followed and crowded upon by coaches all the way she went". Just ten days later, she had "100 boys and girls running looking upon her".[16] By all accounts, Cavendish was something of an early modern celebrity. She even received a mention in one of Marvell's satires of the same year, "Last Instructions to a Painter". Marvell turns his mocking pen to all of the Stuart court, and is mocking Charles II's wife when he writes:

Paint then again Her Highness to the life,
Philosopher beyond Newcastle's wife.[17]

But how had Cavendish achieved such fame? And why were crowds of children – who had surely not read her works of materialist philosophy, or her recently published biography of her husband – also joining in the pursuit?

The answer has less to do with Cavendish's recent writings and skirmishes with the Royal Society than with her spectacular dress. This had also been the case on her first visit to London in 1653: Dorothy Osborne had compared the outlandish nature of her poems to her outfits, and Cavendish herself had coyly remarked that "reports did dress me in a hundred several fashions".[18] By 1667, fashion had changed: the Restoration and the growth in global trade had encouraged new levels of decadence and extravagance, and the shape of dresses had altered to incorporate a longer waist and an off-the-shoulder neckline. But Cavendish was still an outlier: everyone – from the Evelyns to Pepys – commented on her fashion choices. What could she have been wearing which caused such commotion?

Some clue lies in the feverish letter a young man-about-town, Charles North, sent to his father after seeing Cavendish at the premiere of the *The Humorous Lovers*. Writing, as many other correspondents did in the period, of the Anglo-Dutch War which had begun in 1665 (Katherine Jones had claimed that Cavendish was "more discoursed of than the [peace] treaty"), North quickly sidesteps into writing about "the Duchess Newcastle, who is all the pageant now discoursed on". According to his testimony, she had appeared at the theatre in a carriage pulled by eight white bulls, and then had sat with "her breasts all laid out to view" and accessorised with "scarlet trimmed nipples".[19] Even in a decade which had seen bodices "sloping to a deep point in front", this form of display in public was unusual – and certainly enough to be commented on.[20] Cavendish, however, was not simply baring her flesh: her costume was intended as a nod to classical antiquity, and her status as an author. It was also a display of queenly power: both Henrietta Maria and Queen Anne of Denmark had delighted in baring their chests in private settings. Many of the contemporary gossips seem to have missed this point, and likened her dress more to that of the prostitutes, actresses, and mistresses who so dominated court scandal at the time.

This outfit – presumably designed by Cavendish, who wrote in her autobiography that she "took great delight in... fashions I did invent myself, not taking that pleasure in such fashions as was invented by others" – was but one example of her "boldness and profaneness" in presenting herself.[21] Other records from the time continually stress the "black patches" she wore on her face and "about her mouth".[22] These "patches" or "mouches" were to cover "pimples", as Pepys so eloquently puts it, or to make the complexion seem whiter than it was, and had become an item of general fashion since the early 1640s.[23] They could cover scars left by smallpox or the sores and chancres of syphilis, but they were not purely practical: the velvet or silk was cut into the shapes of stars, crescent moons, or diamonds, and they were even used when there was no blemish to hide. In later years, they were seen as a symbol of vanity or sexual disease, and were much mocked in the early eighteenth century in the early incarnation of *The Spectator* as a sign of a particularly female weakness: "virtuous Matrons, who formerly have been taught to believe that this artificial Spotting of the Face was unlawful, are now reconciled by a Zeal for their Cause".[24] In the 1660s, even Pepys had worn one when his "mouth was very scabby" with a cold.[25]

A painting recently came to light that shows the patches on two women during the Interregnum period: one black woman, and one white. On the darker skin tone, the patches are bright white: a crescent moon on the woman's cheek, dots on the other, and what appears to be a sun and a bird on her forehead. The brilliance of the depiction of women of different races on an equal footing is overshadowed by the inscription, which reads:

I black with white bespot, y white with black this evil proceeds from thy proud hart then take her: Devill.

If, in the Restoration years, patches had become a common fashion item, the same was not true of the Interregnum. They were a symbol of evil, and had come close to being banned by Parliament.

But if patches were so common during the 1660s, why were Cavendish's always mentioned? She must have been wearing them more than was usual, or in situations where they were not expected. This is also true of her nipple-baring: it could go unmentioned in an intimate setting, but was scandalous in the public arena of the playhouse. It may have something to do with what else she wore with her patches: in almost all of these descriptions, her "cap" of black velvet is mentioned – the same cap she wore with her (otherwise very fashionable and non-radical) dress in her Peter Lely portrait. This type of hat – a form of velvet, feathered beret-shape – was nothing like the brimmed hats worn by middle-class women in the period, or the cornet which sat on the back of the head or, indeed, the stiff wired structure of a "fontage" which appeared later in the century.[26] Cavendish was not just dressing unusually for a woman, or pre-empting trends that would come later: her hat was far more like the fur-covered caps favoured by men in the period.[27] She was, to all intents and purposes, cross-dressing.

As has been discussed, women dressing as men was hardly unheard of in the period: it is a conceit that appears throughout Cavendish's fiction and plays, as well as the writings of other authors in the period; and it was enough of a concern for Charles I during the Civil War to consider issuing a proclamation against the practice. In the 1620s, there had been such a vitriolic pamphlet war on the subject between a text called *Hic Mulier* ("The Man-Woman") and one titled *Haec Vir* ("The Womanish Man") that scholars have argued it had ramifications throughout the rest of the century.[28] This initial controversy may have been rooted in real anxieties over sex, the mutability of gender, and the growing dominance of certain high-powered women in court life, but in the years of the Restoration it had mutated into something more erotic. In John Dryden and William Davenant's 1669 adaptation of *The Tempest* (called *The Enchanted Island*), Dryden added the following rather disingenuous prologue:

> *Who by our dearth of youths are forc'd to employ*
> *One of our women to present a Boy.*
> *And that's a transformation you will say*
> *Exceeding all the Magick in the Play*
> *Let none expect in the last Act to find,*
> *Her sex transform'd from man to woman-kind*
> *What e're she was before the Play began,*

All you shall see of her is perfect man.
Or if your fancy will be further led,
To find her Woman, it must be abed.[29]

This prologue is the literary equivalent of a striptease. The claim about the "dearth of youths" may be true, but in drawing attention to the sex of the actress "present[ing] a Boy", Dryden is needlessly tugging at her costume to reveal her flesh. Just as Dryden indulges his audience in imagining her body, he denies it: "let none expect in the last act to find, / her sex transformed from man to woman-kind". The only place such a transformation could take place is "abed": her cross-dressing is linked to her sexual availability as an actress – women who were, in this period, very often prostitutes. By the late 1660s, cross-dressing was, almost by definition, erotic.

But the same is not true of Cavendish's cross-dressing: she is described in highly charged erotic language when she bares her nipples at the theatre, but the descriptions of her in her masculine cap or just-au-corps (a male type of coat) seem all but devoid of sexual appeal. She is, instead, something magical and outlandish. For Pepys, this "romance" is not unappealing, but not traditionally sexual. For others, like Mary Evelyn, who likens her to a "chimera" (a fire-breathing Greek monster) it is something ludicrous, threatening, and even possibly contagious (she left hastily in fear of "infection"). Cavendish even confused gender by some of her physical gestures: one description of her meeting the Duke and Duchess of York in 1665 relates how she was not only wearing a masculine "vest", but "made legs and bows to the ground" instead of the feminine curtsey.[30]

* * *

The combination of Cavendish's self-presentation as a thinker (John Evelyn called her "a mighty pretender to learning, poetry, and philosophy") and an outrageous, cross-dressing celebrity culminated, magnificently, in her visit to the Royal Society's home at Arundel House near the Strand. The visit had been much anticipated and debated, and had, in part, been organised by Cavendish's long-time friend Walter Charleton. Many of the men of the Society had dreaded her visit, the first of a woman to the Society; they would not elect a female fellow for almost another three centuries. Cavendish was evidently the subject of much gossip and satire. She had asked for an invitation on 23 May to "see some of [the Society's] experiments": George, Lord Berkeley had relayed her request to the meeting of the fellows, and it had been supported by Edward Howard, Earl of Carlisle and Charleton. Some of the fellows were very reticent about the invitation, well aware that the Society was already open to mockery from traditionalists and religious conservatives, and did not relish the spectre of London's most gossiped-about woman entering their hallowed halls. Nonetheless, the invitation was extended after a vote, and on 30 May the Duchess made the journey down from Clerkenwell.

This would, of course, be no ordinary day of meetings, experiments, and procedural discussions for the Society. Before Margaret had even arrived, a crowd had gathered. Not to be diverted from their regular schedule, the men continued as if nothing out of the ordinary was about to happen: they elected a man called Thomas Harley as a new fellow; they discussed developments in "several magnetical experiments", and Hooke proposed an investigation into the movement of a needle "in the midst of the ruins" of post-Great Fire London. A letter about "worms in the stomachs of cormorants" was read aloud.[31]

Cavendish, when she did arrive, was late: the men had been waiting so long that they had begun to discuss the curious case of a man whose "spleen was cut out" but who, nevertheless, "survived". Cavendish appeared in nothing less than a gilded coach (could this have been a different coach to that which Pepys had noted on May Day as being "silver instead of gold"? Such an extravagance seems unlikely, even for Margaret) drawn by a string of "horses with many a tassle". But the decadence of her mode of transport was nothing compared to her clothes: she wore a dress with a train which, apparently, took up "half a road at least" and had to be carried by her maids of honour – one of whom was the famed Italian beauty Elizabeth Ferabosco. This hyper-feminine display of wealth and extravagance was one moment in which Cavendish's style was slightly ahead of its time: long-trained dresses would not become popular outside court settings until the 1680s. Cavendish's final touch was even more unusual: she finished her outfit with a large, masculine wide-brimmed hat. In a ballad John Evelyn wrote about the visit, he quipped "she looked so like a Cavalier / But that she had no beard".[32] Pepys – having waited some seven weeks to meet Margaret – was rather too shocked to make amusing jokes: "her dress" was "so antick" that he "did not like her at all".[33]

But Cavendish had not, of course, visited the Royal Society to show off her unconventional fashion. Having so attacked the Society's Baconian empiricism and commitment to experimentation, she wanted to see some experiments herself – experiments the fellows had been planning for over a week. Robert Boyle showed her his favourite party trick: the air pump that had made him famous, and that he had written about in *New Experiments Physico-Mechanical, Touching the Spring of the Air, and its Effects* (1660). He showed her how air could be weighed, before moving on to show her how "a red colour" could be made out of "two transparent liquors": a chemical experiment he had recorded in his *Experiments and Considerations Touching Colours* (1664), which Cavendish may well have read about, but nonetheless it must have seemed as magical as Jesus turning water into wine. And despite her published misgivings about basing science on experiments, she was by all accounts delighted by what she saw. Pepys was rather scathing about how she "was full of admiration, all admiration" but, apparently, "said nothing that was worth hearing".[34]

Pepys's comments are rather catty: he had waited seven weeks to see Cavendish, and then judged her on the basis of her public comments to the men who had, despite her criticisms of their work, invited her to the Society. She was unlikely to have been as scathing here as she was in her prose; all parties were no doubt on their best behaviour. (And by all accounts Pepys was rather distracted by "the Ferabosco" who, it was claimed, could "show her face and kill the gallants".) Yet Cavendish's interest in the experiments shows that while she was doubtful about basing an entire school of thought on experimental results, she was not averse to the wonders they could produce. This is true throughout her career – from her early interest in the optical glasses of her husband and brother-in-law, to her Dutch friend Constantijn Huygens asking for her assistance in puzzling out the mystery of "glass drops" that would explode if their tails were broken.[35]* When Virginia Woolf argued that Cavendish "should have had a microscope put in her hand" and "have been taught to look at the stars and reason scientifically", she was missing the point: Cavendish did not live in a cloistered world ignorant of empirical methods and the new frontier of science, but she engaged with it in ways that were original and interesting, as she would show in her most famous work.[36]

* * *

The Royal Society had been founded upon a vision of collective experimental science laid out by Francis Bacon, the natural philosopher who had argued for the benefits of close observation and inductive reasoning at the turn of the seventeenth century. In *The Advancement of Learning* (1605), Bacon had been clear about how he thought scientific writing

---

* These "glass drops" – also known as "Prince Rupert's Drops" – were something of a scientific marvel during the period. They were formed by dripping molten glass into cold water, and letting the resulting tear-shaped glass harden. The drops could withstand greater force than normal glass, but would explode if the tail was broken – a phenomenon that puzzled and delighted contemporary philosophers. Huygens sent Cavendish some of the drops, and asked for her opinions on them.

should be categorised and presented: he wrote that he could find "a number of books of fabulous experiments and secrets, and frivolous impostures for pleasure and strangeness", but could not find "a substantial and severe collection of the heteroclites or irregulars of nature". For him, science writing must be severe – without the "imagination" of "poesy", or the liberties of fiction. The genres should not be mixed in the pursuit of scientific truth, and to do so could be dangerous: because poetry was not "tied to the laws of matter", it could "make unlawful matches and divorces of things".[37] The implication of his reasoning was clear: science should be written or reported in a different way to other forms of text. Bacon did not always strictly follow his own advice. His posthumously published *The New Atlantis* is a description of his vision of a utopian modern science university, described through a form of travel fiction. *The New Atlantis* is not a work of science, but a vision of how science should ideally be conducted.

Writing some six decades after Bacon's command not to mix genres, Cavendish published *The Blazing World*: a piece of prose science fiction that already caused her trouble in its very publication – it was appended to her serious work of natural philosophy, *Observations Upon Experimental Philosophy*. In her preface to the reader, Cavendish immediately recognises this difficulty:

> If you wonder, that I join a work of fancy to my serious philosophical contemplations; think not that it is out of disparagement to philosophy; or out of an opinion, as if this noble study were but a fiction of the mind[38]

She goes on to distinguish between "reason" and "fancy" – "the end of reason, is truth; the end of Fancy, is fiction" – before neatly bridging the apparent difference: she has "joined them as two worlds at the ends of their poles", and has written fiction on "the subject [she] treated of in the former parts".[39]

Her rather verbose description obscures the truth of what she was doing: she – like Francis Godwin with *The Man in the Moone* (1638) – was writing about an alternative utopian world. Unlike Godwin's creation, this new sphere was not the moon: it was "a world of [her] own creating". In creating this new world – and using fiction to elaborate her philosophy – she also created a new genre: *The Blazing World* is among the first recorded works of science fiction, and certainly the first by a woman.

Cavendish ends this bold, genre- and gender-defying preface with the statement that she is "as ambitious as ever any of my sex was, is, or can be":

> Though I cannot be Henry the Fifth, or Charles the Second,
> yet I endeavour to be Margaret the First.

She certainly succeeded: *The Blazing World*'s plot, utopian conception, and hybrid mixture of fiction and philosophy were extremely novel. But she was also working in a tradition that used different genres to explore new forms – even Hobbes's *Leviathan* could be seen as an example – and was closely observing the world around her.

* * *

The text opens with "a young Lady" who is captured by a merchant and then taken away on his ship.[40] She is then, luckily, saved by an act of God: "heaven" frowned "at his theft", and caused "such a tempest" so as to divert the boat towards the North Pole, where all the sailors died of the extreme cold. The girl only survives "by the light of her beauty, the heat of her youth, and the protection of the gods" as the ship makes the journey from the North Pole, through to the "pole of another world, which joined close to it". Cavendish's description of how the two worlds are joined echoes her description of the difference between the genres of "reason" and fiction: both pairs are joined, and closer than everyone might otherwise think.

In this new world, the young heroine enters a zone that appears to be rather like the Arctic: the land is "covered all with snow", and creatures which are "in shape like bears", but walk "upright as men" approach her. Her understandable fear is moderated by their kindness and civility: they take her into their house, and "hold their paws in admiration", before recognising that she is too cold, and carrying her to a warmer clime. She is taken as a gift to the Emperor, and arrives in a city that seems to resemble a magical Venice or, more likely given Cavendish's knowledge of northern Europe, The Hague:

> Rivers did run between betwixt every street, which together with the Bridges, whereof there was a great number, were all paved; the city itself was built of Gold, and their architectures were noble, stately, and magnificent

In this paradisiacal city, the Emperor believes she is a "goddess" and attempts to worship her; her insistence that she is a mere mortal leads to a very modern marriage. The besotted Emperor gives her "an absolute power to rule and govern all that World as she pleased".[41]

The rest of the narrative follows the Empress as she begins to explore her new world and its anthropomorphic animal inhabitants (there are "geese-men", "lice-men", and "ape men") and asks them questions about philosophy, natural science, and religion. There is more than a hint of Jonathan Swift's 1726 *Gulliver's Travels* – in which Swift describes the tiny Lilliputians and the gigantic inhabitants of Brobdingnag – which is, too, a satire on the Royal Society. The anthropomorphic elements, and the frankly psychedelic nature of the story, have also invited comparisons to the British-Mexican surrealist artist, poet, and novelist Leonora Carrington whose stories, with their galloping horses, cat-like women, and unending strangeness have been called "the campy, illegitimate offspring of Margaret Cavendish's romances and Robert Graves's histories".[42] There is more than a passing connection here: both Cavendish and Carrington imagine worlds in which animals are by no means "lesser" than humans (in Carrington's stories, it is humans who bring all sorts of trouble), and describe situations and people where the "real world" is still recognisable, but is warped, or seen at a slant. Some of Carrington's paintings even seem to be set in a snowy world of semi-human creatures (see the ice scene of *Figuras fantásticas a caballo*, 1951–2). It is unlikely, but not impossible, that Carrington had heard of Cavendish but both women share a similar strain of female imagination and an obsession with dream-worlds.

The other-worldly, sheerly *odd* nature of Cavendish's romance shouldn't obscure its satirical intentions. One of the Empress's interactions is with the lice men, who she appoints as her mathematicians. But when they come to demonstrate their skills to her, they fail. They:

> Endeavoured to measure all things to a hairs breadth, and to weigh them to an atom; but their weights would seldom agree, especially in the weighing of Air, which they found a task impossible to be done; at which the Empress began to be displeased, and told them, that there was neither Truth nor Justice in their Profession[43]

Just a year later, the lice men of the Royal Society showed Cavendish the experiment of weighing air: they had evidently understood they were the target of her satire.

Later on in the text, the Empress decides that she wants to write her own work of philosophy (more specifically, she wants to write her own version of "the Jews Cabbala" – a spiritual, mystical text which had gained popularity from the Renaissance onwards). To do this she needs a scribe: she initially asks the spirits with whom she has been discussing her Cabbala, but they manage to escape the task by pleading their ethereality. She then lights upon the idea of using a fellow "soul", and what follows is a process akin to deciding on the guest list for a fantasy dinner party: she reels through the names of "ancient famous writer[s]" – Aristotle, Pythagoras, Plato, and Epicurus – but has to dismiss them all: "They were so wedded to their own opinions, that they would never have the patience to be scribes." The souls of the "most famous modern writers" fail on another issue: they are "so self-conceited, that they would scorn to be scribes to a woman". There is only one woman who is up to the job of writing for the Empress:

> There's a Lady, the *Duchess of Newcastle*, which although she is not one of the most learned, eloquent, witty and ingenious, yet is she a plain and rational writer, for the principle of her writings, is sense and reason, and she will without question, be ready to do you all the service she can

The self-abasing modesty of Cavendish's description of herself belies the force of what she has written: she has not only had the confidence to write herself into her own story, but challenged the whole tradition of thought and philosophy which has come before her. The earlier philosophers – and their contemporary male counterparts – are, she claims, too set in their opinions, too irrational, and too lacking in sense to write the Cabbalistic work she proposes.

And they are certainly missing out. As in the plays she had written a decade earlier in Antwerp, Cavendish describes the relationship between the Duchess's soul and the Empress in ambiguous terms. The Empress is initially happy that the Duchess is a woman because, as she is "one of my own sex", the Emperor will "have no reason to be jealous". The spirits reply to the Empress that "husbands" *do* "have reason to be jealous of platonic lovers":

> For they are very dangerous, as being not only very intimate and close, but subtle and insinuating.

Hearing this, the Empress immediately calls for the Duchess's soul. Is this warning of danger a refutation of the school of thought arguing that love between women was merely "romantic friendship"? It certainly reads like one, if "platonic" is taken to mean a non-sexual relationship (a use of the word that can be traced back to the 1630s). It could, of course, also refer to the Duchess's "platonic" soul. Either way, it is clear that the relationship between the Duchess and the Empress is far from simple.

The pair often share "spiritual" or "immaterial" kisses and embraces, and Cavendish even describes them as "platonic lovers" despite the fact "they were both females". Cavendish comes tantalisingly close to suggesting that her own avatar – her fictional self – engages in lesbianism with another fictionalised embodiment of herself, the "Empress" of philosophy. She shrouds this masturbatory, sapphic fantasy with an insistence upon the incorporeality of the displays of affection – despite her philosophy which has claimed that the minds and souls we can perceive are *not* immaterial – and claims that it is a "platonic friendship". As the spirits' warning suggests, these "subtle and insinuating" friendships may not be what they seem.

There is one moment in which the sexual tension very nearly turns from subtext to text. After spending some time with the Empress, the Duchess begins to miss her husband, and so the two souls return to Welbeck. After a discussion of how badly the Civil War damaged the Duke's houses and land, the Duchess's soul is overcome with worry about her husband, and leaves "her aerial vehicle" and "entered into her Lord":

> The Empress's soul perceiving this, did the like: and then the Duke had three souls in one Body; and had there been but some such souls more, the Duke would have been like the Grand-Signior in his seraglio, only it would have been a platonic seraglio

By 1666, "seraglio" was already used to suggest a harem or otherwise licentious polyamorous situation: Cavendish's assertion that hers was "platonic" is only the faintest nod to propriety. Is it even possible to read something phallic into the moment the Duchess's spirit enters "into" her husband? It is, certainly, a reversal of conventional heterosexual relationships and intercourse.

* * *

From her husband's losses during the Civil War, to the inanities of the men who bored her with their "many debates and contentions", *The Blazing World* is a wonderful summation of all of Cavendish's desires and concerns – made all the more brilliant by their incarnation in a work of imaginative fiction. But it is also a text in which Cavendish reveals a new strand of her intellectual heritage.

Christine de Pizan was a medieval Italian writer at the French court in the early fifteenth century. Her works were incredibly popular at the time – there are more extant copies of her poems and prose than those of Chaucer – and she retained her popularity after her death: Elizabeth I owned copies of her work, which other women may well have read at court. By the seventeenth century, de Pizan's fame had waned (between 1549 and 1838, no editions of her work were published), but she had something of a resurgence when Simone de Beauvoir called her "the first woman to take up a pen to defend her sex".

Some three centuries before de Beauvoir made her a poster girl for woman's writing, Cavendish, too, may have enjoyed her writing about women and her riposte to misogyny. The most important extant manuscript of the complete works of de Pizan is now held in the British Library. This manuscript (MS Harley 4431) was commissioned by Queen Isabel of France in around 1413, and it's a beautiful document: 398 pages of intricate scribal handwriting, adorned with gold-leaf embellishments, intricate illustrations, and decorated initials. The illustrations are attributed to the "Master of the Cité des Dames": the artist who had been the manuscript illuminator for the *City of Ladies* – now de Pizan's most famous work. But on the first page of the manuscript is something not quite so beautifully ornate, or decorative as the rest of the text. In a piece of paper that has been pasted onto the page is the sentence "Henry Duke of Newcastle his booke 1676". The most elaborate and desirable collection of de Pizan's works belonged to Cavendish's step-son, Henry.

1676 was the year that William died, and many of his possessions – including his books – were passed down to Henry. The scholar Cristina Malcomson has argued that it would not have been Henry (by all accounts, a man not very interested in literature) who bought the manuscript but instead William and Margaret during their time abroad. The man who is last recorded as owning it before Henry, in the fifteenth century, was the Flemish soldier, politician, and patron of the arts Louis de Gruuthuse.[44] It is more than likely that William and Margaret owned the manuscript, and that Cavendish – even if she could not read the French – would have learned of the narratives and morality tales in the text from her husband, or would have marvelled at the ornate illustrations. (Some scholars have even suggested that Cavendish's professed ignorance of French was not quite truthful.)[45]

And de Pizan is clearly an influence on Cavendish's work.[46] De Pizan wrote a number of texts in defence of women – additions to the *querelle des femmes* – of which the most famous is her 1405 *La Livre de la Cité des dames* (*The Book of the City of Ladies*). In a lengthy prose-work, de Pizan's narrator describes how she was reading a book that attacked women's moral character, and "sunk into a deep trance" as she recalled all of the many books and esteemed men who had suggested that women were flawed, evil, or otherwise less worthy than men.[47] In her state of despair – "I thought myself very unfortunate that He had given me a female form" – three celestial ladies "crowned and of majestic appearance" materialise in front of her, and instruct her that she is to "construct... a walled city, study and impregnable" in which "ladies who are of good reputation" will be admitted. *The Book of the City of Ladies* is this construction – but, "to those lacking in virtue, its gates will remain forever closed".

De Pizan has been lauded as the first feminist, and has become something of a cult figure. It is easy to see why. Take this passage from early in the text:

> The female sex has been left defenceless for a long time now, like an orchard without a wall, and bereft of a champion to take up arms to protect it.[48]

De Pizan posited herself as this "champion" and later artists, writers, and critics have held her up as the defender of their sex. She featured in Judy Chicago's famous, ground-breaking feminist artwork *The Dinner Party* (1939) alongside the likes of Georgia O'Keefe and Mary Wollstonecraft. And in 2018, she was made the subject of a giant mural in Turin by the Italian artist Camilla Falsini. These tributes to de Pizan are admirable, and she deserves to be as well known as other medieval writers, like Chaucer and her French near-contemporary Charles d'Orleans. But there is also something difficult here. Like Cavendish (and, like other women who wrote about gender in the medieval period or early modernity), she is often either heralded as the pioneer of feminism or hedged around with a whole host of caveats: she is not, we are reminded, a "feminist" in modern terms. Both these arguments are flawed, and reductive: if the history of feminism were limited to women who expressed their beliefs in women's worth more or less as we do now, it would be a far shorter history than the subject deserves. De Pizan – and, by extension, Cavendish, Mary Astell, Bathsua Makin and a whole host of other female writers – are not just "proto-feminists", imperfect thinkers on the road to some platonic ideal of feminism. They are a part of its history, regardless of their contradictions and differences.

Leaving aside the thorny topic of feminist predecessors, how did de Pizan influence Cavendish? Her *City of Ladies* is a separatist, utopian vision of a world that is "more powerful" than the mythical Amazonia: the historical women who live there are safe from male attack, and, in the "new Realm of Femininia" can spend their days in happy mastery of themselves.[49] If Virginia Woolf thought women needed a room of their own to encourage their creativity, Christine de Pizan built them a whole city. The influence upon the Empress's security and happiness in *The Blazing World* – or, the women-only spaces of *The Convent of Pleasure* or *The Female Academy* – is clear. Did Cavendish, too, want a room in the city?

But there are other influences, too: Cavendish's modified empiricism (that is, her recognition that, whilst sense perception should be trusted, experiments based solely on it and new-fangled machines should not be) was matched by a delight in "reason". "Reason", in Cavendish's universe, was adjacent to sense perception: it was the "purer and subtler" rational perception that allowed beings to grasp ideas and objects in a fuller capacity. "Reason" brings about "knowledge", but not in the flashy or fussy way of the Royal Society: it "informs and instructs sense in all its actions".[50] With this form of "reason", scientific discoveries were, Cavendish believed, open to all who could perceive and think, rather than those who had access to experiments. When compared to modern scientific thought – which is based on reason, empirical evidence, and an emphasis on the falsifiable – this type of "knowledge" can sound ludicrous. But there's an emancipatory potential here: for centuries, the debate had raged over whether or not women even had the capacity for rational thought. Here Cavendish was demonstrating her mastery of it, and her preference for it over other types of knowledge. Other scholars have argued that a Cartesian form of reason was particularly inspirational for women in a different way: if body and mind were separate – and the mind was the pinnacle of human existence – then questions of physiology and whether women's bodies were weaker than men's no longer mattered.[51] This is evidently a different form of rationalism to Cavendish's – she denied Descartes's dualism – but the same inspirational, liberating emphasis on pure thought, and pure *wit*, persists.

But some three centuries before Descartes uttered his famous "I think, therefore I am", de Pizan had written of her own all-powerful Lady Reason:

> I am going to reveal my name to you. The very sound of it should reassure you that, if you follow my instructions, you will find me to be an infallible guide to you in all your endeavours. I am called Lady Reason, so rest assured that you are in good hands.[52]

Reason had been attractive to women long before Descartes, and it was not just a Cartesian understanding of the word that inspired them. The nature and meaning of "reason", of course, had space to change between de Pizan's lifetime and Cavendish's, but scholars have recently disagreed with the picture Descartes presented of "moribund scholasticism" and a lack of reason during the late medieval period.[53] There's certainly a similarity between the two women's conceptions of knowledge when de Pizan's Lady Reason tells her to distrust male misogyny and not believe everything she has "read in books" by men.[54] For both Cavendish and de Pizan, Reason was the patron saint of women's intellectual activity.

Scholars have noticed other echoes of de Pizan in Cavendish's writing, including the act of writing herself into her own work in *The Blazing World*. In *L'Advision Cristine* (*Christine's Vision*) – an allegorical story of the difficulties facing the central female narrator – de Pizan added details from her own life. In both texts, the female authors have inserted themselves as a character – and not just any character: a philosopher.

The Blazing World is Cavendish's biting satire of the male intellectual world that excluded her, but it is also something far more positive, and inspiring: a moment of revelling in the heritage of women's contributions to literary and intellectual achievement.

13

What will survive of us is books

MARGARET CAVENDISH'S EXIT from London was not as well chronicled or closely observed as her entrance into the city. After a stay of four months, the couple left in early July, just after the latest humiliating phase of the Anglo-Dutch War (Dutch warships had sailed up the Thames and ransacked the Medway ports) was over. William's son, Henry, had been involved in raising forces and strengthening defences in the North.[1] But by all accounts, London's interest in Cavendish as a spectacle had ended rather sooner: she does not appear in John Evelyn's diary after her visit to the Royal Society at the end of May 1667, and nor does Pepys mention her – except when he reads her *Life of William*, and remarks that she is a "mad, conceited, ridiculous woman", and he "an asse to suffer her what she writes to him".[2] For Pepys, the romance and mystery of Margaret had unravelled as soon as he met her.

Pepys's world-weariness may have reflected the attitude of a certain section of London society, but it was far from universal. Once the couple were once again safely ensconced in their country retreat at Welbeck, they were visited by the politician and merchant Thomas Povey, who was making a tour of the Midlands and the north east, through "Warwickshire, Staffordshire, Cheshire, and Derbyshire". In his letter to a fellow politician, John Williamson, he recounts his journey – "I have seen the wonders of the Peak... and beautiful Chatsworth" – before describing his next visit:

... and thence to see the Queen of Sheba and her more considerable Prince, the Duke of Newcastle, and his palace, stables, riding-house and horses, the most extraordinary in Europe[3]

Povey's comments demonstrate perfectly how the popular conception of Cavendish as an eccentric, mythical figure often precluded any real engagement with her: she was a figure of fun, and her husband was alternately an "asse" or noble angel for putting up with her.

Aside from his rather patronising conception of her unconventional character, Cavendish might have taken umbrage at other elements of Povey's description. Far from returning like the Queen of Sheba bearing, as the biblical story had it, "a very great train, with camels that bare spices, and very much gold, and precious stones", Cavendish had come back to Welbeck impoverished by the couple's excesses in the capital, and with an ever-keener sense of how wronged she and her husband had been by their loyalty to the crown during the Civil Wars.[4] Her biography of William – *The Life of the Thrice Noble, High, and Puissant Prince William Cavendish* – had been published that year, and it included an unflinching catalogue of all the monetary losses her husband had suffered as a result of his loyalty: a figure no less than £941,303, by Margaret's calculation. However large this sounds – an estimation of its current value is between £99 million and £172 million – it was not inconsistent with the sums calculated by other penniless Royalists.[5] It was not the financial claims that had shocked her readers, but the passages of the book which had been inked out and redacted prior to the book going on sale: sections that suggested direct disagreement with the king – or the failure of other Royalist leaders during the wars – were crudely blacked out. In some editions, the passages can still be read if the page is held up to the light; Cavendish's readers must have been able to see what she had, with false modesty, excised from her text, even if she made sure the offending passages were not included in the Latin translation.*

Thomas Povey was not, then, coming to see a rich and bounteous Queen of Sheba, but nor was he going to meet a "more considerable Prince": while William was still, as ever, spending money on his horses, he had taken to rather more underhand means to repair his fortunes. The English countryside had suffered from significant deforestation during the Civil Wars – something John Evelyn had discussed in his paper presented to the Royal Society, *Sylva* – but, despite this, William still began to cut down trees in the royal lands of Sherwood Forest. He appears in court records for failing to pay his "creation moneys" – that is, money newly created lords had to pay to the king. He also faced the indignity of asking to be paid his salary as a gentleman of the bedchamber, which he hadn't claimed since his appointment in 1660 – probably because, not living in London, he rarely carried out the duties that normally went with the post.[6] Despite these financial crises, William found the funds to publish his second work on horsemanship – *A New Method, And Extraordinary Invention, to Dress Horses* – in 1667 (certainly a busy year for the couple). It would be translated into French and German in later years.

The ideal of a happy, rural life, complete with ruddy-cheeked swains and buxom young maidens, was a powerful notion throughout the seventeenth century and into the eighteenth, especially after John Dryden's 1697 translation of Virgil's *Georgics*. In her 1663 edition of *Philosophical and Physical Opinions*, Cavendish had played into this tradition: she

---

* James Fitzmaurice, in his article "Margaret Cavendish on Her own Writing: Evidence from Revision and Handmade Correction", draws attention to two covered-up passages in the text: one in which Cavendish suggests that William's troops worked whilst not being paid by the king, and another in which she accused two other generals of "invigilancy and carelessness". In the Latin edition, translated for her by Walter Charleton, neither of these asides or names are included.

suggested that William had retired to "a shepherd's life", and that she was his "shepherdess".[7] Her role as a "shepherdess" was not just decorative: she described how she "was resolved" to "employ all [her] thoughts and industry in good huswifry", "knowing" the extent of William's "great debts". The self-effacing, semi-fictional tone of this preface obscures the truth: in the latter part of the 1660s, and especially after 1667, Cavendish took on ever more of the management of William's estates. In 1668 and 1670, he had increased the amount of land and wealth she would inherit after his death (which had caused the servants to rail that "her whole care and studie was nothing more than to inrich herselfe for a second husband").[8] But Margaret was unlikely to be concerned with just one aspect of power – or, indeed, to be interested in another husband – so she made efforts to increase her direct control over the estates. She liaised with Sir Francis Topp and became involved on a minute level with the management of the land: she was the recipient of accounts from some of the tenants and, in 1671, even contributed to rural panic about the confiscation of "unbranded cattle" by the king, by being "very severe in punishing those of the Forest in Nottinghamshire" who had not branded their livestock.[9]

This close involvement in the estate came back to haunt Cavendish. Her relationships with Henry Cavendish and William's other children were fraught, as they resented her growing power and the weakening of their father. But Margaret doted on her grandchildren, and wrote in one rather amusing letter to "Harry" (Henry, William's seven-year-old grandson) that she was "sorry he hath got a knock upon his forehead", and that, if he were married "it would be a dangerous bump".[10] Cavendish's joy in children – and her ability to make jokes about cuckold's horns – reveals a different side to her character: a light-hearted family woman, rather than a cloistered intellectual or an eccentric princess.

In 1671, a different type of "dangerous bump" would appear in Cavendish's life. As was mentioned in Chapter 10, a group of disgruntled servants resented the fact that "the Duchess did so narrowly of late inspect his Grace's affairs", and sent him a "libell" which suggested she had been having an affair with Topp. The libel was dismissed by William out of hand – and he made efforts to get back at the accusers by suggesting that Andrew Clayton (one of the conspirators, and the long-serving steward at Welbeck) had committed fraud by embezzling the Newcastle accounts. While Newcastle's defence of his wife ("abused Peg") was robust, the conspiratorial document suggests the couple were not quite as content as some historians and biographers have liked to insist: Clayton described being "often involved in sharpe and passionate quarrels between their graces".[11] Just as Margaret was exerting more control, and was finally, after decades of writing, able to engage with other scholars and philosophers, William was ageing and weakening. The imbalance must surely have affected their relationship.

* * *

Far from dedicating herself exclusively to a life of cattle-branding disputes, tenancy squabbles, and concerns over forestry rights, Cavendish was still writing and reading during this period. Her treatment in London – oscillating between fawning and idolising; and patronising and insulting – confirmed something she must have known for a while: despite her intellect, bravery, and her novel ideas, many of her contemporaries saw her simply as an eccentric: a lady writer who wrote silly books.

Cavendish, by all accounts, played into this perception of eccentricity with her dress and her mannerisms: it may have been a way to hide her shyness and anxiety, and a means of ensuring the attention she was convinced she deserved. Since 1663, however, she had moved away from this performance in her writing.

Comparatively recent scholarship about Cavendish has argued that "her lack of knowledge or grammar and her total inability to revise were serious impediments in her writing"; her work is "impulsive and undisciplined"; and that she "lazily" published her books when she realised the effort needed to update and refine her thoughts was "too Herculean a task".[12] Cavendish's early publications *were* marked by haste, careless printers' errors, and unusual prefaces, but from 1663 onwards she had embarked on a campaign of re-editing and republishing all but one of her pre-Restoration works. Her 1655 *Philosophical and Physical Opinions* (itself already a revised edition of 1653's *Philosophical Fancies*) was the first to receive such treatment, when it was revised and republished in 1663. In this edition, the long letter that Cavendish's husband had written defending her authorship was no longer necessary: Cavendish was now famous as a writer. In its place is a letter to her husband in which she thanks him for the "leave to publish them": "a favour few husbands would grant their wives".[13] She has not quite shed the habit of numerous prefaces – there are still nearly forty pages before the work properly begins – but they are no longer of an apologetic tone. Instead of excusing herself for not being "rational and probable", she is now bold enough to ask that those readers who wish to "write such or the like" would "be pleased to consider, and remember mine as the original".[14] The contents of the book are altered, too: in the place of long, winding sentences broken up only by italicised words and semi-colons is a terse, tight prose style, and an authorial voice that is in control of her medium ("As I said in my first chapter...").[15] Gone are explanatory marginalia: the text is clear enough not to need them. As Cavendish said in her preface, she was now aiming at a "more exact and perfect fabrick" to give her thoughts "as much and as clear lights" as possible.

The first edition of *Philosophical and Physical Opinions* was marked by its unusual style: passages of prose would regularly give way to rhymed couplets on the same subject. In Chapter 8 of the 1655 edition, Cavendish writes this on the nature of infinite matter:

For *Infinite* cannot be confined, or prescribed, settle, ruled, or disposed [...] and what is infinite, hath no absolute power: for what is *absolute*, is finite.[16]

Just below it is this verse:

Finite cannot tell how Infinite doth flow,
Nor how infinite matter moveth to and fro.
For infinite of matter, more, or less:
Nor infinite of causes cannot finde
The infinite effects of every Kinde.

Cavendish's use of irregular pentameter is typical of her poetry in the period – as, indeed, is her use of verse to express her philosophical opinions (in 1653, she had written that "poetry" was a genre "most properly belonging to women").[17] By the 1663 edition, her thoughts on the nature of infinite and finite matter were not supplemented by poetry. Instead, she writes:

The infinite and only matter cannot have an exact form or figure, by reason it is infinite.[18]

All of a sudden, it is far easier to understand what Cavendish had meant in her first volume. As other scholars have noted, this was more than just a shift in her way of writing: it marks a move towards the "plain style" advocated by the Royal Society for their own scientific writings. Whilst Cavendish disagreed with much of what the Society stood for – and would, in *The Blazing World*, eschew this turn towards "plain" writing in favour of fiction once more – she was, at least in part, setting herself up to engage with them on their own terms.[19]

* * *

Cavendish's first publication – her *Poems and Fancies* – also received a similar treatment: it was republished as *Poems and*

Phancies in 1664, and *Poems, Or Several Fancies, in Verse: With the Animal Parliament* in 1668.[20] Cavendish had evidently been dissatisfied with her first book for some time. On an early page in the copy of the first edition in the British Library, is the following note, written in Cavendish's unmistakable handwriting:

> ... reader let me intreat you to consider only the fancyes in this my book of poems and not the languesh numbers nor rimes nor fals printing for if you doe you will be one condemning judg who will deprive my muse[21]

Cavendish's concern is touching: she evidently felt that her poetry lacked poise and polish. And yet, despite that, she still believed in her ideas and her philosophy: her "fancyes".

In 1664, she had the chance to correct what she saw as this mismatch between her style and her ideas. The "second impression, much altered and corrected" is, indeed, very different to the first: spelling is modernised and regularised as the double letters and silent "e"s are dropped; her metre is regularised so that there are far fewer lines which are not in pentameter; and her rhyme is altered so that there are fewer half-rhymes and near-rhymes.[22] More broadly, her syntax has often been revised to make her sense clearer, and the lines easier to parse, and the organising structure of the volume has been rejigged, with sections now numbered, and formal titles added. It is also in this edition when William's dedication ("I saw your poems, and then wish'd them mine") appears more often in the opening pages (as is often the way with early modern books, there are still variations even within print runs).[23]

In the first section of poems about the nature of the world and atoms in the 1653 edition, are these lines:

There may be many Worlds like Circles round,
In after Ages more Worlds may be found.

If we into each Circle can but slip
By Art of Navigation in a Ship
This World compar'd to some, may be but small:
No doubt that Nature made degrees of all.[24]

In the 1664 edition, these lines become:

There may be many Worlds like Circles round,
And many more in After-ages found;
If we by Art of Shipping could into
Each Circle slip, we might perhaps it know.
This World compar'd to some it may be but small,
No doubt, for Nature made degrees of all;[25]

It is difficult to see why these changes have been made: the 1653 version was not, by Cavendish's standards, very difficult to understand. Nor were there any non-pentameter lines. Nonetheless, the syntax of the third and fourth line in the 1664 edition has been altered – it is now marginally easier to understand that Cavendish is discussing a sea-voyage (the rest of the poem goes on to discuss "Drake"). At the expense of this, the rhyme of "slip" and "ship" has been replaced with "-to" and "know" – but, in early modern pronunciation, it is likely to have sounded more natural than it does to modern ears. There was another alteration: for reasons difficult to discern, an extra syllable has been added to the line "this world compar'd to some...". Given that it is almost impossible to scan this with an unstressed final syllable "small" (that is, a "feminine ending"), it seems that the alterations have created a hypermetrical line: all of a sudden, the idea that the world is but one amongst many is prosodically dominant. That these alterations are so fiddly and small does not mean they should be overlooked. Someone paid enough attention to Cavendish's ideas and prosody to justify these shifts and changes – and the resulting extra-metrical emphasis on multiple worlds.

There is a more famous example of the changes to which other scholars have already drawn attention, but nonetheless deserves quoting. At the beginning of the second "clasp" – that is, the intermediary passages – Cavendish writes in the 1653 edition:

> Give Mee the Free, and Noble Stile
> Which seems uncurb'd, though it be wild:
> Though it runs wild about, It cares not where;
> It shewes more Courage, then It doth of Feare.
> Give me a Stile that Nature frames, not Art:
> For Art doth seem to take the Pedants part.
> And that seems Noble, which is Easie, Free,
> Not to be bound with ore-nice Pedantry.[26]

In the 1664 edition, this becomes:

> Give me a free and noble Style, that goes
> In an Uncurbed Strain, though Wild it shows;
> For though it Runs about it cares not where,
> It shews more Courage than it doth of Fear:
> Give me a Style that Nature frames, not Art,
> For Art doth seem to take the Pedants part;
> And that seems Noble, which is easie, free,
> And not bound up with o're nice Pedantry.[27]

The 1668 edition is almost identical to the 1664 version. For a poem about a "free" style, Cavendish has systematically regularised her writing: instead of the opening tetrameter couplet in the 1653 version, an extra foot has been added to each line to make the whole poem pentameter. And the rhyme has been regularised as "goes" / "shows" to replace the partial rhyme of "stile" / "wild". But the regularising effects of these alterations are not just "o're nice pedantry". In altering the syntax of the second line, it suddenly becomes far easier to parse: in the new edition, her style travels in an "uncurbed strain", whilst appearing "wild". In the first edition, the meaning is all but obscured.

Here, it is easy to prefer the first version: its irregularities are of a piece with the meaning of the poem, and there is the uncomfortable sense of an older hand altering the later edition. This is an argument similar to those who refuse to accept the changes William Wordsworth made to *The Prelude* in his later life; it is an argument that puts the poet on a pedestal, and lauds her or his first creation over everything else, as if it were something divine and unalterable. It's a distinctly Romantic notion, but one that should, I think, be avoided with Cavendish: her decision not just to edit, but subsequently to republish her work, reveals a continued interest in her writing, and her self-presentation as writer.

Her changes also have interesting ideological implications. In the preface to her 1653 edition, she memorably wrote that the book was her "child", and that she wanted to "shew her the world, in hopes some may like her".[28] This child is gendered feminine, but in the 1664 and 1668 editions, the pronouns are swapped: the book-child becomes "it". Could Cavendish, as one academic has suggested, been "less keen to depict her poems either as such a direct embodiment of herself, or as explicitly and necessarily feminine"?[29]

There is another gender difference between the editions. In the prefatory poem "The Poetresses Hasty Resolution", in the 1653 edition Cavendish describes "reason" as female:

> *Reason observing which way I was bent,*
> *Did stay my hand, and ask't me what I meant;*
> *Will you, said shee, thus waste your time in vaine*[30]

This female figure – like Cavendish's female Nature – is directing Cavendish, and showing her the way. But in the 1664 edition, this figure of reason becomes male: "will you, said *He*" (emphasis added). There is some argument to suggest that

Cavendish here was making the imaginative realm masculine and that this was part of a plan to engage with a wider readership, who need not see her works as explicitly feminine.[31] If this was the case, she had changed her mind when she republished the volume in 1668. Reason, "she", is once again a woman – and so is Cavendish's mental world. These changes are more than minor swaps in pronouns: they mark a change in how Cavendish was trying to present herself during the years of scholarly debate in the mid-1660s. After publishing *The Blazing World* and enjoying or enduring her London celebrity, she was continuing to develop her gynocentric view of the world and intellectual life.

* * *

These edits and alterations have become the subject of some debate, with some biographers suggesting that Cavendish could not have made them herself (her earliest biographer, Grant, wrote "it is impossible to believe that Margaret undertook the revisions herself, a task so absolutely at variance with her impatient and wandering temperament"), and that, as a result, the altered texts should not be as prized as the originals.[32] But even if it were not Cavendish who personally sent off marked-up versions of her texts to the printers (although I believe that she probably did edit her own texts), the changes made are still to *her* works, and are a part of her long-term project.

After her trip to London in 1667, her programme of revisions and new editions stepped up: she published her Latin version – the language of scholars and European universities – of her *Life of William* in 1668 (translated by Walter Charleton); new editions of her *Observations Upon Experimental Philosophy* and *Orations of Divers Sorts* in 1668; and new versions of *The Worlds Olio* and *Natures Pictures* in 1671. The changes to the latter are most revealing. *The Worlds Olio* appears without its "epistles" between her essays – the epistles in which she defended her books against the charge of "not being her own", and declared her originality (she "never converst in discourse" with any philosophers). After her published works engaging with other thinkers, and her appearance at the Royal Society, such claims were no longer necessary or apposite. At the end of her life, Cavendish was trying to move away from the image of the secluded, unschooled thinker; but she is, still, often known by her earliest declarations. She also edited the text for its post-Restoration audience, by removing her essays criticising the monarchs James I and Henry VII.[33]

The changes to *Natures Pictures* are even more substantial: the 1671 edition appears without the autobiographical fragment that had been appended to it in 1656. It was here where she had told her readers of her early childhood, her education, and about her meeting William when they were both in exile. Now a duchess – and a public figure – was such a statement about her life, and her relationship, considered unbecoming? Such an argument seems unlikely, given that parts of her *Life of William* read almost like a joint biography. Its erasure is still interesting: as with the epistles in *The Worlds Olio*, Cavendish was excising aspects of her authorial voice that seemed too immature, uneducated, and naïve. She was preparing her work to be read in a new light.

As for the more minute edits, there is every chance that Cavendish herself *did* make them. As she was growing more skilled as a writer, reader, and thinker, she could not stop herself from changing her previous works. There is evidence that Cavendish could operate on such a precise level. One scholar, James Fitzmaurice, studied a copy of Cavendish's *Plays* (1662) which is now in the Princeton University Library: throughout the text, someone with "handwriting very like that to be found in the letters written by Cavendish in 1645" had systematically corrected the typographical printing errors, and made revisions and changes "with a view towards a new edition".[34] Cavendish was far from the haphazard writer many believe her to be. In presentation copies of some of her *Sociable Letters* sent to universities and famous scholars, she – or someone instructed by her – even made sure that corrected textual errors appeared as if they were in print.

* * *

It is an interesting scene to imagine: Cavendish, in her late forties, putting aside the business of managing her husband's estates to focus on editing her work for reissue; scrutinising her much younger musings; and marking up copies of her books to be sent to the printers. But this was not her only use of her time. Just a few months after her *Plays Never Before Printed*, Cavendish's last original work was published in 1668: *Grounds of Natural Philosophy* was, notionally, a revised edition of *Philosophical and Physical Opinions* but it was so much changed and altered that it now counted as an entirely separate work.

Almost every part of *Grounds of Natural Philosophy* is marked by a serious, sober engagement with the philosophers and ideas of the day. Even the book's title is a statement, as "grounds" replace "opinions". Gone are the elaborate, apologetic prefaces: in their place is one letter, "to all the universities in Europe", asking them to consider her work. She has moved far beyond just pandering to Oxford and Cambridge. In this, her last published preface, there is a touching nod to her first book. Here, as with *Poems and Fancies*, she describes her book as a baby: "this beloved Child of my brain". But instead of an image of the beautiful child being bashful, or crying, is something rather more robustly physical: she describes "obstinately, suckl[ing] it myself".[35] It is this "bring[ing] it up alone, without the help of any Scholar" which caused "many imperfections" in her prior editions. In this edition, "by many alterations and additions", she has tried to correct this oversight. Her insistence on ending the letter with a declaration of being "too illiterate" is nothing more than a modest topos. Here is Cavendish asking the world to take her seriously:

But, if you will be contented with pure Wit, and the effects of mere contemplation; I hope, that somewhat of that kind may be found in this Book, and in my other Philosophical, Poetical, and Oratorical Works[36]

And it is difficult *not* to take this book seriously: after the letter, Cavendish inserts a lengthy table of contents, with numbered sections and chapters for each and every part of the book. She then goes on to expound the philosophy she has developed throughout her life, but in radically clearer language than before, and with nods to "learned persons" who disagree with her.[37] She has adopted the language and argumentative styles of the philosophers she has been reading, but still makes them her own. One aspect of science which fascinated Cavendish throughout her life was whether a "vacuum" could exist in nature – it was a much-debated subject in contemporary science, with people either following the views of Aristotle (to whom the saying "nature abhors a vacuum" has been attributed), or disagreeing with him. Boyle and Hooke even built an air-pump to explore the phenomenon. Cavendish had never been certain about this debate. In her earliest work, *Poems and Fancies*, she had tried to debate it in atomistic terms; in her 1655 *Philosophical and Physical Opinions* she had described it in poetry; and in her 1663 edition, she had admitted the difficulty:

To treat of Vacuum, whether there be any or not, is very Difficult, for there is as much to be said of one side as of the other.[38]

By 1668, she was done with sitting on the fence. She declared "in my opinion, there cannot possibly be any *Vacuum*". This was because, she argued, if "nature's parts could wander and stray in and out" of a vacuum, "there would be a confusion".[39] Her decision – based on pure "reason" rather than experimentation – is significant: it is Cavendish's long-lasting desire for order in the world that resolved one of her lengthiest debates with herself. Her hatred of chaos and "confusion" cast a long shadow.

There are other alterations to her philosophical opinions in *Grounds*, too. Throughout her philosophy, Cavendish's view of free will had mutated and altered. In her earliest atomism, there had been little to no possibility of free will but, since her vitalist materialism, her compatibilist position moved between (only occasionally libertarian) freedom, and a view of constraint within nature. In *Grounds*, however, she reaches a synthesis: all matter has "free-will to move after whatever manner they please", but each aspect of the world can only function with the "consent of associating parts", and perform "proper actions, as actions proper to their compositions".[40] This is modified compatibilism – there is a libertarian strain, and a sense of necessity – but it is a view of order and harmony, and one very different from Hobbes's view of base, nasty human nature. Perhaps in a bid to clear up the aspersions that had been following her for some time, she also included an appendix laying out her thoughts on religion, and its compatibility with her vitalist philosophy: "God is an Eternal Creator; Nature his Eternal Creature."[41]

Apart from her grand political ideas and scientific speculations a new note is introduced. As with all of her philosophical and scientific writings, *Grounds* has passages on illnesses and diseases – how they are caused by the humours, and how they manifest themselves. But now, for the first time, Cavendish also writes specifically about "women's health". She had long since discussed how children were born as a part of her argument explaining how "sensitive animate matter" grew "by degrees", but in 1668 she writes about "mischances, or miscarriages of breeding creatures".[42] She describes how miscarriages happen when there are "irregularities of the corporeal motions, or parts of the child" or, instead, "parts of the mother". Her language is more scientific – and she is talking about all animals, not just humans – but her concerns about the possibility of "false conceptions" links her to the women who wrote about their own miscarriages, or the midwifery books that were so popular in the seventeenth century. She is now more cautious about describing diseases (and she no longer proposes cures).[43] Its inclusion is striking: did Cavendish want to tie herself to a tradition of woman's writing she would surely have known about? Even her step-daughter Elizabeth had written verse about a child who had only lived for a number of days.[44]

This is, of course, merely one chapter in *Grounds of Natural Philosophy*, a book that demonstrates Cavendish's mature style – succinct, idiosyncratic, and engaged. Despite the sense of summation, she must have hoped to go on developing and coming into her own. Cavendish was only forty-five when the book was published, and there was no reason to expect that the "parts of [her] mind" would stop "argu[ing] amongst themselves".

* * *

How were these re-editions and new volumes financed? All evidence points to Cavendish's first few books – that is 1653's *Poems and Fancies* and *Philosophical Fancies* – being, at least in part, a financial risk to the printers (in one poem she describes the fear that the printer will "loose ill by your poetry").[45] But, by 1667, when Walter Charleton wrote to Cavendish to praise her "bestow[ing] great money in printing" her books – and making them such "elegant volumes" – something had evidently changed.[46]

Frustratingly few records of the financial relationship between publishers, printers, and authors in this period exist, and none of Cavendish's books were entered into the best-surviving record of publishing at the time, the Stationers' Register that was kept by the guild of publishers and booksellers. The absence of Cavendish's books is, in itself, not particularly unusual – many books were not entered – but it does tell us something about Cavendish's financial situation. Publishers tended to enter books that were likely to be the most lucrative – and might have resulting copyright difficulties as other publishers rushed to copy the successful text. Cavendish's publishers certainly entered other texts they printed into the register: the names "Thomas Warren", "William Wilson", and "Anne Maxwell" appear throughout the volumes. In a particularly interesting historical oddity, when the publisher was a woman, they were often still referred to as a "master" – that is, they had the freedom to sell books; "master" was a status gained through a long apprenticeship – and the person entering their name simply put "[sic]" after the title. Alice Warren (one of Cavendish's two female publishers) is entered alternately as "Mistress Alice Warren", and "Master *(sic)* Alice Warren".[47]

Combined with Charleton's comment, the absence of Cavendish's books in this register suggests that after 1653, Cavendish's means of printing her books had changed: she, like her husband, likely now paid for publication. This was far from unusual in the period, a time in which it was even harder than our own to make money from publishing, and was not necessarily an indication of the quality, or popularity, of the work. From squabbles and difficulties recorded in the Royal Society's papers, it seems that their printers, Martin and Allestree, also sometimes refused to print books without payment: on one occasion, when the Society asked the printers if they would "be at the charge" – that is, be liable for the cost of – an "astronomical manuscript", the two men refused, and the Society had to consider choosing someone else.[48]

Paying for publication did mean that, as Charleton notes, Cavendish had more control over how her books appeared. She published beautiful, "elegant" volumes that often had engraved frontispieces pasted in, and were printed in a larger format than many other books in the period: she printed her works in "folio", meaning that the paper was folded fewer times to make each "quire" (a selection of pages), and each page was larger. But, there's also something distinctly poignant about this means of publication: despite her fame in 1666 – and the crowds who besieged her every move – she could not rely on an audience who were as interested in her writings as they were her reported "eccentricities". And, given the large number of her own books she sent to scholars, librarians, and academics, there is every chance that she was, tragically, her own biggest customer.

* * *

After her last revised works had been published in 1671, Cavendish was far from retiring to a peaceful rural life without intellectual debate or engagement. She and William were still very much involved in the literary world. In the late 1660s, they were the patrons of several playwrights: Richard Flecknoe, Thomas Shadwell, and John Dryden all enjoyed their assistance or companionship (even if they might not have got on together: Dryden's long poem *Mac Flecknoe* is a savage attack on Shadwell). Shadwell even helped William with one of his own plays, and wrote to Margaret to ask her permission to dedicate one of his works to her. In response, Margaret sent him a "noble present" of her books, and he wrote back thanking her for "favours" he had received at Welbeck. Shadwell's 1676 play, *The Virtuoso*, was a scathing satire of the Royal Society which owed much to Cavendish's *Blazing World*. The culture of literary exchange and patronage that the couple had cultivated in Paris and Antwerp was far from dwindling in these years.

Margaret was not just supporting the efforts of other writers: she was still deeply engaged in her own work. "Ghost manuscripts" by Cavendish seem to have appeared in the eighteenth century, in St John's College, Cambridge. These manuscripts have not been found in recent years but, given that Cavendish burned her handwritten work after her books had gone to print, could these have been the now-lost remains of some new project? She was certainly still interested in many philosophical and scientific problems. In *Grounds of Natural Philosophy*, she had touched upon "the loadstone": that is, a naturally occurring magnetised mineral. Lodestones were a scientific problem then much in vogue – everyone from Francis Bacon to Descartes had written about them, and the Royal Society held one they called "a terrella" (a "little earth") that the king had presented to them in 1661. Writing in 1668, Cavendish had admitted her fascination with the concept – "the *loadstone*, it is not more wonderful in attracting Iron, than Beauty" – but admitted her ignorance: "I dare not venture to treat of the Nature... neither have I had much experience of it".[49] Cavendish's momentary capitulation to the Royal Society's emphasis on experiment and observation is not complete – she still hazards some opinions about this mysterious stone – but her interest in it as a phenomenon demonstrates the way her thought had changed in the course of her life. In the summer of 1672, she was engaged in her own experiments with magnetism and iron filings, and sent her husband's agent Benoist off with her findings to London to see if he could corroborate them with any other scholars.

Cavendish would never get a chance to write about this issue which had confounded "so many learned men". On 15 December 1673, she died when she was only fifty years old.

* * *

There are many oddities about Margaret's demise despite the fact that, for the period, she had lived to (or exceeded) the average life expectancy. For a woman whose medical history is so well chronicled, there are no records of a doctor's concerns preceding her death. She certainly did not die in childbirth (as William's daughter, Elizabeth, had done in 1663); nor did she, as with William's other daughter, Jane, die of having "become epileptic". Cavendish's death must have been something remarkably sudden: a heart attack, or a stroke. She had, unfortunately, done nothing to ensure her health in old age with her love of purging cures, bleeding, and limiting her exercise in favour of writing.

Despite their squabbles and disagreements, Cavendish's death must have come as a dreadful shock to William: he was nearing his eightieth birthday, and had been preparing for his own death for some time. Not only had he made sure that Margaret would be well provided for in his absence, he had also begun the preparations for his own burial: he had asked for, and been granted, permission to be buried in Westminster Abbey. It could not have been anything short of heart-breaking to know that Margaret – thirty years his junior, and his partner for the last two decades – would enter their shared tomb before him. William would not be there to see it happen: he was too weak, and ill, to make the journey to London.

Cavendish had not been to the capital since her triumphant season in 1667 but, on 3 January 1674, her "mourning hearse" finally arrived in the city, and was laid out in state at Newcastle House.[50] Without William to accompany her for this last public performance it was, instead, a retinue of servants who travelled with her into London, and a train of marshals and nobility who paraded behind her body as it wound its way through the city and into Westminster Abbey. Her body entered the church on the evening of 7 January. It was a gloomy, almost gothic scene: the all-black costumes of the mourners, the horses, and the hearse were only visible in the darkness by the light of burning torches.

The pageant was a cruel parody of Cavendish's earlier fame: once the woman who had been dressed in black velvet and chased by crowds, it was now her servants and horses who had adopted her costume, and the crowd was only her "near relations" and other nobles. Not one to skimp on ceremony, her body was carried into the Abbey with her duchess's coronet on its very own black velvet cushion, and some of the attendants from the College of Arms even wore armour.[51] Amidst all the pomp, Cavendish was accompanied by her favourite sister Catherine (the sister who the young Cavendish had been anxious about dying in her sleep, or eating food which could poison her) who was now Lady Pye. Catherine's children were also present, as were Margaret's other sister, Anne Lucas, and William's son

Henry and his wife Frances, and Elizabeth's surviving husband, the Earl of Bridgewater. Surrounded by this crowd of relations – some of whom she loved, but had spent much of her life divided from, and others with whom she had quarrelled and fought – she was laid to rest in a vault in the Abbey's north transept.

Now, if you visit the Abbey, she can be found under an elaborate marble monument commissioned by William while he was still alive. The effigies of husband and wife lie side by side, with their eyes closed and their bodies nearly, but not quite, touching. Cavendish is in full ceremonial dress, complete with a coronet, and William has his wig and heraldic medal. It's a chilling monument. The stony image of husband-and-wife has more than a hint of Larkin's poem "An Arundel Tomb" and its hollow last line "what will survive of us is love".[52] In Margaret's left hand is a book and an ink-pot, and the inscription below attests that she was a "wise wittie & learned Lady, which many of her Bookes do well testify". But the epitaph, most likely written by William, could not refrain from mentioning that she left behind "noe issue". What will survive of us, it seems, is books.

14

Doubt of an after being

CAVENDISH HAD NEVER been coy, even in her first publication, about her desire to be loved by posterity. After declaring at the opening of *Poems and Fancies* that "all I desire is Fame", she went on to write that this "fame" will build her "a Pyramid, a praise to [her] memory".[1] It will not be "so high as Babels Tower" but, nonetheless, she is "sorry it doth not touch at heaven". In her later writings, this link between fame and an afterlife became even clearer. In her second book, *Philosophical Fancies*, she declared that "if any like my fancies when they'r read, / My times rewarded, though my body's dead" and, in her first book of essays, *The Worlds Olio*, she begins with nothing less than a meditation on the "desire for fame".[2] According to her – and, in a moment that makes her distance from traditional Christian theology clear – "the desire for fame proceeds from doubt of an after being". Cavendish's longing for renown after her death did not stem from confidence, but rather from fear: a fear that she would be forgotten, and that she may "write, and write, and't may never be read; / My books, and I, all in a grave lie dead".[3]

Cavendish's worst fear of murky obscurity sounds prophetic in light of Virginia Woolf's accusation that her work stands "congealed in quartos and folios that nobody ever reads", but, for Cavendish, there was no alternative to this continual push for renown.[4] In her *Plays*, it is only a woman called "Lady

Ignorant" who dissents, and argues that "women care not for wide mouthed fame" but "take more delight to speak our selves whilst we live, than to be talked of when we are dead".[5] Cavendish's opinion was far closer to that of the Empress in *The Blazing World*, who declared that she would "rather die in the adventure of noble achievements, than live in obscure and sluggish security". In her view "the shortest liv'd fame lasts longer than the longest life of man".[6]

But far from the picture of cloistered eccentricity some commentators have liked to imagine, Cavendish was well aware that much of her work was not being truly appreciated by her readers, and was more ridiculed than revered. She believed that later ages might well understand her more, and, in a short poem at the end of *Natures Pictures*, wrote:

> *But say that Book should not in this Age take*
> *Another age of great esteem may make*
> *If not the second, then a third may raise*
> *It from the Dust, and give it wondrous praise:*
> *For who can tell but my poor Book may have*
> *Honour'd renown, when I am in the Grave*
> *And when I dye, my Blessing I will give,*
> *And pray it may in after ages live*[7]

The poignant thing here is not that Cavendish was able to see that her work was not best suited to her own time, or even that she shamelessly desired for centuries of renown after her death, but that she says this without a hint of regret: she was happy to die, if it meant that her books might live.

The ghost of Cavendish would have been happy, then, to see what William prepared for her after her death. The octogenarian William would not join Cavendish in their shared tomb for a further three years and, during this time, he was able to publish a book of posthumous tributes to his wife. *Letters and Poems in Honour of the Incomparable Princess, Margaret, Duchess of*

Newcastle appeared in 1676, just months before William died. Like the later volume published in 1678 (which included letters to both of them), it was a compilation of laudatory letters thanking Margaret for presents of her books, or praising her for her knowledge and brilliance. Alongside the fawning letters (many of which were written in Latin) were poems: some, like that from the Restoration playwright George Etherege, praised her "matchless Book[s]", whilst others lauded her unconventional, unfeminine life.[8]

In one anonymous poem on her "closet" – that is, the private room in which she could entertain one or two people – the poet compares it to a "sacred cell" where "holy hermits anciently did dwell".[9] In a note of surprise, the poet remarks, "Is this a ladys closet? 'tcannot be / For nothing here of vanity you see". Any pretence the poem has to being objective, or accurate, falls to pieces: Cavendish's vanity and attention to her dress would never have allowed her to forgo a mirror in favour of the "mirror of the mind".[10] Towards the end of the volume are a collection of elegies: Thomas Shadwell (who was supported by William until his own death) laments that "she is gone who did inspire ye all", whilst the priest Knightly Chetwood favoured an image of female "Nature" intruding into Cavendish's "privy chambers" to choose "one of her sex" to be her emissary.[11] There are, again, a flurry of Latin elegies – scholarly praise which would have pleased Cavendish, despite her inability to read it. The chaplain at Welbeck, Clement Ellis, wrote a moving (if poetically mediocre) elegy, which begun with the couplet:

> *She's dead, and here she lies; the vulgar cry:*
> *Fools know not that great Wits can never dye.*[12]

Given that he had known Cavendish since her return to England, it is no surprise that her desire for posthumous renown reverberates throughout his poem, which ends with the statement that, by her cleverness, Cavendish had made "the honour of our sex" (that is, men), "seem lost":

> *Wit was Hermaphrodite, when one in twain*
> *But now 'tis only Masculine again.*[13]

It is, of course, not surprising that a volume bankrolled by her husband contains much praise of Cavendish – and this forms the basis for the later 1678 collection. But what about other opinions of the authoress and empress of the whole world?

Not all the elegies were quite so kind. Cavendish had been the subject of mocking poems in the last years of her life (one was even written by her friend and acquaintance, John Evelyn). "The Session of the Poets" was written around the time of her London season – a satirical ballad that attacked every poet of the period, from William Davenant to John Dryden. Cavendish's inclusion is proof that she was considered to be one of the established writers, but her depiction is, nonetheless, cruel. William appears at Apollo's court with all the other poets, but has his "wife's poems, plays, essays & speeches" artfully concealed in his "breeches".[14] Apollo will have none of Cavendish's scribblings, and instructs William to "provide her fresh straw, and a chamber that dark is" – that is, to treat her as if she were insane. And in an anonymous epitaph that circulated in the years after her death (and was unearthed by her 2003 biographer, Katie Whitaker), this cruel tone continues as the speaker describes wanting to replace the inscription on Cavendish's grave with one of his own devising:

> *"Shame of her sex, Welbeck's illustrious whore,*
> *The true man's hate and grief, plague of the poor,*
> *The great atheistical philosophraster,*
> *That owns no God, no devil, lord nor master;*
> *Vice's epitome and virtue's foe,*
> *Here lies her body, but her soul's below"*[15]

The man who recorded the epitaph, John Stainsby, often travelled around the North and the Midlands, where this poem must have been written. Its knowledge of Cavendish's estate dealings ("plague of the poor") and the accusation of her unchastity ("Welbeck's illustrious whore") has echoes of Cavendish's 1671 libel case – could it have been written by one of the conspirators, or another one of the servants or tenants on the estate? Or had details from the case leaked, despite William's best attempts? Either way, its vitriol provides a harsh point of comparison to the letters and poems collected in the published volume: in the years immediately following her death, Cavendish was far from universally adored.

* * *

Such a revelation would have hardly shocked her: she was well aware that she was often not respected, and bet her hopes on the future. How, then, has her reputation fared in the four centuries since her death?

As both the fawning letters and the cruel epitaph reveal, almost as soon as she died, Cavendish's life was overtaken by myth. The first of these myths began to develop in the late seventeenth century, just two decades after Cavendish's death, with the publication of Gerard Langbaine's *An Account of the English Dramatick Poets* in 1691. It is, of course, significant that Cavendish was included: out of over 500 pages, she was one of only six women to make the cut. But the contents of her entry would set the tone – and scope – of interest in her for many decades to come. According to Langbaine, Cavendish was the perfect wife for William: "so great a consort for so great a wit".[16] His appraisal of her relies on her relationship to her husband – the fact that "her soul" sympathised "with his in all things", and that in the "crown of her labours" (her *Life of William*) she "described all his Glorious Actions".[17] What little praise there is of her is qualified:

I know there are some that have but a mean Opinion of her
Plays; but if it be consider'd that both the Language and
Plots of them are all her own: I think she ought with Justice
to be preferr'd to others of her Sex, which have built their
Fame on other People's Foundation[18]

And the catalogue of her other works is partial: after focusing
on her *Life of William*, he lists only a handful of other volumes.
Already it seems that Cavendish has been subsumed by others'
condescending opinions, and her published works are hard to
find.

This cloying focus on how brilliant a wife Cavendish was
to William continues into the early eighteenth century, as
Giles Jacob (in his *The Poetical Register*, 1719) followed
Langbaine's assessment. For him, Margaret, the "consort
to the forementioned Duke", could only make up for the
"inconsiderable faults in her numerous productions" by her
originality.[19] Langbaine and Jacob find echoes in the two other
"poetic encyclopaedia" projects of the century: George Ballard's
Memoirs of Several Ladies of Great Britain (1752), and
Theophilus Cibber's *The Lives of the Poets of Great Britain and
Ireland* (1753). Cibber takes the relationship between husband
and wife one step further, and invents a romantic story about
how Margaret's "gallant brother, Lord Lucas" asked William,
when they were fighting together, to look out for his sister "on
whom he could bestow no fortune, and whose beauty exposed
her to danger".[20] All of a sudden, Cavendish's life has been
transformed into a romance. Not content with one falsehood,
Cibber invented the story that Cavendish "kept a great many
young ladies about her person", who had to sleep near to her to
be ready "at the call of her bell, to rise any hour of the night,
to write down her conceptions".[21] Cavendish's depiction as a
raving madwoman was all but complete. To make his (false)
biography perfectly malicious, Cibber ended with a damning
assessment of her character and her lack of children: "she is

said to have been very reserved and peevish, perhaps owing to the circumstance just mentioned of having never been honoured with the name of mother".

Ballard's depiction was marginally more accurate. He had the assistance of Thomas Birch (the historian and writer who had recorded the history of the Royal Society) who had sent him a "memoranda relating to women" who were known "for their writings, or skill in learned languages". Alongside Katherine Philips and Julian of Norwich, Birch had recorded some of Cavendish's writings, and had told Ballard where to find her biography "in her own breath".[22] Ballard's project is fascinating: it is a collection of brief biographies of many female writers written because, in his words, Great Britain has "very many ingenious women" who are "unknown to the public in general" and "have been passed by in silence by our greatest biographers".[23] But if his aims were laudable, his product was less so: because existing editions of works by Cavendish were now so rare, he struggles to find many of her books; he gets crucial facts about her life wrong (he claims her father is 'Sir Charles Lucas'); and once again places her on a false pedestal of perfect femininity. According to him, she was "truly pious, charitable and generous... and a perfect pattern of conjugal love and duty".[24] This image of the "perfect wife" would persist long into the twentieth century, when newspaper articles about her in 1922 could unironically write that "Margaret Cavendish set a good example to other Margarets by making her husband her only hero, and she has no gossip to record of their friends and acquaintances".[25]

Some of the best eighteenth-century criticism of Cavendish is found not in literary biographies but in a weekly newspaper called *The Connoisseur* that only lasted for 140 issues. Writing in response to an edited anthology, *Poems by Eminent Ladies* (1755) – after Ballard, the interest in women's writing continued – the anonymous columnist of *The Connoisseur* described a fanciful dream in which he imagined a debate being held in

Parnassus (in ancient mythology, the home of the muses) about whether "English ladies, who had distinguished themselves in poetry, should be allowed to hold the same rank, and have the same honours paid them, with the men".[26] After a debate between Juvenal and Sappho, Apollo stepped in and "decreed that all those females, who thought themselves able to manage *Pegasus*" – that is, a symbol of the muses' creativity – "should immediately show their skill and dexterity in riding him". There is, of course, barely disguised sexual mockery in the passage. As all the women argued about who should be the first to mount him, one lady advanced. Cavendish – with "something rather extravagant in her air" and "an old-fashioned habit, very fantastic" – "sprang into the saddle with surprising agility". She rode without fear, "giving an entire loose to the reins", and the winged horse "ran away with her quite out of sight".[27]

Here is the familiar description of Cavendish not being fully in control of her talent (admittedly written in more imaginative terms), but it is subtly different: Cavendish "kept a firm seat, even when the horse went at his deepest rate". And when she came to dismount, "Shakespeare and Milton very kindly offered their hand to help her down". It's such a laudatory image that it's tempting to suspect it was intended ironically. But there is, apparently, no irony present – the author goes on to quote approvingly from Cavendish's "Dialogue between Melancholy and Mirth". Nonetheless, one wonders how well he knew his Civil War history. It is difficult to imagine the staunch Republican Milton offering his hand to the royalist duchess.

The choice of poem in *The Connoisseur* offers another glimpse into how Cavendish was perceived in the century after her death. By far her most favoured poem was "A Dialogue between Melancholy and Mirth" – a long work found in the "Dialogues" section of *Poems and Fancies* that focuses on the interior thoughts of the speaker as she is faced with choosing between the "fat white arms" and embraces of mirth, and the "sad and sober face" – but greater knowledge – of melancholy. It was even argued that the poem had inspired Milton's *L'Allegro* and *Il Penseroso*, despite the fact that Milton had written his poems a decade earlier. (If there was any influence, it must have been the other way round.) Alongside *The Connoisseur*, this poem appears in the 1755 edition of *Poems by Eminent Ladies*, and would crop up again in anthologies all the way through the nineteenth century. The literary critic, essayist, and editor of *The Examiner* Leigh Hunt even marked a passage of the poem in his copy of Alexander Dyce's *Specimens of British Poetesses* (1827).[28]

But if this poem was singled out, it was at the expense of others – and of a full understanding of Cavendish as a poet. It was included when her scientific, atomistic works were not, and was often placed alongside her "Fairie" poems from *Poems and Fancies*. These fairy poems were included as part of an editorial process of making Cavendish a "woman" writer – a woman who had written about her own emotions and, in a flight of fancy, about harmless fairies. If the selection were not narrow enough already, her poems were bowdlerised: in the 1755 anthology, passages from the poem in which she describes what the fairies eat (cobwebs, flies, and ants' eggs) are excised without any mention from the editors at all. Not only was Cavendish away with the fairies, she wasn't even allowed to write them as mischievous and malevolent figures like those found in Shakespeare's *A Midsummer Night's Dream* or Robert Herrick's work. By 1813, Samuel Egerton Brydges (a descendant of William) felt compelled to include the poem in its entirety, but still remarks, "a few flat or coarse circumstances occur". In his notes to "Melancholy and Mirth", he went further. After a description of how Mirth's "pores are open, whence streams out a sweat", Brydges embarrassedly adds "in these days it seems a little wonderful that a lady of rank so high, and mind so cultivated, could use language so coarse and disgusting as is seen here".[29] In our own day, it seems a little wonderful that the first selected edition of Cavendish's could exclude so many of Cavendish's most important works, and utterly divorce her from the historical, philosophical, and scientific context within which she wrote. In too many editors' hands, Cavendish became little more than a quaint eccentric who wrote harmless, if uninteresting, musings about "fairyland".

Unfortunately, this trend of anthologising, editing, and denigrating Cavendish's work got far worse before it got better. In the late eighteenth century, Horace Walpole gave Cavendish a kicking when he claimed that she and her husband were a "picture of foolish nobility".[30] Despite disagreeing with Walpole's attempt to make her "appear as ridiculous as possible", Alexander Dyce still didn't do Cavendish any favours in his edited anthology when he described her "Pastime and recreation of the Fairies" as being an "extraordinary mixture of imagination and coarse absurdity".[31] Writing two decades later, Louisa Stuart Costello's *Memoirs of Eminent Englishwomen* (1844) shows a remarkable turn of phrase and imagination in her description of Cavendish, but is still far from complimentary:

> In almost every age there has been some such self-esteemed Phoenix, whose harmless conceit does but little injury, but is, nevertheless, a general annoyance, except to the tradesmen she employs to print and bind the countless volumes with which she delights to adorn her own library[32]

Ouch. The criticism is only tempered by the fact that all Costello had to go on were previous (often false) descriptions of Cavendish's eccentricities, and the few anthologised and edited works. Cavendish's own volumes were now vanishingly rare – stuck, uncatalogued and uncared-for, in private collections.

There was one nineteenth-century champion of her work: the essayist Charles Lamb refers to Cavendish repeatedly throughout his *Essays of Elia*, calling her "dear Margaret Newcastle", and "that princely woman".[33] While his praise was verbose, his knowledge of her work was limited: he, like many writers before him, focused only on her biographical writing. For him, "no casket is rich enough, no casing sufficiently-durable, to honour and keep safe such a jewel" as her *Life of William*.[34] And his delight in her work did little to change the perception of her as a harmless eccentric: the "somewhat fantastical, and original brain'd, generous Margaret Newcastle".[35]

In 1872, Cavendish's reputation took another blow when it was edited by the Liberal Party MP and author of several satirical novels, Edward Jenkins. After an introduction in which he railed against having to read her works – "a discouraging progress" – and remarked that "she had a frenzy for creation, and was not very careful whether she produced a goldfinch or a tadpole", he moves on to her writing.[36] Not content with just excising offending passages, he edited her poems to "improve" them, casually remarking on "The Pastime of the Queen of the Fairies" that "my corrections and alterations have been rather numerous" as "parts of it are exceedingly clumsy and feeble". Perhaps his most offensive edits are to the passages he excerpts from *The Convent of Pleasure*. Like Samuel Egerton Brydges before him, he quotes a speech the disguised Princess makes to Lady Happy when they are both dressed as shepherdesses. And, like Brydges, he cuts off the interaction before there is any hint of illicit sapphic love. The next line after the included excerpt reads, "May I live in your favour, and be possest with your Love and Person, is the height of my ambitions".[37] Such a declaration of love – and physical "possession" – between two women was evidently far too much for the nineteenth century.

But Jenkins chose more of the play for his anthology, including the song that Lady Happy sings when she is dressed as a sea-goddess in one of the Convent's plays. In a speech directly to the Princess (who is still disguised as a woman), Lady Happy says:

My cabinets are oyster-shells
In which I keep my orient pearls
To open them I use the tide,
As keys to locks, which open wide[38]

It's a sensual and overtly sexual image. The idea of a lock and key as a sexual metaphor had long since been in use (and appears, memorably, in the casket scenes in Shakespeare's *The Merchant of Venice*), and oysters had been associated with all things yonic since antiquity (they are also the image Sir Edward Denny chose when he accused Lady Mary Wroth of unchastity when publishing her works: "common oysters such as thine gape wide / And take in pearles or worse at every tide").[39] It is hard not to read something sexual in Cavendish's description of shells "open[ing] wide" – but there is also something knowing about the gender dynamics here. Whilst Lady Happy invokes the phallic image of the lock and key, she also tosses it away in favour of "the tide". As ever, any gender division in *The Convent of Pleasure* is immediately, brilliantly complicated.

But, when this speech is rendered in Jenkins's edition, it is completely altered. The first four lines now read as a composite quatrain, made from lines 1–2, and 5–6:

My cabinets are oyster-shells,
In which I keep my orient pearls:
And modest coral I do wear,
Which blushes when it touches air.[40]

The sexy, knotty, difficult lines have been completely excised, and the poem continues as if they never happened. In a note at the end, Jenkins writes that he has "been obliged for the sake of both symmetry and harmony to leave out several verses in this song". In fact, the only lines he has left out are those about the oysters and the tide: the resulting poem *is* more symmetrical (Jenkins imposes a false structure of quatrains), but, it is also flattened, and wrung-out of its complexity and interest. It is also difficult to believe that Jenkins made these cuts simply for the case of poetic harmony. He may have been a forward-thinking politician and writer, but the excitements of unfiltered Cavendish proved too much for him.

The late nineteenth century was not a high point for the study of women's poetry from earlier periods. While the interest in the eighteenth century had been flawed, as the over-edited anthologies reveal, it was, at least, part of a genuine desire to read these female poets. By the nineteenth century, this interest seems to have been replaced by a desire to catalogue and examine the "poetesses" as if they were particularly repugnant animals in a zoo. In his particularly laughable commentary, *English Poetesses*, Eric Robertson begins with a bold opening note:

> Ladies who write verse now-a-days do not dare to be called "Poetesses"; yet, as they have not had the wit to find a better designation for themselves, the name must serve[41]

From that high point, the book only gets worse. After remarking that all women are made to be mothers ("the springs of maternal feeling within her bosom are the secret of her life") and arguing that women would rather be Niobe – that is, the weeping figure from antiquity whose children were all slain – than "the artist who carved her", Robertson makes a sweeping statement about women's poetry: "take away lover, and husband and child, from the poetry written by women, and what have you left?". This book is less a study of poetry written by women, than a concerted attempt to inscribe sex-difference, and the corresponding difference in skill, in writing. For Robertson, women's poetry is not something to be esteemed ("Did Katherine Philips rival Otway? Did Mrs. Hemans rival Wordsworth, or Landor, or Keats, or Shelley?"), but instead a means of understanding these women's lives: "the beauty of noble lives led by pure and able women".[42]

Given that Cavendish did not have a "child" – and little of her writing, other than her *Life of William*, is about her husband or lover – how did Robertson approach her work? By the time he reached Cavendish, he had already attacked Aphra Behn ("so unsexed a writer"), and attempted to approach her in the same, unflinchingly rude terms: "The Duchess of Newcastle is one of whose qualities it is exceedingly difficult to form an exact estimate." He despairs over her lack of modesty – "the frankness of her disclosures with respect to her self" – and derides her work: "she possesses an abundance of sense, but very little of it common sense". Given the selection of her work he chose to quote – again, her poem about fairies, and an unremarkable passage of prose about the dangers of sending women to boarding schools – his lack of respect for her is almost understandable. By 1883, Cavendish had become completely divorced from the bulk of her work and thought, and was little more than a paper-thin flimsy figure of an early woman writer: someone to be remembered, but certainly not emulated. She even had a new nickname, coined by the Victorian antiquarian Mark Anthony Lower: "Mad Madge of Newcastle".[43]

* * *

It is, then, ironic that the first book-length critical study of Cavendish coincided with – or, maybe, *caused* – the low point in her reputation. In 1918, Henry Ten Eyck Perry published his joint biography of William and Margaret, *The First Duchess of Newcastle and her Husband as Figures in Literary History*. Despite the title of his book, Perry puts Cavendish's "eccentricity" above her writings: "There can be no doubt that Margaret Cavendish is an unusual and engaging personality, whatever one may think of her as an authoress."[44] Like other writers before him, he stresses the importance of her biography of William above all else, and denigrates her other books: their length is "discouraging to the uninitiated and exasperating to those who do peruse".[45] These opinions and complaints were, by now, standard in Cavendish studies, but what Perry wrote next was novel. Taking the gossips' comments from Cavendish's lifetime, and combining them with the new-found nickname of "Mad Madge", Perry came to the belief that Cavendish was "more warped and lopsided than modern psychology tells us that we all are".[46] After reading *The Blazing World*, his criticism went further: Cavendish was, apparently, "dangerously far from sanity".[47] From Dorothy Osborne's catty comments in 1653 – "there are soberer people in Bedlam" – through the partial acclaim in her lifetime and limited posthumous interest, opinions on Cavendish had, finally, come full circle: she was an insane woman, as her dedication to writing books proves.

It is, perhaps, unfair to blame Perry for this development in Cavendish studies: while his book focused on her autobiography it did, at least, mention the scientific elements in her poems and prose (even if he insisted on remarking that it "is not science at all, but fancy, pure and simple").[48] But his accusation of insanity stuck: even as late as 1979 – only forty-three years ago – one literary study argued that *The Blazing World* was evidence of the author's "schizophrenia".[49] One of Cavendish's most successful, ambitious, and radically ground-breaking works was little more than a sign of psychological distress. Wherever her posthumous fame has taken her in the afterlife, let's hope William distracted her so she didn't have to hear that.

Virginia Woolf's famous criticism of Cavendish appeared in the decade after the Perry study, in *The Common Reader* (1925) and *A Room of One's Own* (1929). In light of the critical history that preceded her, and the fact that so few of Cavendish's works were anthologised and in print, her attacks make more sense:

> Though her philosophies are futile, and her plays intolerable, and her verses mainly dull, the vast bulk of the Duchess is leavened by a vein of authentic fire. One cannot help following the lure of her erratic and loveable personality, as it meanders and twinkles through page after page. There is something noble and Quixotic and high-spirited, as well as crack-brained and bird-witted, about her.[50]

What appears brilliantly original in Woolf's account on a first reading seems, after tracing Cavendish's critical history, to be little more than a wonderfully witty mash-up of Lamb's appreciation of her eccentricity, and the derogatory comments of all those who had edited and anthologised her. When she wrote *A Room of One's Own* (1929), Woolf's criticism was more important: when she railed against the "empty shelves" of women's writing, she was not revealing her ignorance of early modern women writers but, instead, the way they had been constrained, altered, and all but eradicated by the edited editions and anthologies in which they appeared. As the brilliant scholar of early modern women's writing Margaret Ezell put it, the women in these anthologies were not "muses for other women writers" but, instead, "antiquarian artifacts in difficult type".[51] It is no surprise, then, that when speaking to the keen female undergraduates at Cambridge, Woolf felt the need to imagine an inspiring female poetic figure: Shakespeare's unappreciated sister. But when Woolf ended with her feminist call to arms – "she lives in you and in me... for great poets do not die" – did she realise that she was quoting Margaret Cavendish?[52]

* * *

In more recent years, as feminist criticism and interest in women's writing has picked up, Cavendish's reputation is still highly contested. The first biography of Cavendish was Douglas Grant's *Margaret the First* (1957) – but whilst it made use of her letters and archival material, Grant persisted in deriding and mocking his subject. According to him, Cavendish never performed any scientific experiments (despite letters which prove otherwise), and was temperamentally incapable of editing her work. Grant's biography was followed by Kathleen Jones's, *A Glorious Fame*, in 1988. At the time when it was written, Jones could still remark that "only one of [Cavendish's] books has been reprinted for sale to the general public since her death".[53] That "one book" was, of course, Cavendish's biography of her husband. Jones had no problem in placing Cavendish in a group of female "minor writers", and saw her success only in terms of what came after her: she was one of the tricky "first stumbling steps of feminist awareness". The most scholarly, and *fair*, book on Cavendish appeared in 2003: Katie Whitaker's meticulous *Mad Madge*. But despite her even-handed approach to Cavendish – and her wealth of archival research – Whitaker still made use of that cruel nickname.

Away from biographies, there have been creative responses to Cavendish's life and work. In 2018, Danielle Dutton published *Margaret the First*, a brilliantly inventive novel of her life. Siri Hustvedt's *The Blazing World* (2014) is a novel about a female artist who struggles to prove that it was she who created her work: surely there is a trace of Cavendish, and her struggles, here? It is certainly a better use of Cavendish's title than the 2021 sci-fi film of the same name.

In the last half-century, Cavendish's fate has been a patchy one: her feminist credentials led to her inclusion in the outburst of academic feminist criticism around second-wave feminism, but her contradictions – her Royalism; her authoritarianism; her occasional vitriolic attacks on her own sex – made her far from an easy poster girl for the movement. In her groundbreaking work of feminist criticism, *A Literature of their Own* (1977), Elaine Showalter called her "melancholy, guilt-ridden, suicidal" (and argued that Woolf was of her kind). Hilda L. Smith, in her book *Reason's Disciples: Seventeenth-Century English Feminists* (1982), includes Cavendish in this group, but insists that "no work of a seventeenth-century feminist poses so many interpretative problems".[54] In insisting that Cavendish fit within the boundaries of what is now "feminism", Smith – and other writers – found only problems, rather than the opportunities and delights of her contradictions. Writing in 1995, Germaine Greer tried to turn this new strain of feminist criticism on its head, and argued that much of women's writing from pre-1900 was, in fact, inferior to men's, and we should not be afraid of admitting this. Rather disingenuously, she asked: "Homer and Milton were blind; can we really claim that being female is a worse handicap than being blind?"[55] But despite calling Cavendish "the crazy Duchess", Greer does quote approvingly from one of her poems about war from *Poems and Fancies*.[56]

More recently, Cavendish studies have moved on from the repeated myths: essays are less likely to stress that Cavendish was completely uneducated, or that she was insane. Her plays are read and studied – some have even been performed – and her political philosophy and natural science writings have appeared in academic editions, or have been studied in monographs. There is even soon to be a twenty-volume edition of her complete works.[57]

All the same, this uptick in attention has not been without a certain type of condescension: as one academic has put it, "more than any other early modern woman writer" (or, we might argue, any writer at all), "Cavendish has prompted critical disclaimers, qualifications, and apologies".[58] Her works are still attacked for being contradictory and confusing (nobody ever says the same about Alexander Pope's *The Dunciad*); too anti-feminist for her supposed feminist credentials (does this stop anyone reading Mary Wollstonecraft?); and too rooted in a scientific and philosophical context different to our own to be relevant (it is hard to find someone who would argue this about Thomas Hobbes, or John Locke).

But away from the chattering of critics, it's important to place Cavendish within a broader tradition of women's writing. Whilst she was much gossiped-about and rarely appreciated in her lifetime, only half a century after her death a public forum of women's writing – and writing *for* women – was beginning to develop. Cavendish died just forty years before the advent of the *Female Tatler* (a literary periodical written for women, and supposedly by the anonymous woman "Mrs Crackenthorpe") – and its style of letters, with characters only identified by their initials, is remarkably close to *Sociable Letters*. Thirty years after the *Tatler*, Eliza Haywood, the English actress and professional author, published *The Female Spectator*.

The eighteenth century was awash with literary women, from Charlotte Smith (who wrote poems to alleviate the money troubles caused by her husband whilst she was in debtors' prison), to Delarivier Manley, whose libellous novel *The New Atlantic* (1709) put her in legal difficulty. In publishing their work for public consumption – and risking their reputations as they did so – did these women know they were following in Margaret's shoes? It is hard to imagine they didn't: the spectre of Cavendish would not vanish until the nineteenth century, when many women, once again, resorted to anonymity and the use of pseudonyms to earn money from their work.

As tempting as it is to laud Cavendish as a pioneer, a trendsetter and a feminist icon who should be on posters and tote bags everywhere, we should not do so at the expense of ignoring her difficulties, her contradictions, and her complex individuality. To do so would be the inverse, but have the same flattening effect, of simply calling her an "eccentric". Instead, we should take her for all she was: in her own words: "I am as I am, MARGARET NEWCASTLE."[59]

Appendix 1

Works by Margaret Cavendish

Work*	Abbreviation†
Poems and Fancies (London: T. Roycroft for J. Martin and J. Allestree, 1653)	*PaF 1653*
Philosophical Fancies (London: T. Roycroft for J. Martin and J. Allestree, 1653)	*PF 1653*
The Worlds Olio (London: J. Martin and J. Allestree, 1655)	*WO 1655*
Philosophical and Physical Opinions (London: J. Martin and J. Allestree, 1655)	*PPO 1655*
Natures Pictures (London: J. Martin and J. Allestree, 1656)	*NP 1656*
Plays written by the thrice noble, illustrious and excellent princess, the Lady Marchioness of Newcastle (London: A. Warren for J. Martin, J. Allestree, and T. Dicas, 1662)	*Plays*
Orations of Divers Sorts (London: W. Wilson, 1662)	*ODS 1662*
Orations of Divers Sorts (London: W. Wilson, 1663)	*ODS 1663*

---

* As much detail as is certain is given; for more, see Cameron Kroetsch, "List of Margaret Cavendish's Texts, Printers, and Booksellers (1653 – 1675)".
† Attempts have been made to distinguish abbreviations for subsequent editions from entirely new works of a similar name – see *Plays*, and *PNBP*.

Philosophical and Physical Opinions (London: W. Wilson, 1663)	*PPO 1663*
Poems and Fancies (London: W. Wilson, 1664)	*PaF 1664*
Sociable Letters (London: W. Wilson, 1664)	*SL*
Philosophical Letters (London: 1664)	*PL 1664*
Observations Upon Experimental Philosophy (London: A. Maxwell, 1666)	*OUEP 1666*
The Blazing World (London: A. Maxwell, 1666)	*BW 1666*
Life of William (London: A. Maxwell, 1667)	*LoW 1667*
Plays Never Before Printed (London: A. Maxwell, 1668)	*PNBP*
Grounds of Natural Philosophy (London: A. Maxwell, 1668)	*GNP*
De Vita et Rebus Gestis Nobilissimi Illustrissimique Principis Guilielmi (*Life of William*, Latin edition) (London: T. Milbourne, 1668)	*LoW Latin*
The Blazing World (London: A. Maxwell, 1668)	*BW 1668*
Observations Upon Experimental Philosophy (London: A. Maxwell, 1668)	*OUEP 1668*
Orations of Divers Sorts (London: A. Maxwell, 1668)	*ODS 1668*
Poems and Fancies (London: A. Maxwell, 1668)	*PaF 1668*
The Worlds Olio (London: A. Maxwell, 1671)	*WO 1671*
Natures Pictures (London: A. Maxwell, 1671)	*NP 1671*
Life of William (London: A. Maxwell, 1671)	*LoW 1671*

Appendix 2

Other abbreviated works

Work	Abbreviation
A Collection of Letters and Poems Written by several Persons of Honour and Learning, Upon Divers Important Subjects, to the Late Duke and Dutchess of Newcastle (London: Langly Curtis, 1678)	*Letters 1678*
Calendar for the Committee for Compounding, ed. Mary Anne Everett Green, 5 parts, (London: Her Majesty's Stationery Office, 1889–92)	*CCC [vol.]*
Calendar of State Papers Domestic: Charles I, 1625–1638, ed. John Bruce (London: Her Majesty's Stationery Office, 1858–71)	*CSPD*
Calendar of State Papers Domestic: Charles I, 1639–1649, ed. William Douglas Hamilton (London: Her Majesty's Stationery Office, 1871–93)	*CSPD*
Calendar of State Papers Domestic: Charles II, 1660–1669, ed. Mary Ann Everett Green (London: Her Majesty's Stationery Office, 1860–94)	*CSPD*
Calendar of State Papers Domestic: Interregnum, ed. Mary Ann Everett Green (London: Her Majesty's Stationery Office, 1875)	*CSPD*

Calendar of State Papers Relating to English Affairs in the Archives of Venice, ed. Allen B. Hinds, 38 vols (London: Her Majesty's Stationery Office, 1864 – 1947)	*CSPV*
Letters and Poems in Honour of the Incomparable Princess, Margaret, Duchess of Newcastle (London: Thomas Newcombe, 1676)	*Letters 1676*
The Diary and Correspondence of John Evelyn, ed. William Bray, 2 vols (London: M. Walter Dunne, 1901)	*Evelyn [vol.]*
The Diary of Samuel Pepys, ed. R. C. Latham & W. Matthews, 11 vols (London: HarperCollins, 1995)	*Pepys [vol.]*
The Life of William Cavendish, to which is added The True Relation of My Birth, Breeding, and Life, ed. C. H. Firth (London: John C. Nimmo, 1886)	*Life and True Relation*

Appendix 3

Abbreviations

	Abbreviation
Bodleian Libraries, Oxford	*Bodleian*
British Library	*BL*
English Broadsheet Broadside Ballad Archive	*EBBA*
Historical Manuscripts Commission	*HMC*
University of Nottingham Manuscripts and Special Collections	*NUL*
Princeton University Library	*PUL*
Public Records Office	*PRO*

Bibliography

Archival sources

Bodleian Libraries, Oxford

Bodleian MS Ashmole 1463
Bodleian MS Ashmole 36
Bodleian MS North c.4
Bodleian MS Wood D. 16
Bodleian MS Rawlinson Poet 16

British Library, London

BL Add MS 12514
BL Add MS 32497
BL Add MS 4244
BL Add MS 61414
BL Add MS 61415
BL Add MS 70118
BL Add MS 70499
BL Add MS 78357
BL Add MS 78439
BL Add MS 70500
BL Add MS 75345
BL Add MS 75345
BL Add MS 12514
BL C.39.h.27
BL Harley MS 2043
BL Harley MS 4955

BL Harley MS 6083
BL Harley MS 6804
BL MS Egerton 206
BL MS Egerton 607
BL MS Sloane 1950

College of Arms

MS I.31

University of Nottingham Manuscripts and Special Collections

NUL MS PwV 90
NUL Ne 4 1/9
NUL Ne C15366
NUL Ne X 611
NUL Pw 1/316
NUL Pw V 90/5

Princeton University Library

PUL RCT01, Item 226

Public Records Office

PRO, SPD 29/ 450, r02

Yale University Library

MS b.233

Newsbook sources

Mercurius Aucilus, First Week (Oxford: 1 January 1643),
   Thomason / E.732 [15]
Mercurius Pragmaticus, Thomason / E.407 [309]
—— 15 (London: 11 July 1648)
—— 18 (London: 1 August 1648)
—— 19 (London: 8 August 1648)

—— 21 (London: 24 August 1648)

—— 23 (London: 5 September 1648)

—— 45 (London: 20 February 1649)

Mercurius Rusticus, [...] from the beginning of this unnatural war, to the 25th of March, 1646 (London: 1685)

A Continuation of Certain Special and Remarkable passages from both Houses of Parliament, from Thursday 25th August till Tuesday the 30th, 1642, 4 (London: 30 August 1642), Thomason / E.121 [24]

The Great Eclipse of the Sun (London: 1644)

Mercurius Britannicus, Thomason E. 67 [26]

—— 44 (London: 22 July 1644)

—— 19 (London: 4 January 1644)

Perfect Occurrences of Parliament, 25 (London: 14 June 1645), Thomason / E.252 [25]

A More Exact and Perfect Relation of the Great Victory (by Gods providence) obtained by the Parliaments forces [...] on Saturday 14 June 1645 (London: 1645), Thomason / E.288 [28]

An Ordinance of the Lords and Commons [...] for the Great Victory (London: 1645), Thomason / E.288 [26]

Works by Margaret Cavendish

Bell in Campo & The Sociable Companions, ed. Alexandra G. Bennett (Toronto, Canada: Broadview Editions, 2002)

The Blazing World (London: A. Maxwell, 1666)

The Blazing World (London: A. Maxwell, 1668)

The Blazing World and Other Writings, ed. Kate Lilley (London: Penguin Classics, 1994)

The Cavalier and his Lady, Selections from the Works of the First Duke and Duchess of Newcastle, ed. Edward Jenkins (London: Macmillan and Co., 1872)

The Convent of Pleasure and Other Plays, ed. Anne Shaver (Maryland: John Hopkins University Press, 1999), Introduction.

De Vita et Rebus Gestis Nobilissimi Illustrissimique Principis

Guilielmi (*Life of William,* Latin edition) (London: T. Milbourne, 1668)

Grounds of Natural Philosophy (London: A. Maxwell, 1668)

Life of William (London: A. Maxwell, 1667)

Life of William (London: A. Maxwell, 1671)

The Life of William Cavendish, to which is added The True Relation of My Birth, Breeding, and Life, ed. C. H. Firth (London: John C. Nimmo, 1886)

The Lives of William Cavendishe, Duke of Newcastle, and of His Wife, Margaret, Duchess of Newcastle, ed. Mark Anthony Lower (London: 1872)

Margaret Cavendish, ed. Michael Robbins (New York: NYRB, 2019)

Margaret Cavendish: Essential Writings, ed. David Cunning (Oxford: Oxford University Press, 2019)

Margaret Cavendish's Poems and Fancies: A Digital Critical Edition, ed. Liza Blake (Online: 2019)

Natures Pictures (London: A. Maxwell, 1671)

Natures Pictures (London: J. Martin and J. Allestree, 1656)

Observations Upon Experimental Philosophy (London: A. Maxwell, 1666)

Observations Upon Experimental Philosophy (London: A. Maxwell, 1668)

Observations Upon Experimental Philosophy, ed. Eileen O'Neill (Cambridge: Cambridge University Press, 2001)

Orations of Divers Sorts (London: A. Maxwell, 1668)

Orations of Divers Sorts (London: W. Wilson, 1662)

Orations of Divers Sorts (London: W. Wilson, 1663)

Paper Bodies: A Margaret Cavendish Reader, ed. Sylvia Bowerbank and Sara Mendelson (Toronto, Canada: Broadview Editions, 2000)

Philosophical and Physical Opinions (London: J Martin and J. Allestree, 1655)

Philosophical and Physical Opinions (London: W. Wilson, 1663)

Philosophical Fancies (London: T. Roycroft for J. Martin and J. Allestree, 1653)

Philosophical Letters (London: 1664)

Plays (London: A. Warren for J. Martin, J. Allestree, and T. Dicas, 1662)

Plays Never Before Printed (London: A. Maxwell, 1668)

Poems and Fancies (London: A. Maxwell, 1668)

Poems and Fancies (London: T. Roycroft for J. Martin and J. Allestree, 1653)

Poems and Fancies (London: W. Wilson, 1664)

Poems and Fancies with the Animal Parliament, ed. Brandie R. Siegfried (New York: Iter Press, 2018)

Political Writings, ed. Susan James (Cambridge: Cambridge University Press, 2003)

Sociable Letters (London: W. Wilson, 1664)

Sociable Letters, ed. James Fitzmaurice (Toronto, Canada: Broadview Editions, 2004)

The Select Poems of Margaret Cavendish, ed. Samuel Egerton Brydges (Kent: Lee Priory Press, 1813)

The Worlds Olio (London: A. Maxwell, 1671)

The Worlds Olio (London: J. Martin and J. Allestree, 1655)

Other works

Adcock, Rachel, Sara Read, and Anna Ziomek, eds, *Eliza's Babes in Flesh and Spirit: An Anthology of Seventeenth-Century Women's Writing* (Manchester: Manchester University Press, 2014)

A Comparison Between the Two Stages (London: 1702)

The Connoisseur, 2 vols (London: 1774)

A Collection of Ordinances and Regulations for the Government of the Royal Household (London: Society of Antiquaries, 1790)

The Valiant Commander with his Resolute Lady (London: 1664)

Astell, Mary, *A Serious Proposal to the Ladies* (London: R. Wilkin, 1694)

Bacon, Francis, *The Advancement of Learning, in The Two Books of Francis Bacon* (London: 1605)

Ballard, George, *Memoirs of Several Ladies of Great Britain* (London: W. Jackson, 1752)

Battigelli, Anna, *Margaret Cavendish and the Exiles of the Mind* (USA: Kentucky University Press, 1998)

Begley, Justin, "Margaret Cavendish, The Last Natural Philosopher" (unpublished doctoral thesis, University of Oxford, 2016)

Bell, R., ed., *Memorials of the Civil War* (Fairfax Papers), 2 vols (London: 1849)

Bending, Stephen, *Green Retreats: Women, Gardens and Eighteenth-Century Culture* (Cambridge: Cambridge University Press, 2013)

Birch, Thomas, *The History of the Royal Society of London*, 4 vols (London: A. Millar, 1757)

Bordinat, Philip, "A Study of Salisbury Court Theatre" (unpublished doctoral thesis, University of Birmingham, 1952)

Bostridge, Ian, *Witchcraft and its Transformations c. 1650–1750* (Oxford: Oxford University Press, 1997)

Bowerbank, Sylvia, "The Spider's Delight: Margaret Cavendish and the 'Female' Imagination", *English Literary Renaissance*, 14 (1984), 392–408

Bradstreet, Anne, *Several Poems Compiled* (Boston: 1678)

Breasted, Barbara, "Comus and the Castlehaven scandal", *Milton Studies*, 3 (1971), 2014–2224

Broad, Jacqueline and Karen Green, "Fictions of a feminine philosophical persona: Christine de Pizan, Margaret Cavendish and philosophia los", in *The Philosopher in Early Modern Europe: The Nature of a Contested Identity*, ed. Conal Condren, Stephen Gaukroger, and Ian Hunter, pp. 229–54

Brontë, Charlotte, *Villette*, ed. Helen M. Cooper (London: Penguin Classics, 2004)

Bruce, John, ed., *Calendar of State Papers Domestic: Charles I, 1625–1638* (London: Her Majesty's Stationery Office, 1858–71)

Buckingham, George Villiers, Duke of, ed., *Poems on Affairs of State* (London: 1697)

Cain, Tom and Ruth Connolly, eds, *The Poems of Ben Jonson*, (London: Routledge, 2021)

Carey, John, ed., *Milton: The Complete Shorter Poems*, 2nd edn (London: Pearson Longman, 2007)

Cavendish, William, ed., *Letters and Poems in Honour of the Incomparable Princess, Margaret, Duchess of Newcastle* (London: Thomas Newcombe, 1676)

—— *The Phanseys Of William Cavendish Marquis Of Newcastle Addressed To Margaret Lucas and Her Letters In Reply*, ed. Douglas Grant (London: Nonesuch Press, 1956)

Chalmers, Hero, *Royalist Women Writers 1650–1680* (Oxford: Clarendon Press, 2004)

Chisenhall, Edward, *A Journal of the Siege of Lathom House* (London: 1823)

Cibber, Theophilus, *The Lives of the Poets of Great Britain and Ireland: to the Time of Dean Swift* (London: R. Griffiths, 1753)

Clarendon, Edward Hyde, *The History of the Rebellion and Civil Wars in England*, ed. W. Dunn Macray, 6 vols (Oxford: Clarendon Press, 1888)

Clark, Sandra, "'*Hic Mulier*', '*Haec Vir*', and the Controversy over Masculine Women", *Studies in Philology*, 82 (1985), 157–183

Clucas, Stephen, ed., *A Princely Brave Woman: Essays on Margaret Cavendish* (London: Routledge, 2003)

—— "The Atomism of the Cavendish Circle: A Reappraisal", *The Seventeenth Century*, 9 (1994), 247–73

A Collection of Letters and Poems Written by several Persons of Honour and Learning, Upon Divers Important Subjects, to the Late Duke and Dutchess of Newcastle (London: Langly Curtis, 1678)

Collins, Jane, *Susanne Du Verger* (London: Routledge, 1996).

Costello, Louisa, *Memoirs of Eminent Englishwomen*, 4 vols (London: Richard Bentley, 1884)

Coward, Barry, *The Cromwellian Protectorate* (Manchester: Manchester University Press, 2003)

Crawford, Patricia, *"Women's published writings 1600–1700"*, in *Women in English Society 1500–1800* (London and New York: Methuen, 1985), ed. Mary Prior, pp. 211–82

Creaser, John, *"Milton's 'Comus': The Irrelevance of the Castlehaven Scandal"*, *Milton Quarterly*, 21 (1987), 24–34

Cunning, David, *Cavendish* (London: Routledge, 2016)

Cunnington, Philips and C. Willis, *The Handbook of English Costume in the Seventeenth Century* (London: Faber and Faber, 1963)

Davenant, William and John Dryden, *The Tempest, or The Enchanted Island* (London: J.M, 1670)

Dawson, Hannah, ed., *The Penguin Book of Feminist Writing* (London: Penguin Classics, 2021)

De Lisle, *Leanda, Henrietta Maria: Conspirator, Warrior, Phoenix Queen* (London: Penguin, 2022)

de Pizan, Christine, *The Book of the City of Ladies*, trans. Rosalind Brown-Grant (London: Penguin, 1999)

Dearing, Vinton A., Earl Miner, and H. T. Swedenberg, eds, *The Works of John Dryden*, 20 vols (Berkeley; Los Angeles; London: 1956–2000)

Donoghue, Emma, *Passions Between Women* (London: Bello, 2014)

Douglas Hamilton, William, ed., *Calendar of State Papers Domestic: Charles I, 1639–1649* (London: Her Majesty's Stationery Office, 1871–93)

Dugaw, Dianne, *Warrior Women and Popular Balladry, 1650–1850* (Cambridge: Cambridge University Press, 1989)

Duncan-Jones, Katherine, ed., *Sir Philip Sidney* (Oxford: Oxford University Press, 1989)

Dyce, Alexander, *Specimens of British Poetesses* (London: T. Rodd, 1825)

Emre, Merve, "How Leonora Carrington Feminized Surrealism", *New Yorker*, 28 December 2020

English Broadside Ballad Archive, *Pepys Ballads* (online)

Evelyn, John, trans., *A Character of England as it was lately presented in a letter to a noble man in France* (London: Jo Crooke, 1659)

Evelyn, John, *Numismata* (London: 1697)

—— *The Diary and Correspondence of John Evelyn*, ed. William Bray, 4 vols (London: H. Colburn, 1857)

—— *The Diary and Correspondence of John Evelyn*, ed. William Bray, 2 vols (London: M. Walter Dunne, 1901)

Eyre, George Edward Briscoe, ed., *A Transcript of the Registers of the Worshipful Company of Stationers 1640–1708 AD*, 3 vols (London: 1913)

Ezell, Margaret J. M. and Frances N. Teague, eds, *Educating English Daughters: Late Seventeenth-Century Debates* (Ontario: Iter Academic Press, 2016)

Ezell, Margaret, *"'To Be Your Daughter in Your Pen': The Social Functions of Literature in the Writings of Lady Elizabeth Brackley and Lady Jane Cavendish"*, Huntington Library Quarterly, 51 (1988), 281–96

—— *Writing Women's Literary History* (Baltimore: Johns Hopkins University Press, 1993)

Faderman, Lillian, ed., *Chloe Plus Olivia: An Anthology of Lesbian Literature from the Seventeenth Century to the Present* (London: Viking, 1994)

—— *Surpassing the Love of Men* (New York: Quill, 1981)

Fanshaw, Richard, trans., *The Faithful Shepherd* (London: 1647)

Fanshawe, Ann, *Memoirs of Lady Fanshawe* (London: John Lane The Bodley Head, 1907)

Faulkner, P. A, *Bolsover Castle, Derbyshire* (London: Her Majesty's Stationery Office, 1972)

Firestone, Shulamith, *The Dialectic of Sex* (New York: Bantam Books, 1970)

Firth, C. H., "London during the Civil War", *History*, 11 (1926), 25–36

Firth, C. H. and J. H. Leslie, "The Siege and Capture of Bristol by the Royalist Forces in 1643", *Journal of the Society for Army Historical Research*, 4 (1925), 180–203

Fitzmaurice, James, "Margaret Cavendish on Her own Writing: Evidence from Revision and Handmade Correction", *The Papers of the Bibliographical Society of America*, 85 (1991), 297–307

—— *The Cavendishes, the Evelyns, and Teasing in Verse and Prose*, Quidditas 16 (1995–6)

Fogle, French R. and Louis A. Knafla, eds, *Patronage in Late Renaissance England* (California: University of California, 1983)

—— "'The Lotterie': A Transcription of a Manuscript Play Probably by Margaret Cavendish", *Huntington Library Quarterly*, 66 (2003), 155–67

Foxton, Rosemary, *Hear the Word of the Lord: A Critical and Bibliographical Study of Quaker Women's Writing, 1650–1700* (Melbourne: Bibliographical Society of Australia and New Zealand, 1994)

Fraser, Antonia, *Cromwell Our Chief of Men* (London: Weidenfeld and Nicolson, 1973)

—— *The Weaker Vessel* (London: Orion, 1984)

Gelbart, Nina, "The Intellectual Development of Walter Charleton", *Ambix*, 18 (1971), 149–68

Goulding, Richard W., *Letters Written by Charles Lamb's "Princely Woman, the Thrice Noble Margaret Newcastle" to her Husband* (London: John Murray, 1909)

Gowing, Laura, *Common Bodies: Women, Touch and Power in Seventeenth-Century England* (New Haven: Yale University Press, 2003)

—— *Ingenious Trade: Women and Work in Seventeenth-Century London* (Cambridge: Cambridge University Press, 2021)

Grant, Douglas, *Margaret the First* (London: Rupert Hart-Davis, 1957)

Green, Mary Ann Everett, ed., *Calendar of State Papers Domestic: Interregnum* (London: Her Majesty's Stationery Office, 1875)

—— *Calendar of State Papers Domestic: Charles II, 1660–1669* (London: Her Majesty's Stationery Office, 1860–94)

—— *Calendar for the Committee for Compounding, 5 parts* (London: Her Majesty's Stationery Office, 1889–92)

—— *Letters of Queen Henrietta Maria* (London: R. Bentley, 1857)

Greer, Germaine, Susan Hastings, Jeslyn Medoff, and Melinda Sansone, eds, *Kissing the Rod: An Anthology of Seventeenth-Century Women's Verse* (London: Little, Brown, 1988)

Greer, Germaine, *Slip-Shod Sibyls* (London: Penguin, 1996)

—— *The Female Eunuch* (London: Paladin, 1970)

Grymeston, Elizabeth, *Miscelanea. Mediations. Memoratives* (London: Melch. Bradwood for Felix Norton, 1604)

Halifax, George Savile, *Advice to a Daughter* (London: M. Gillyflower and James Partridge, 1688)

Hamilton, Anthony, *Memoirs of Count Grammont* (Philadelphia: E. L. Carey & A. Hart, 1836)

Hayden, Judy A, ed., *The New Science and Women's Literary Discourse* (New York: Palgrave Macmillan, 2011)

Henderson, Jeffrey, ed., and M. D. Macleod, trans., *Lucian*, 8 vols (London: Harvard University Press, 1961)

Hervey, Helen, "Hobbes and Descartes in the Light of Some Unpublished Letters of the Correspondence between Sir Charles Cavendish and Dr John Pell", *Osiris*, 10 (1952), 67–90

Higgins, Patricia, "The Reactions of Women, with special reference to women petitioners", *Politics, Religion and the English Civil War*, ed. Brian Manning (London: Edward Arnold, 1973)

Historical Manuscripts Commission, 5th Report (London: 1876)

—— *6th Report* (London: 1877)

—— *10th Report*, Appendix 6 (London: 1885)

—— *12th Report*, Appendix 9 (London: 1891)

—— *13th Report*, Part II (London: 1892)

—— *Report on the Manuscripts of the Late Reginald Rawdon Hastings* (London: 1928)

Hill, Christopher, *The World Turned Upside Down: Radical Ideas During the English Revolution*, rev. edn (London: Penguin, 2019)

Hinds, Allen B., ed., *Calendar of State Papers Relating to English*

Affairs in the Archives of Venice, 38 vols (London: Her Majesty's Stationery Office, 1864–1947)

Hobby, Elaine and Chris White, eds, *What Lesbians Do in Books* (London: The Women's Press, 1991)

Hooke, Robert, *Micrographia* (London: 1665)

hooks, bell, *Art on My Mind* (New York: The New Press, 1995)

Hopkins, Lisa and Tom Rutter, eds, *A Companion to the Cavendishes* (Yorkshire Arc Humanities Press, 2000)

Hopkins, Lisa, "Play Houses: Drama at Bolsover and Welbeck", *Early Theatre*, 2 (1999), 25–44

Hutchinson, Lucy, *Memoirs of the Life of Colonel Hutchinson*, ed. James Sutherland (London: Oxford University Press, 1973)

Hutton, Sarah and Marjorie Hope Nicolson, eds, *The Conway Letters: The Correspondence of Anne, Viscountess Conway, Henry More, and their Friends 1642–1684*, rev. edn (Oxford: Oxford University Press, 1992)

Jackson, Clare, *Charles II* (London: Penguin Books, 2018)

Jacob, Giles, *The Poetical Register* (London: E. Curll, 1719)

Jenkins, Edward, ed., *The Cavalier and his Lady, Selections from the Works of the First Duke and Duchess of Newcastle* (London: Macmillan and Co., 1872)

Jones, Kathleen, *A Glorious Fame: The Life of Margaret Cavendish, Duchess of Newcastle, 1623-1673* (London: Bloomsbury, 1988)

Keay, Anna, *The Restless Republic: Britain Without a Crown* (London: William Collins, 2022)

Keeble, N. H., *The Restoration* (Oxford: Blackwell Publishing, 2002)

Kerrigan, William, *The Sacred Complex* (Harvard: Harvard University Press, 1983)

Kroetsch, Cameron, "List of Margaret Cavendish's Texts, Printers, and Booksellers (1653–1675)", *Digital Cavendish Project* (Online: 2013)

Kyte, Holly, *Roaring Girls* (London: HQ, 2019)

Lamb, Charles, *Essays of Elia* (London: 1823)

Langbaine, Gerard, *An Account of the English Dramatick Poets* (London: L.L. for George West and Harry Clements, 1691)

Lanyer, Aemilia, *Salve Deus Rex Judaeorum* (London: Valentine Simmes for Richard Bonian, 1611)

Larkin, Philip, *Collected Poems* (London: Faber and Faber, 1988)

Latham, R. C. and W. Matthews, *The Diary of Samuel Pepys*, 11 vols (London: HarperCollins, 1995)

Leigh, Dorothy, *The Mother's Blessing* (London: John Budge, 1616)

Leonard, John, "Saying 'No' to Freud: Milton's A Mask and Sexual Assault", *Milton Quarterly*, 25 (1991), 129–40

Lewis, Thomas Taylor, ed., *Letters of the Lady Brilliana Harley* (London: Camden Society, 1854)

Littleton, Adam, *A Sermon at the Funeral of the Right Honourable the Lady Jane* (London: 1669), p. 20

Love, Harold and Arthur F. Marotti, "Manuscript Transmission and Circulation", in *The Cambridge History of Early Modern English*, ed. David Lowenstein and Janel Mueller (Cambridge: Cambridge University Press, 2003), pp. 55–80

Love, Harold, *Scribal Publication in Seventeenth-Century England* (Oxford: Clarendon Press, 1993)

Lovelace, Richard, *Lucasta Posthume Poems of Richard Lovelace, Esq.* (London: 1659)

Lucas, Charles, *Sir Charles Lucas: His Last Speech at the place of Execution, where hee was shot to Death* (London: R. Smithhurst, 1648)

MacArthur, Ellen, "Women Petitioners and the Long Parliament", *The English Historical Review*, 24 (1909), 698–709

Makin, Bathsua, "An Essay To Revive the Antient Education of Gentlewomen", in *Religion, Manners, Arts & Tongues* (London: J. D. for Tho. Parkhurst, 1673)

Malcolm, Noel, Simon Schaffer, Quentin Skinner and Sir Keith Thomas, eds, *The Clarendon Edition of the Works of Thomas Hobbes*, 25 vols (Oxford: Oxford University Press, 1984–2014)

Malcomson, Cristina and Mihoko Suziki, eds, *Debating Gender in Early Modern England 1500–1700* (New York: Palgrave Macmillan, 2002)

Manuel, Frank E. and Frizie P. Manuel, *Utopian Thought in the Western World* (Oxford: Blackwell, 1979)

Milton, John, *Paradise Lost, in Milton: Paradise Lost*, ed. Alastair Fowler, 2nd edn. (London: Routledge, 2017)

Mintz, Samuel I., "The Duchess of Newcastle's Visit to the Royal Society", *The Journal of English and Germanic Philology*, 51 (1952), 168–72

Morley, Henry, ed., *The Spectator*, 3 vols (London: George Routledge, 1891)

Motteville, Françoise, *Memoirs for the History of Anne of Austria*, translated from the Original French, 5 vols (London: 1726)

Murphy, Andrew, "The History of the Book in Britain, c. 1475–1800", in *The Oxford Companion to the Book*, ed. Michael F. Suarez and H. R. Woudhusyen, 2 vols (Oxford; New York: Oxford University Press, 2010) I, pp. 172–9

Nate, Richard, "'Plain and Vulgarly Express'd': Margaret Cavendish and the Discourse of the New Science", *Rhetorica*, 19 (2001), 403–17

Norbrook, David, "Lucy Hutchinson Versus Edmund Waller: an Unpublished Reply to Waller's 'A Panegyrick to My Lord Protector'", in *The Seventeenth Century*, 11 (1996), 61–86

Oren-Magidor, Daphna, *Infertility in Early Modern England* (London: Palgrave Macmillan, 2017)

—— "Literate Laywomen, Male Medical Practitioners and the Treatment of Fertility Problems in Early Modern England", in *Social History of Medicine* 29 (2016)

Parry, Edward Abbott, ed., *Letters from Dorothy Osborne to Sir William Temple, 1652–54* (London: J. M. Dent & Sons, 1890)

Perry, Henry Ten Eyck, *The First Duchess of Newcastle and her Husband as Figures in Literary History* (Boston, London: Ginn and Company, 1918)

Perry, Ruth, "Radical Doubt and the Liberation of Women", *Eighteenth-Century Studies*, 18 (1985), 472–93

Pinney, Thomas, ed., *Essays of George Eliot* (London: Routledge, 1963)

Plant, Marjorie, *The English Book Trade: an Economic History of the Making and Sale of Books*, 3rd edn, (London: Allen & Unwin, 1974), pp. 217–18

Poole, Elizabeth, *A Vision: wherein is manifested the disease and cure of the Kingdome* (London: 1648)

Poynting, Sarah, "Deciphering the King: Charles I's letters to Jane Whorwood", *The Seventeenth Century*, 21 (2006), 128–40

Quehen, Hugh de, ed., *Lucy Hutchinson's Translation of Lucretius: De rerum natura* (London: Duckworth, 1996)

Raven, James, *The Business of Books* (New Haven and London: Yale University Press, 2007)

Raylor, Timothy, "Newcastle's Ghosts: Robert Payne, Ben Jonson, and the 'Cavendish Circle'", *Literary Circles and Cultural Communities in Renaissance England*, ed. Claude J. Summers and Ted-Larry Pebworth (Columbia: University of Missouri Press, 2000), pp. 92–114

Rich, Barnaby, *My Ladies Looking Glass* (London: 1616)

Robbins, Robin, ed., *The Complete Poems of John Donne* (London: Routledge, 2013)

Roberts, Josephine, ed., *The Poems of Lady Mary Wroth*, rev. edn (Louisiana: LSU Press, 1992)

Robertson, Eric, *English Poetesses* (London: Cassell and Company, 1883)

Rogers, John, *The Matter of Revolution: Science, Poetry, and Politics in the Age of Milton* (Ithaca, NY: Cornell University Press, 1996)

Rogers, Katherine, *Feminism in Eighteenth Century England* (Urbana: University of Illinois Press, 1982)

Rostenberg, Leona, *The Library of Robert Hooke* (Santa Monica: Modoc Press, 1989)

Sarasohn, Lisa T. and Brandie R. Siegfried, *God and Nature in the Thought of Margaret Cavendish* (London: Routledge, 2014)

Sarasohn, Lisa T., "A Science Turned Upside Down: Feminism and the Natural Philosophy of Margaret Cavendish", *Huntingdon Library Quarterly*, 47 (1984), 289–307

—— "Thomas Hobbes and the Duke of Newcastle: A Study in the Mutuality of Patronage before the Establishment of the Royal Society", *Isis*, 90 (1999), 715–37

—— *The Natural Philosophy of Margaret Cavendish: Reason and Fancy during the Scientific Revolution* (Baltimore: John Hopkins University Press, 2010)

Saunders, J. W., "The Stigma of Print: A Note on the Social Bases of Tudor Poetry", in *Essays in Criticism*, 1 (1951), 139–64

Scott-Baumann, Elizabeth, "Margaret Cavendish as Editor and Reviser", in *Forms of Engagement: Women, Poetry, and Culture, 1640–1680* (Oxford: Oxford University Press, 2013), pp. 60–80

Semler, L. E., "Stories of Selves and Infidels: Walter Charleton's Letter to Margaret Cavendish (1655)" in *Storytelling: Critical and Creative Approaches*, ed. Jan Shaw, Philippa Kelly, L. E. Semler (London: Palgrave Macmillan, 2013)

Semler, L. E., "Stories of Selves and Infidels: Walter Charleton's Letter to Margaret Cavendish (1655)", in *Storytelling: Critical and Creative Approaches*, ed. Jan Shaw, Philippa Kelly, L. E. Semler (London: Palgrave Macmillan, 2013), pp. 191–210

Serre, Puget de la, *Histoire de l'Entrée de la Reine Mere du Roy Tres Christien dans la Grand Bretagne* (London: John Raworth for George Thomason, 1639)

Sharp, Jane, *The Midwives Book* (London: Simon Miller, 1671)

Shattock, Joanne, ed., *The Oxford Guide to British Women Writers* (Oxford: Oxford University Press, 1993)

Siegfried, Brandie R. and Lisa Walters, *Margaret Cavendish: An Interdisciplinary Perspective* (Cambridge: Cambridge University Press, 2022)

Slaughter, Thomas P., *Ideology and Politics on the Eve of Restoration: Newcastle's advice to Charles II* (California: American Philosophical Society, 1984)

Smith, David Nichol, *Characters from the Histories and Memoirs of the Seventeenth Century* (Oxford: Clarendon Press, 1920)

Smith, Hilda L., ed., and Susan Cardinale, comp., *Women and the Literature of the Seventeenth Century: An Annotated Bibliography Based on Wing's Short-title Catalogue* (Connecticut: Greenwood Press, 1990)

Smith, Hilda L., "'A General War amongst the Men but None amongst the Women': Political differences between Margaret and William Cavendish", in *Politics and the Political Imagination in Later Stuart Britain*, ed. Howard Nenner (Rochester: University of Rochester Press, 1998), pp. 143–160

—— "Margaret Cavendish and the False Universal", in *Virtue, Liberty, and Toleration: Political Ideas of European Women, 1400–1800*, ed. Jacqueline Broad and Karen Green (Dortrecht: Springer, 2007), pp. 95–110

—— *Reason's Disciples: Seventeenth-Century English Feminists* (Chicago; London: University of Illinois Press, 1982)

Smith, Nigel, ed., *The Poems of Andrew Marvell* (London: Pearson Longman, 2006), line 20

Spence, Ferrand, trans., *Lucian's Works*, translated from the Greek (London: 1684)

Springborg, Patricia, ed., *Mary Astell: A Serious Proposal to the Ladies* (London: Pickering & Chatto, 1997)

Starr, Nathan Comfort, "The Concealed Fansyes: A Play by Lady Jane Cavendish and Lady Elizabeth Brackley", *PMLA*, 46 (1931), 802–38 (pp. 805–6)

Stokes, Mark, "'Give me a Souldier's Coat': Female Cross-Dressing during the English Civil War", in *History*, 103 (2018), 5–26

Straub, Valerie, *The Renaissance of Lesbianism in Early Modern England* (Cambridge: Cambridge University Press, 2002)

Strickland, Agnes, *The Lives of the Queens of England*, 2nd edn, 8 vols (London: Colburn & Co., 1851)

Stubbes, Henry, *Campanella Revived* (London: 1670)

—— *The Plus Ultra reduced to a Non Plus* (London: 1670)

Suzuki, Mihoko, ed., *The History of British Women's Writing, 1610–1690* (London: Palgrave Macmillan, 2011)

Swetnam, Joseph, *The Arraignment of Lewd, Idle, Froward and Unconstant Woman* (London: Thomas Archer, 1615)

Teague, Frances N., *Bathsua Makin, Woman of Learning* (United States: Bucknall University Press, 1998)

Thomas, Keith V., "Women and the Civil War Sects", *Past and Present* (1958)

Thomas, Patrick, ed., *The Collected Works of Katherine Philips*, 3 vols (Essex: Stump Cross Books, 1990)

Thompson, E. M., *Hatton Correspondence*, 2 vols (London: Camden Society, 1878)

Todd, Janet, ed., *The Works of Aphra Behn*, 7 vols (London: Routledge, 1995–6)

—— *The Critical Fortunes of Aphra Behn* (South Carolina: Camden House, 1998)

Travitsky, Betty S., ed. and comp., *Bibliography of English Women Writers 1500–1640* (Online: Iter Press, 2010)

Verger, Susan du, *Du Verger's Humble Reflections upon Some Passages of the Right Honourable the Lady Marchioness of Newcastle's Olio* (London: 1657)

Walen, Denise, "Constructions of Female Homoerotics in Early Modern Drama", *Theatre Journal*, 54 (2002), 411–30

Walker, Katherine A., "The Military Activities of Charlotte de La Tremouille, Countess of Derby, During the Civil War and Interregnum", *Northern History*, 38 (2001), 47–64

Wall, Wendy, *The Imprint of Gender: Authorship and Publication in the English Renaissance* (Ithaca and London: Cornell University Press, 1993)

Walpole, Horace, *A Catalogue of the Royal and Noble Authors of England* (London; Edinburgh: 1796)

Walter, John, *Understanding popular violence in the English Revolution: The Colchester Plunderers, John Walter* (Cambridge; New York: Cambridge University Press, 1999)

Walters, Lisa, *Margaret Cavendish: Gender, Science, Politics* (Cambridge: Cambridge University Press, 2014)

Warwick, Philip, *Memoirs of the Reign of King Charles I* (London: 1702)

Welch, Evelyn, ed., *Fashioning the Early Modern: Dress, Textiles, and Innovation in Europe, 1500–1800* (Oxford: Oxford University Press, 2017)

Wheatley, H. B., "Signs of Booksellers in St. Paul's Churchyard" in *The Library*, TBS–9 (1906), 67–106

Whitaker, Katy, *Mad Madge* (London: Chatto & Windus, 2003)

Whitelocke, Bulstrode, *Memorials of the English Affairs* (London: 1682)

Wiesner, Merry, "Luther and Women: The Death of Two Marys" in *Feminist Theology: A Reader*, ed. A. Loades (London: SPCK, 1990), pp. 123–34

Winchelsea, Anne Finch, *The Poems of Anne, Countess of Winchelsea*, ed. Myra Reynolds (Chicago: University of Chicago Press, 1903)

Wollstonecraft, Mary, *A Vindication of the Rights of Women*, ed. Janet Todd (Oxford: Oxford University Press, 1994)

Wood, Anthony à, *The Life and Times of Anthony à Wood*, 5 vols (Oxford: Clarendon Press, 1891)

Woolf, Virginia, *The Essays of Virginia Woolf*, 4 vols, ed. Andrew McNeillie (London: The Hogarth Press, 1994)

—— *A Room of One's Own and Other Essays*, ed. Hermione Lee (London: The Folio Society, 2000)

—— *A Writer's Diary* (London: Hogarth Press, 1953)

Worsley, Lucy, *Bolsover Castle* (Swindon: English Heritage, 2000)

Woudhuysen, Henry, *Sir Philip Sidney and the Circulation of Manuscripts* (Oxford: Clarendon Press, 1996)

Wroth, Mary, *The Countess of Montgomery's Urania* (London: John Marriott and John Grimsand, 1621)

Notes

Note: in seventeenth-century books, and especially in Margaret Cavendish's works, pagination is often irregular or incorrectly numbered. I have made every effort to make it clear what page is being referred to, even where the pagination is disrupted.

Introduction

1. *Bodleian MS North c.4*, f. 146
2. *Pepys VIII*, pp. 163–4
3. *Pepys VIII*, p. 196
4. *Pepys VIII*, p. 209
5. *The Diary and Correspondence of John Evelyn*, ed. William Bray, 4 vols (London: H. Colburn, 1857), IV, p. 8–9 (N. B. This edition, including Mary's correspondence, is not the same one that is referred to throughout the rest of the notes unless otherwise specified.)
6. *Bodleian MS North c.4*, f. 146
7. *Pepys VIII*, pp. 242–4. For more details of Cavendish's visit to the Royal Society, see *Evelyn II*, pp. 33–4; Thomas Birch, *The History of the Royal Society of London*, 4 vols (London: A. Millar, 1757), II, pp. 176–7; and Samuel I. Mintz, "The Duchess of Newcastle's Visit to the Royal Society", *The Journal of English and Germanic Philology*, 51 (1952), 168–72
8. Mintz, p. 176
9. *PaF 1653*, sig. A3r
10. *Plays*, "Bell in Campo", p. 580
11. Virginia Woolf, *A Room of One's Own*, in *A Room of One's Own and Other Essays*, ed. Hermione Lee (London: The Folio Society, 2000), pp. 21–105; pp. 65–7
12. Virginia Woolf, "The Duchess of Newcastle" in *The Common Reader*, in *The Essays of Virginia Woolf*, ed. Andrew McNeillie, 4 vols (London: The Hogarth Press, 1994), pp. 81–91; pp. 87–8

13. *A Princely Brave Woman: Essays on Margaret Cavendish*, ed. Stephen Clucas (London: Routledge, 2003), p. 1
14. *PNBP*, "The Convent of Pleasure", p. 32
15. *BW 1666*, sig. "To the Duchesse of Newcastle on her New Blazing World"
16. *BW 1666*, p. 121 (mispaginated; refers to page as marked)

Chapter 1

1. The date of Margaret Cavendish's death was December 1673, as stated in the Depositum in *BL Add MS 12514*, ff. 290/297; the bill for her funeral on ff. 282–90 of the same manuscript dates the ceremony to 7 January.
2. *BL Add MS 12514*, ff. 290/297
3. Epigraph on the tomb of Margaret Cavendish in Westminster Abbey.
4. Katy Whitaker, *Mad Madge* (London: Chatto & Windus, 2003), p. 8
5. *Life and True Relation*, p. 276
6. *SL 1664*, p. 145
7. For more on the status of the Lucas family, and the lands surrounding St John's Abbey, see Douglas Grant, *Margaret the First* (London: Rupert Hart-Davis, 1957), pp. 27–34
8. *Life and True Relation*, p. 277
9. Bathsua Makin, *An Essay To Revive the Antient Education of Gentlewomen, in Religion, Manners, Arts & Tongues* (London: J. D. for Tho. Parkhurst, 1673), p. 3. A contemporary edition is edited by Frances Teague and Margaret J. M. Ezell in *Educating English Daughters: Late Seventeenth-Century Debates* (Ontario: Iter Academic Press, 2016), pp. 28–51
10. Mary More, *The Woman's Right* (c. 1674–80). A contemporary edited edition is available in *Educating English Daughters*, pp. 129–43
11. Mary Astell, *A Serious Proposal to the Ladies* (London: R. Wilkin 1694), pp. 60–1, p. 77. A contemporary edition is edited by Patricia Springborg (London: Pickering & Chatto, 1997)
12. Frances N. Teague, *Bathsua Makin, Woman of Learning* (United States: Bucknall University Press, 1998), p. 43
13. Makin, p. 52
14. Joseph Swetnam, *The Arraignment of Lewd, Idle, Froward and Unconstant Woman* (London: Thomas Archer, 1615), p. 4

15. Woolf, *A Room of One's Own*, p. 65
16. Makin, p. 60
17. See Sylvia Bowerbank, "The Spider's Delight: Margaret Cavendish and the 'Female' Imagination", *English Literary Renaissance*, 14 (1984), 392–408; and L. E. Semler, "Stories of Selves and Infidels: Walter Charleton's Letter to Margaret Cavendish (1655)", in *Storytelling: Critical and Creative Approaches*, ed. Jan Shaw, Philippa Kelly, L. E. Semler (London: Palgrave Macmillan, 2013), pp. 191–210
18. *Life and True Relation*, pp. 277–80
19. *SL 1664*, p. 267
20. *SL 1664*, p. 338
21. Lucy Hutchinson, *Memoirs of the Life of Colonel Hutchinson*, ed. James Sutherland (London: Oxford University Press, 1973), p. 16
22. Ann Fanshawe, *Memoirs of Lady Fanshawe* (London: John Lane The Bodley Head, 1907), p. 32
23. George Savile Halifax, *Advice to a Daughter* (London: M. Gillyflower and James Partridge, 1688), p. 148
24. *Life and True Relation*, p. 277
25. Anthony Hamilton, *Memoirs of Count Grammont* (Philadelphia: E. L. Carey & A. Hart, 1836), p. 132
26. *Memoirs of Colonel Hutchinson*, p. 62
27. *Life and True Relation*, p. 312
28. *Life and True Relation*, p. 285
29. *SL 1664*, p. 184
30. *Life and True Relation*, p. 314
31. *SL 1664*, p. 423

Chapter 2

1. *HMC 12th Report*, Appendix 9, MSS of the Duke of Beaufort, pp. 27–8
2. Descriptions of the siege of Colchester can be found in *Mercurius Pragmaticus*, Numbers 15 and 18 (July–August 1648)
3. *Mercurius Pragmaticus* 19, 1– 8 August 1648
4. *Mercurius Pragmaticus* 15, 4–11 July 1648
5. *Mercurius Pragmaticus* 21, 17–24 August 1648
6. *Mercurius Pragmaticus* 23, 29 August – 5 September 1648. The numbering system for these newspapers is sometimes contradictory, and there are two 23s.
7. *Sir Charles Lucas: His Last Speech at the place of Execution, where hee was shot to Death* (London: R. Smithhurst, 1648), p. 1

8. Accounts of Sir Charles Lucas's death are also found in Clarendon, *The History of the Rebellion and Civil Wars in England*, ed. W. Dunn Macray, 6 vols (Oxford: Clarendon Press, 1888), IV, p. 388

9. John Walter, *Understanding popular violence in the English Revolution: The Colchester Plunderers* (Cambridge; New York: Cambridge University Press, 1999), p. 1

10. Descriptions of the siege at St John's Abbey can be found in *HMC 10th Report*, Appendix 6, pp. 146–7 and *Mercurius Rusticus, [...] from the beginning of this unnatural war, to the 25th of March, 1646* (London: 1685). A record of Margaret's mother, Elizabeth, asking to be allowed to search townspeople's houses for her lost possessions is in *HMC 5th Report*, p.46.

11. *HMC 5th Report*, p. 45

12. As Whitaker, p. 43, makes clear, one contemporary newsletter describes "great violence seized upon him, his mother, wife, and sisters children"; see also *A Continuation of Certain Special and Remarkable passages from both Houses of Parliament, from Thursday 25th August till Tuesday the 30th, 1642*, p. 3

13. For details of Henrietta Maria's warlike machinations, I am much indebted to Leanda de Lisle's book *Henrietta Maria: Conspirator, Warrior, Phoenix Queen* (London: Penguin, 2022)

14. *The Great Eclipse of the Sun* (London: 1644)

15. *Mercurius Britannicus*, Number 44, 15–22 July 1644

16. *Letters of Queen Henrietta Maria*, ed. Mary Anne Everett Green (London: R. Bentley, 1857), p. 205, quoted in de Lisle, p. 247; see also David Nichol Smith, *Characters from the Histories and Memoirs of the Seventeenth Century* (Oxford: Clarendon Press, 1920), quoted in de Lisle, p. 237

17. *Letters of Queen Henrietta Maria*, p. 219, quoted in de Lisle p. 255

18. Edward Hyde Clarendon, *The History of the Rebellion and Civil Wars in England*, ed. W. Dunn Macray, 6 vols (Oxford: Clarendon Press, 1888), I, p. 264

19. Anthony à Wood, *The Life and Times of Anthony à Wood*, 5 vols (Oxford: Clarendon Press, 1891), I, p. 69

20. *Memoirs of Lady Fanshawe*, pp. 24–5

21. *NP 1656*, p. 220

22. *Life and True Relation*, p. 284

23. *NP 1656*, p. 88

24. *WO 1655*, p. 51

25. *Memoirs of the Life of Colonel Hutchinson*, p. 279

26. *Mercurius Aulicus*, issue First Week (Oxford: 1643), p. 6; p. 5

27. *WO 1655*, p. 32; p. 2
28. *NP 1656*, p. 317
29. *PaF 1653*, p. 173
30. *WO 1655*, p. 95

Chapter 3

1. *Life and True Relation*, pp. 287–8
2. Description of this visit is taken from Puget de la Serre, *Histoire de l'Entrée de la Reine Mere du Roy Tres Christien dans la Grand Bretagne* (London: John Raworth for George Thomason, 1639)
3. For more details of the capital during this period, see C. H. Firth's "London during the Civil War", *History*, 11 (1926), 25–36
4. *BW 1666*, p. 121
5. For an account of the attack on Bridlington, see Françoise de Motteville, *Memoirs for the History of Anne of Austria, Translated from the Original French*, 5 vols (London: 1726), I, pp. 219–21
6. *Mercurius Britannicus*, Issue 19, 28 December 1643 – 4 January 1644
7. *Letters of Henrietta Maria*, p. 220; p. 222
8. *Life and True Relation*, pp. 35–7
9. *Memoirs of the Life of Colonel Hutchinson*, pp. 46–7
10. *Memoirs for the History of Anne of Austria*, I, p. 220
11. For an account of the rules governing the households of both the king and queen, see *A Collection of Ordinances and Regulations for the Government of the Royal Household* (London: Society of Antiquaries, 1790), pp. 340–50
12. *Life and True Relation*, p. 287
13. *PNBP*, "The Presence", p. 4; p. 19
14. *PNBP*, "The Presence", p. 14
15. *PNBP*, "The Presence", p. 14
16. *PNBP*, "The Presence", p. 30
17. *Plays*, "Bell in Campo", p. 579
18. *Plays*, "Bell in Campo", p. 589
19. *Plays*, "Bell in Campo", p. 591
20. *Plays*, "Bell in Campo", p. 616
21. *Plays*, "Bell in Campo", p. 588
22. *Plays*, "Bell in Campo", p. 584
23. Dorothy Leeke's letter is quoted in Mark Stokes, "'Give me a Souldier's Coat': Female Cross-Dressing during the English Civil War", in *History*, 103 (2018), 5–26 (p. 17)

24. For descriptions of the mutilations at Naseby, see *Perfect Occurrences of Parliament*, 13 June 1645 (London: 1645), *A More Exact and Perfect Relation of the Great Victory* (London: 1645), and *An ordinance of the Lords and Commons [...] for the Great Victory* (London: 1645)

25. Mark Stokes's 2018 article is the best example of recent scholarship on the subject, but Antonia Fraser's *The Weaker Vessel* (London: Orion, 1984) also discusses many of the women who played a role.

26. Elizabeth Poole, *A Vision: wherein is manifested the disease and cure of the Kingdome* (London: 1648), p. 6

27. Fraser, pp. 165–6

28. Details of the siege are found in *A Journal of the Siege of Lathom House*, which exists in two manuscript copies – *Bodleian MS Wood D. 16* and *BL Harley MS 2043* – and countless print editions. I quote from *A Journal of the Siege of Lathom House* (London: 1823). See also Katherine A. Walker, "The Military Activities of Charlotte de La Tremouille, Countess of Derby, During the Civil War and Interregnum", *Northern History*, 38 (2001), 47–64

29. *A Journal of the Siege of Lathom House*, p. 47

30. *Memorials of the Civil War* (Fairfax Papers), ed. R. Bell, 2 vols (London: 1849), I, 194–5

31. *Letters of the Lady Brilliana Harley*, ed. Thomas Taylor Lewis (London: Camden Society, 1854), pp. 207–9

32. Accounts of Lady Cunningham are found in *CSPD 1639*, pp. 144–6; pp. 282–3 and *HMC 6th Report*, p. 352

33. *CSPD 1639*, p. 282

34. *CSPD 1639*, p. 146

35. The depositions of Dorothy Hazard and Joan Batten were transcribed in Charles Firth and J. H. Leslie, "The Siege and Capture of Bristol by the Royalist Forces in 164", *Journal of the Society for Army Historical Research*, 4 (1925), 180–203

36. These draft proclamations – found in *BL Harley MS 6804* – are quoted in Stokes, pp. 18–19

37. *The Valiant Commander with his Resolute Lady* (London: 1664), quoted in Stokes, p. 6

38. For discussion of this famous ballad, see Dianne Dugaw, *Warrior Women and Popular Balladry, 1650–1850* (Cambridge: Cambridge University Press, 1989), pp. 15–40

39. Stokes, p. 14

40. Stokes, p. 22

41. The classic study on this subject is Sandra Clark's article "'Hic

Mulier', 'Haec Vir', and the Controversy over Masculine Women",
Studies in Philology, 82 (1985), 157–183

42. Barnaby Rich, *My Ladies Looking Glass* (London: 1616), p. 21

43. *Mercurius Pragmaticus*, 45, 13–20 February 1649

44. Sarah Poynting, "Deciphering the King: Charles I's letters to Jane Whorwood", *The Seventeenth Century*, 21 (2006), 128–40

Chapter 4

1. *NP 1656*, pp. 220 –72

2. *NP 1656*, p. 230

3. *SL 1664*, pp. 244–6

4. *NP 1656*, pp. 243–4

5. *PaF 1653*, p. 155

6. Bulstrode Whitelocke, *Memorials of the English Affairs* (London: 1682), p. 88; quoted in de Lisle, *Henrietta Maria*, p. 273

7. Agnes Strickland, *The Lives of the Queens of England*, 2nd edn, 8 vols (London: Colburn & Co., 1851), V, p. 314

8. *Memoirs of Anne of Austria*, pp. 121–2

9. *Memoirs of Anne of Austria*, p. 122

10. *Life and True Relation*, p. 288

11. *Memoirs of Anne of Austria*, p. 122

12. *PPO 1663*, pp. 391–2

13. *Life and True Relation*, p. 279

14. *Life and True Relation*, pp. 86–7

15. *Life and True Relation*, p. 79

16. Philip Warwick, *Memoirs of the Reign of King Charles I* (London: 1702), p. 258; partially quoted in Whitaker, p. 72

17. *Letters of Henrietta Maria*, p. 261

18. *Life and True Relation*, pp. 206–7

19. *Life and True Relation*, p. 288

20. All the letters can be found in *BL Add MS 70499*, ff. 259–97. They are also transcribed in Richard W. Goulding, *Letters Written by Charles Lamb's "Princely Woman, the Thrice Noble Margaret Newcastle" to her Husband* (London: John Murray, 1909), and in Anna Battigelli, *Margaret Cavendish and the Exiles of the Mind* (USA: Kentucky University Press, 1998). *BL Add MS 70499*, f. 259r

21. *BL Add MS 70499*, f. 261r

22. *BL Add MS 70499*, f. 263r

23. *BL Add MS 70499*, f. 274r

24. William Cavendish, *The Phanseys Of William Cavendish Marquis Of Newcastle Addressed To Margaret Lucas and Her Letters In Reply*, ed. Douglas Grant (London: Nonesuch Press, 1956), "The Onely Shee", p. 21

25. *BL Add MS 70499*, f. 265r–v

26. *Phanseys*, "The Marriage Songe", p. 29; *BL Add MS 70499*, f. 285r

27. *Phanseys*, "Loves Fier", p. 95

28. *BL Add MS 70499*, f. 270r

29. *Life and True Relation*, p. 5

30. Whitaker, p. 66

31. *Life and True Relation*, p. 288–9

32. *BL Add MS 70449*, ff. 259–97

33. George Savile, Marquis of Halifax, *Advice to a Daughter*, p. 25

34. *PaF 1653*, p. 159

35. *Phanseys*, "The Unparalel'd Love", p. 68

36. *BL Add MS 70449*, f. 299r

37. *PaF 1653*, p. 156

Chapter 5

1. *EBBA, Pepys Ballads*, 1.44–45

2. *Pepys I*, p. 148

3. *Evelyn I*, pp. 26–7

4. Jane Sharp, *The Midwives Book* (London: Simon Miller, 1671), p. 4

5. Sharp, p. 43

6. Sharp, p. 96

7. *Life and True Relation*, p. 87–8

8. *NUL MS PwV 90*, f. 21v

9. *Life and True Relation*, pp. 88–9

10. *NUL MS PwV 90*, f. 14v

11. *NUL MS PwV 90*, f. 19v

12. *NUL MS PwV 90*, f. 21v

13. *NUL MS PwV 90*, f. 20r

14. *PaF 1653*, sig. A7r

15. *PaF 1664*, sig. A2r. This prefatory verse is found in some of the 1653 editions. See *Margaret Cavendish's Poems and Fancies: A Digital Critical Edition*, ed. Liza Blake (Online: 2019), "Textual Introduction"

16. Anne Bradstreet, *Several Poems Compiled* (Boston: 1678), p. 236; *Eliza's Babes in Flesh and Spirit: An Anthology of Seventeenth-Century Women's Writing*, ed. Rachel Adcock, Sara Read, &

Anna Ziomek (Manchester: Manchester University Press, 2014), p. 127

17. *SL 1664*, pp. 94–5
18. *SL 1664*, pp. 183–4
19. *Life and True Relation*, p. 89
20. Sharp, pp. 97–100
21. Mary Whitelocke, *Memoir,* PUL RCT01, Item 226. The manuscript is unpaginated. For more discussion of Whitelocke, see Daphna Oren-Magidor, *Infertility in Early Modern England* (London: Palgrave Macmillan, 2017)
22. *Geneva Bible 1560*, I Timothy 2.14–15
23. Merry Wiesner, "Luther and Women: The Death of Two Marys" in *Feminist Theology: A Reader*, ed. A. Loades (London: SPCK, 1990), pp. 123–34, p. 123
24. *BL Add MS 61415*, f. 34r
25. *BL Add MS 61415*, f. 35v
26. *BL Add MS 61414*, f. 37r. See also Daphna Oren-Magidor, "Literate Laywomen, Male Medical Practitioners and the Treatment of Fertility Problems in Early Modern England", in *Social History of Medicine* 29 (2016), 290–310
27. *BL Add MS 61415*, ff. 39–40
28. Laura Gowing, *Common Bodies: Women, Touch and Power in Seventeenth-Century England* (New Haven: Yale University Press, 2003), p. 125
29. *Pepys V*, p. 145
30. *Pepys V*, p. 134
31. *CSPD 1629*, p. 548
32. *CSPV XXII, 1629*, p. 65–72; "Enclosure"
33. *The Letters of Henrietta Maria*, p. 12–13
34. Lady Mary Carey, "Upon the Sight of my abortive Birth the 31st of December 1657", in *Flesh and Spirit*, p. 49
35. Lady Mary Carey, "Written by me at the Death of my 4th Son, & 5th Child Peregrine Payler", in *Flesh and Spirit*, p. 48
36. *BL Add MS 78439*, ff. 18 – 19
37. *BL MS Egerton 206*, f. 22v, f. 28r
38. *BL MS Egerton 206*, f. 35r
39. *BL MS Egerton 206*, f. 114r– 115v
40. *NUL MS PwV 90* ff. 81v – 82v; quoted in Whitaker, p. 113
41. *NUL MS PwV 90*, f. 28r

Chapter 6

1. John Milton, *A Masque Presented at Ludlow Castle*, in *Milton: The Complete Shorter Poems*, ed. John Carey, 2nd edn (London: Pearson Longman, 2007), pp. 173–233

2. *A Masque Presented at Ludlow Castle*, lines 739, 65, 77, 916, 879, 915

3. See Barbara Breasted, "Comus and the Castlehaven scandal", *Milton Studies*, 3 (1971), 2014–2224, and John Creaser, "Milton's 'Comus': The Irrelevance of the Castlehaven Scandal", *Milton Quarterly*, 21 (1987), 24–34. For Freudian readings and debates, see William Kerrigan *The Sacred Complex* (Harvard: Harvard University Press, 1983), John Leonard, "Saying 'No' to Freud: Milton's *A Mask* and Sexual Assault", *Milton Quarterly*, 25 (1991), 129–40

4. Virginia Woolf, *A Writer's Diary* (London: Hogarth Press, 1953), p. 6

5. *Phanseys*, 'Loves Fate', p. 35

6. For more information on the circle around the Cavendish brothers, see Lisa T. Sarasohn, "Thomas Hobbes and the Duke of Newcastle: A Study in the Mutuality of Patronage before the Establishment of the Royal Society", *Isis*, 90 (1999), 715–37, and Whitaker pp. 115–19. For Charles Cavendish's scientific and mathematical notebooks, see *BL Harley MS 6083*

7. Sarasohn, p. 731

8. See Lisa Hopkins, "Play Houses: Drama at Bolsover and Welbeck", *Early Theatre*, 2 (1999), 25–44

9. For more on the Cavendish–Jonson relationship, see Tom Rutter, "The Cavendishes and Ben Jonson", in *A Companion to the Cavendishes*, ed. Lisa Hopkins, Tom Rutter (Arc Humanities Press, 2000), pp. 107–25

10. Here I am quoting from Timothy Raylor's transcription, found in "Newcastle's Ghosts: Robert Payne, Ben Jonson, and the 'Cavendish Circle'", *Literary Circles and Cultural Communities in Renaissance England*, ed. Claude J. Summers and Ted-Larry Pebworth (Columbia: University of Missouri Press, 2000), pp. 92–114 (p. 107). Raylor makes it clear how much of the poem Payne, as Cavendish's secretary, had to alter.

11. *BL Harley MS 4955*

12. *BL Harley MS 4955*, ff. 95v – 96r

13. *Life and True Relation*, p. 97

14. *Life and True Relation*, p. 97

15. Helen Hervey, "Hobbes and Descartes in the Light of Some Unpublished Letters of the Correspondence between Sir Charles Cavendish and Dr John Pell", *Osiris*, 10 (1952), 67–90 (p. 70)

16. Hervey, p. 84

17. *BL Harley MS 6083*, f. 177v. Cavendish records his brother's correspondence with Hobbes – "part of Mr Hobbes answers to my brother's...".

18. Andrew Marvell, "Flecknoe, an English Priest at Rome", *The Poems of Andrew Marvell*, ed. Nigel Smith (London: Pearson Longman, 2006), line 20

19. *WO 1655*, unpaginated "epistle" between pp. 46 and 47

20. Whitaker, pp. 116–17

21. Margaret Ezell, "'To Be Your Daughter in Your Pen': The Social Functions of Literature in the Writings of Lady Elizabeth Brackley and Lady Jane Cavendish", *Huntington Library Quarterly*, 51 (1988), 281–96 (p. 285), and *Patronage in Late Renaissance England*, ed. French R. Fogle and Louis A. Knafla (California: University of California, 1983), pp. 1–29

22. Ezell, p. 293. For more discussion of Jane Cavendish and Elizabeth Brackley's writing, see Sara Mueller, "Jane Cavendish and Elizabeth Brackley's Manuscript Collections", *A Companion to the Cavendishes*, pp. 199–215

23. Alison Findlay, quoted in Tom Rutter, "The Cavendishes and Ben Jonson", *A Companion to the Cavendishes*, pp. 107–125, p. 119

24. See both *Bodleian Rawlinson MS Poet 16*, and Beinecke Osborne Collection *MS b.233*

25. Ezell, p. 289

26. Nathan Comfort Starr, "The Concealed Fansyes: A Play by Lady Jane Cavendish and Lady Elizabeth Brackley", *PMLA*, 46 (1931), 802–38 (pp. 805–6)

27. Starr, p. 809

28. Starr, p. 818

29. *Life and True Relation*, p. 141

30. *WO 1655*, unpaginated "epistle" between pp. 46 and 47

31. *WO 1655*, unpaginated "epistle" between pp. 46 and 47

32. *WO 1655*, sig. A3r

33. *WO 1655*, p. 1

34. *WO 1655*, p. 46

35. *WO 1655*, sig. A3r

36. *CCC III*, p. 1732

37. *Life and True Relation*, pp. 108–9

38. *Life and True Relation*, p. 109
39. John Evelyn, trans., *A Character of England as it was lately presented in a letter to a noble man in France* (London: Jo Crooke, 1659), p. 60
40. *Evelyn I*, p. 281
41. CCC III, p. 2022; *Life and True Relation*, pp. 110–11
42. *Life and True Relation*, pp. 297–8
43. For more information on this, see Ellen MacArthur, "Women Petitioners and the Long Parliament", *The English Historical Review* 24 (1909), 698–709 and, more recently, Patricia Higgins, "The Reactions of Women, with special reference to women petitioners", *Politics, Religion and the English Civil War*, ed. Brian Manning (London: Edward Arnold, 1973), pp. 179–224
44. *Life and True Relation*, pp. 302–3
45. Hero Chalmers, *Royalist Women Writers 1650–1680* (Oxford: Clarendon Press, 2004), pp. 20–1
46. *Life and True Relation*, p. 302
47. For more on "scribal publication" see, amongst others, Harold Love, *Scribal Publication in Seventeenth-Century England* (Oxford: Clarendon Press, 1993). This method of transmission is discussed in more detail in Chapter 7.
48. Chalmers, pp. 20–1
49. *WO 1655*, p. 5

Chapter 7

1. *Letters from Dorothy Osborne to Sir William Temple, 1652–54*, ed. Edward Abbott Parry (London: J. M. Dent & Sons, 1890), pp. 81–2
2. James Raven, *The Business of Books* (New Haven and London: Yale University Press, 2007), p. 56; H. B Wheatley, "Signs of Booksellers in St. Paul's Churchyard" in *The Library*, TBS–9 (1906), 67–106
3. *PaF 1653*, sig. A1r
4. *Letters from Dorothy Osborne*, p. 82
5. *Letters from Dorothy Osborne*, p. 100
6. *Letters from Dorothy Osborne*, p. 100
7. See Patricia Crawford, "Women's published writings 1600–1700", in *Women in English Society 1500–1800* (London and New York: Methuen, 1985), ed. Mary Prior, pp. 211–82, p. 265. More recent bibliographic studies of the period affirm these numbers, even if there are slight deviations: see *Women and the Literature of the*

Seventeenth Century: An Annotated Bibliography Based on Wing's Short-title Catalogue, ed. Hilda L. Smith, comp. Susan Cardinale (Connecticut: Greenwood Press, 1990), and *Bibliography of English Women Writers 1500–1640,* ed. and comp. Betty S. Travitsky (Online: Iter Press, 2010)

8. For more on the proliferation of Quaker women's writing, see Rosemary Foxton, *Hear the Word of the Lord: A Critical and Bibliographical Study of Quaker Women's Writing, 1650–1700* (Melbourne: Bibliographical Society of Australia and New Zealand, 1994)

9. Andrew Murphy, "The History of the Book in Britain, c. 1475–1800", in *The Oxford Companion to the Book,* ed. Michael F. Suarez and H. R. Woudhusyen, 2 vols (Oxford; New York: Oxford University Press, 2010) I, pp. 172–9, p. 173

10. Raven, p. 46

11. Wendy Wall, *The Imprint of Gender: Authorship and Publication in the English Renaissance* (Ithaca and London: Cornell University Press, 1993), p. 4

12. *BL Harley MS 4955.* See the discussion of the manuscript in Chapter 6. The manuscript is thought to have been finished being compiled in 1634 – which would, of course, invite the possibility that the poems were copied from the 1633 edition, but the tradition of manuscript copying and circulation also invites the very strong possibility that at least some of the other poems were accumulated from other sources.

13. Henry Woudhuysen, *Sir Philip Sidney and the Circulation of Manuscripts* (Oxford: Clarendon Press, 1996), p. 17

14. J. W. Saunders, "The Stigma of Print: A Note on the Social Bases of Tudor Poetry", in *Essays in Criticism,* 1 (1951), 139–64; quoted in Woudhuysen, pp. 13–14

15. Harold Love and Arthur F. Marotti, "Manuscript Transmission and Circulation", in *The Cambridge History of Early Modern English,* ed. David Lowenstein and Janel Mueller (Cambridge: Cambridge University Press, 2003), pp. 55–80, p. 56

16. As quoted in Wall, p. 1

17. See Wall, pp. 1–2

18. *A Comparison Between the Two Stages* (London: 1702), p. 26

19. Richard Lovelace, *Lucasta Posthume Poems of Richard Lovelace, Esq.* (London: 1659), p. 84

20. Janet Todd, *The Critical Fortunes of Aphra Behn* (South Carolina: Camden House, 1998), p. 5

21. Todd, p. 6
22. Foxton, pp. 4–7
23. *BL Add MS 70118*
24. Dorothy Leigh, *The Mother's Blessing* (London: John Budge, 1616), sig. A7v
25. Elizabeth Grymeston, *Miscelanea. Mediations. Memoratives* (London: Melch. Bradwood for Felix Norton, 1604), sig. A3r
26. Lady Mary Wroth, *The Countess of Montgomery's Urania* (London: John Marriott and John Grimsand, 1621), sig. Ar
27. Philip Sidney, "Astrophel and Stella", in *Sir Philip Sidney*, ed. Katherine Duncan-Jones (Oxford: Oxford University Press, 1989), p. 156
28. *The Poems of Lady Mary Wroth*, ed. Josephine Roberts, rev. edn (Louisiana: LSU Press, 1992), Sir Edward Denny, "To Pamphilia from the father-in-law of Seralius", pp. 32–3
29. *The Poems of Lady Mary Wroth*, p. 35
30. Aemilia Lanyer, *Salve Deus Rex Judaeorum* (London: Valentine Simmes for Richard Bonian, 1611), sig. *b*3r
31. Lanyer, sig. D r
32. *WO 1655*, unpaginated "epistle" between pp. 46 and 47
33. *PaF 1653*, sig. A7r
34. *Life and True Relation*, p. 304
35. Raven, pp. 88–91; see also Marjorie Plant, *The English Book Trade: an Economic History of the Making and Sale of Books*, 3rd edn, (London: Allen & Unwin, 1974), pp. 217–18
36. In February 1656, William Cavendish wrote that the printing for his book "will cost above £1300". See *Life and True Relation*, p. 357
37. *PaF 1653*, sig. A8r; Whitaker, p. 382, pp. 154–9
38. *PaF 1653*, p. 156
39. *PF 1653*, sig. B6r
40. For more information on the pair, see Leona Rostenberg, *The Library of Robert Hooke* (Santa Monica: Modoc Press, 1989), pp. 13–25
41. *PaF 1653*, sig. A4r
42. See n15 to Chapter 5
43. *PaF 1653*, sig. A4v
44. *PaF 1653*, sig. A3
45. *PaF 1653*, p. 213
46. *PaF 1653*, sig. A2v
47. *PaF 1653*, sig. A3r
48. *PaF 1653*, sig. A5v

49. *PaF 1653*, sig. A6r
50. Ben Jonson, "To the Reader", *The Poems of Ben Jonson,* ed. Tom Cain and Ruth Connolly (London: Routledge, 2021)
51. *PaF 1653*, p. 1
52. For more on atomism and the new science, see Lisa T. Sarasohn, "A Science Turned Upside Down: Feminism and the Natural Philosophy of Margaret Cavendish", *Huntingdon Library Quarterly,* 47 (1984), 289–307; Alvin Snider, "Hutchinson and the Lucretian Body", *The New Science and Women's Literary Discourse,* ed. Judy A. Hayden, (New York: Palgrave Macmillan, 2011), pp. 29–64; Steven Clucas, "The Atomism of the Cavendish Circle: A Reappraisal", *The Seventeenth Century,* 9 (1994), 247–73; and Nina Gelbart, "The Intellectual Development of Walter Charleton", *Ambix,* 18 (1971), 149–68. More recent scholarship is collected in *A Princely Brave Woman: Essays on Margaret Cavendish,* ed. Stephen Clucas (London: Routledge, 2003) and *Margaret Cavendish: An Interdisciplinary Perspective,* ed. Lisa Walters and Brandie R. Siegfried (Cambridge: Cambridge University Press, 2022)
53. See Alvin Snider, "Hutchinson and the Lucretian Body", in *The New Science and Women's Literary Discourse,* pp. 29–46, and *Lucy Hutchinson's Translation of Lucretius: De rerum natura,* ed. Hugh de Quehen (London: Duckworth, 1996), pp. 23–7
54. John Milton, *Paradise Lost,* in *Milton: Paradise Lost,* ed. Alastair Fowler, 2nd edn (London: Routledge, 2017), II.900; 898
55. *PaF 1653*, p. 158
56. *PaF 1653*, p. 151
57. *PaF 1653*, p. 17
58. *PaF 1653*, pp. 45–6
59. Sarasohn, p. 291
60. Sarasohn, pp. 292–3
61. *PaF 1653*, pp. 156–7
62. *PaF 1653*, p. 155
63. *PaF 1653*, pp. 191–8
64. *PaF 1653*, p. 194
65. *PaF 1653*, p. 196
66. *PaF 1653*, p. 199
67. *PaF 1653*, p. 211
68. *PaF 1653*, p. 16

Chapter 8

1. Charlotte Brontë, *Villette*, ed. Helen M. Cooper (London: Penguin Classics, 2004), p. 545
2. Charlotte Brontë, *Villette*, p. 546
3. *BL Add MS 32497*, f. 71r
4. *BL Add MS 32497*, f. 73v
5. *BL Add MS 32497*, f. 87v
6. *BL Add MS 32497*, f. 74r
7. *CSPD 1652–1653*, Warrants of the Council of State, Generals of the Fleet &c., p. 467, p. 469; Whitaker, p. 163
8. *BL Add MS 32497*, f. 99v
9. *BL Add MS 32497*, ff. 93v–94r
10. *BL Add MS 32497*, ff. 100r; 99v; 99r
11. *BL Add MS 32497*, f. 93r
12. *BL Add MS 32497*, ff. 100v; 108v
13. *BL Add MS 32497*, f. 100v
14. *BL Add MS 32497*, f. 97v
15. *PF 1653*, sig. A2v; p. 1
16. *PF 1653*, pp. 12–13
17. *PF 1653*, sig. B4r
18. *ODS 1662*, p. 125
19. *ODS 1662*, p. 183
20. *SL 1664*, p. 427
21. *BL Add MS 32497*, ff. 98r; 100r
22. *BL Add MS 32497*, f. 101r
23. *Letters 1678*, p. 66
24. *Letters 1678*, p. 87
25. Whitaker, p. 166
26. *PF 1653*, p. 85
27. *PF 1653*, pp. 24–5
28. *PF 1653*, p. 78; p. 80
29. *WO 1655*, p. 1
30. *Life and True Relation*, p. 112
31. *Life and True Relation*, p. 295
32. Charlotte Brontë features in *The Penguin Book of Feminist Writing*, ed. Hannah Dawson (London: Penguin Classics, 2021), p. 38. Dawson does include one feminist from this period: Mary Astell, and her tract *Some Reflections Upon Marriage* (1700)
33. George Eliot, "Silly Novels by Lady Novelists", in *Essays of George Eliot*, ed. Thomas Pinney (London: Routledge, 1963), pp. 300–24

34. Mary Wollstonecraft, *A Vindication of the Rights of Women,* ed. Janet Todd (Oxford: Oxford University Press, 1994), p. 73

35. See Christopher Hill, *The World Turned Upside Down: Radical Ideas During the English Revolution,* rev. edn (London: Penguin, 2019), particularly Chapter 15 "Base Impudent Kisses", pp. 234–47, and Keith V. Thomas, "Women and the Civil War Sects", *Past and Present* (1958), 42–62

36. Hill, p. 244

37. *Paf 1653,* sig. A3v

38. *ODS 1662,* p. 221

39. For more on this period of feminism, see Hilda L. Smith, *Reason's Disciples: Seventeenth-Century English Feminists* (Chicago; London: University of Illinois Press, 1982)

40. Mary Astell, *Some Reflections Upon Marriage,* in Dawson, p. 14

41. *ODS 1662,* p. 198

42. *ODS 1662,* p. 168

43. *ODS 1662,* p. 170; p. 175

44. *ODS 1662,* p. 182

45. Germaine Greer, *The Female Eunuch* (London: Paladin, 1970), p. 15

46. *SL 1664,* p. 95

47. Shulamith Firestone, *The Dialectic of Sex* (New York: Bantam Books, 1970), pp. 10–11

48. *ODS 1662,* p. 226

49. *ODS 1662,* p. 229

50. *ODS 1662,* p. 246

51. Lisa Walters, in her *Margaret Cavendish: Gender, Science, Politics* (Cambridge: Cambridge University Press, 2014), explores the limits of assuming Cavendish was as much a Royalist as her husband, William. But, in trying to argue that Cavendish was a Republican, the book is flawed.

52. See Hilda L. Smith, "'A General War amongst the Men but None amongst the Women': Political differences between Margaret and William Cavendish", in *Politics and the Political Imagination in Later Stuart Britain,* ed. Howard Nenner (Rochester: University of Rochester Press, 1998), pp. 143–160

53. *ODS 1662,* p. 202

54. Anne Finch, Countess of Winchelsea, "The Unequal Fetters", *The Poems of Anne, Countess of Winchelsea,* ed. Myra Reynolds (Chicago: University of Chicago Press, 1903), p. 150

55. Smith, *Reason's Disciples: Seventeenth-Century English Feminists,* p. 118

56. Astell, in Dawson, p. 14
57. *SL 1664*, p. 28

Chapter 9

1. *The Collected Works of Katherine Philips*, ed. Patrick Thomas, 3 vols (Essex: Stump Cross Books, 1990), I, p. 73; Clare Jackson, *Charles II* (London: Penguin Books, 2018), p. 3
2. *The Collected Works of Katherine Philips*, I, p. 71
3. *Evelyn I*, pp. 332–3
4. *Memoirs of the Life of Colonel Hutchinson*, p. 366
5. *The Collected Works of Katherine Philips*, I, p. 73
6. Antonia Fraser, *Cromwell Our Chief of Men* (London: Weidenfeld and Nicolson, 1973), p. 676
7. *Memoirs of the Life of Colonel Hutchinson*, p. 336
8. N. H. Keeble, *The Restoration* (Oxford: Blackwell Publishing, 2002), p. 19
9. *Pepys I*, p. 86
10. *Pepys I*, p. 75
11. *Memoirs of the Life of Colonel Hutchinson*, p. 335–6
12. David Norbrook, "Lucy Hutchinson Versus Edmund Waller: an Unpublished Reply to Waller's 'A Panegyrick to My Lord Protector'", in *The Seventeenth Century*, 11 (1996), 61–86 (p. 65)
13. *Evelyn I*, p. 332
14. Thomas P. Slaughter, *Ideology and Politics on the Eve of Restoration: Newcastle's advice to Charles II* (California: American Philosophical Society, 1984), p. 5
15. *Life and True Relation*, p. 127
16. *Life and True Relation*, p. 127
17. *Life and True Relation*, p. 128
18. *NUL Ne C15366*
19. *NP 1656*, p. 218
20. *NP 1656*, p. 93, p. 159
21. *PPO 1655*, sig. Av, sig. B3v, sig. B2v
22. *PPO 1655*, sig. (a3)v
23. *PPO 1655*, p. 106, p. 129
24. *NUL Ne 4 1/9*
25. Whitaker, p. 171
26. *Life and True Relation*, pp. 308–309
27. *Life and True Relation*, p. 307
28. Whitaker, p. 183

29. *Life and True Relation*, p. 307
30. *PPO 1655*, p. 128
31. *Plays*, sig. "To the Readers"
32. *SL 1664*, p. 289
33. *Letters 1678*, pp. 142–3
34. See L. E. Semler, "Stories of Selves and Infidels: Walter Charleton's Letter to Margaret Cavendish (1655)" in *Storytelling: Critical and Creative Approaches*, ed. Jan Shaw, Philippa Kelly, L. E. Semler (London: Palgrave Macmillan, 2013), pp. 191–210
35. *NP 1656*, sig. b2r
36. Barry Coward, *The Cromwellian Protectorate* (Manchester: Manchester University Press, 2003), p. 69
37. *Life and True Relation*, p. 130
38. *Life and True Relation*, p. 130

Chapter 10

1. Philip Bordinat, "A Study of Salisbury Court Theatre" (unpublished doctoral thesis, University of Birmingham, 1952), pp. 1–2
2. Bordinat, p. 63
3. *Pepys II*, pp. 25–6
4. *Life and True Relation*, p. 131
5. Grant, p. 182–3
6. *Life and True Relation*, p. 131
7. Lucy Worsley, *Bolsover Castle* (Swindon: English Heritage, 2000), pp. 2–3; see also P. A. Faulkner, *Bolsover Castle, Derbyshire* (London: Her Majesty's Stationery Office, 1972)
8. *CSPD 1649*, p. 217
9. *CSPD 1655*, p. 137
10. Whitaker, p. 243
11. *NUL Pw V 90/5*, f. 20v
12. Quoted in Whitaker, p. 231
13. Quoted in Whitaker, p. 232
14. *Phanseys*, "The Unparalel'd Love", p. 68
15. Whitaker, p. 279
16. Grant, p. 231
17. Quoted in Whitaker, p. 279
18. *HMC 5th Report*, p. 155
19. *PNBP*, "The Convent of Pleasure", p. 49
20. *NUL Pw 1/316*, f. 1r
21. *NU Pw 1/316*, f. 2v

22. Hilda L. Smith, "'A General War amongst the Men but None amongst the Women': Political differences between Margaret and William Cavendish", p. 145

23. Adam Littleton, *A Sermon at the Funeral of the Right Honourable the Lady Jane* (London: 1669), p. 20

24. *SL 1664*, p. 295

25. See Cameron Kroetsch, "List of Margaret Cavendish's Texts, Printers, and Booksellers (1653–1675)", *Digital Cavendish Project* (Online: 2013)

26. For a recent study of this, see Laura Gowing, *Ingenious Trade: Women and Work in Seventeenth-Century London* (Cambridge: Cambridge University Press, 2021)

27. *Plays*, sig. A4r

28. *Plays*, "The Several Wits", p. 84; p. 87; p. 82

29. *Plays*, "Youths Glory, and Deaths Banquet", p. 125

30. *Plays*, "The Unnatural Tragedy", p. 330

31. *Plays*, "The Female Academy", p. 679

32. See *The Convent of Pleasure and Other Plays*, ed. Anne Shaver (Maryland: John Hopkins University Press, 1999), Introduction

33. *PNBP*, "The Bridals", p. 41

34. *PNBP*, "The Bridals", p. 71

35. Sharp, p. 44

36. Sharp, p. 45

37. Emma Donoghue, *Passions Between Women* (London: Bello, 2014), p. 40–1

38. Lucian, *Dialogues of the Courtesans*, in *Lucian*, ed. Jeffrey Henderson, trans. M. D. Macleod, 8 vols (London: Harvard University Press, 1961), VII, p. 385

39. Ferrand Spence, *Lucian's Works translated from the Greek* (London: 1684), p. 304

40. Richard Fanshaw, trans., *The Faithful Shepherd* (London: 1647), p. 46

41. Valerie Straub, *The Renaissance of Lesbianism in Early Modern England* (Cambridge: Cambridge University Press, 2002), p. 2

42. John Donne, "Sappho to Philaenis", in *The Complete Poems of John Donne*, ed. Robin Robbins (London: Routledge, 2013), p. 929. N.B., the poem is in "Dubia".

43. Denise Walen, "Constructions of Female Homoerotics in Early Modern Drama", *Theatre Journal*, 54 (2002), 411–30 (p. 414)

44. *The Collected Works of Katherine Philips*, I, p. 142

45. *The Works of Aphra Behn*, ed. Janet Todd, 7 vols (London: Routledge, 1995–6), I, pp. 393–4

46. Elaine Hobby, "Katherine Philips: Seventeenth-Century Lesbian Poet", in *What Lesbians Do in Books*, ed. Elaine Hobby and Chris White (London: The Women's Press, 1991), pp. 183–204, p. 201

47. Lillian Faderman (ed.), *Chloe Plus Olivia: An Anthology of Lesbian Literature from the Seventeenth Century to the Present* (London: Viking, 1994), p. 33

48. Lillian Faderman, *Surpassing the Love of Men* (New York: Quill, 1981), p. 68

49. Germaine Greer, Susan Hastings, Jeslyn Medoff, Melinda Sansone (eds), *Kissing the Rod: An Anthology of Seventeenth-Century Women's Verse* (London: Little, Brown, 1988), p. 188

50. Hobby, p. 190

51. *PNBP*, "The Convent of Pleasure", p. 6

52. See Stephen Bending, *Green Retreats: Women, Gardens and Eighteenth-Century Culture* (Cambridge: Cambridge University Press, 2013)

53. *PNBP*, "The Convent of Pleasure", p. 11

54. *PNBP*, "The Convent of Pleasure", p. 14

55. bell hooks, "Women Artists: The Creative Process", *Art on My Mind* (New York: The New Press, 1995), pp. 125–32, p. 125

56. hooks, p. 131

57. *PNBP*, "The Convent of Pleasure", p. 22

58. *PNBP*, "The Convent of Pleasure", p. 32

59. *PNBP*, "The Convent of Pleasure", p. 33

60. *PNBP*, "The Convent of Pleasure", p. 45

61. *PNBP*, "The Convent of Pleasure", p. 51

62. Traub, p. 180

Chapter 11

1. *OUEP 1666*, p. 94

2. *BW 1666*, unpaginated title page

3. HMC *13th Report*, Part II, p. 145

4. HMC *Report on the Manuscripts of the Late Reginald Rawdon Hastings*, p. 152

5. It even graces the front cover of Duncan Grant's biography, *Margaret the First*, and was sold in 1929 as a portrait of Cavendish.

6. Whitaker, p. 266

7. *Evelyn II*, p. 8

8. See Whitaker, p. 255, and Grant, p. 200

9. The former printed by W. Wilson, who had been responsible for

her *Orations of Divers Sorts* (1662), and the latter (probably) by D. Maxwell, whose widow would go on to publish all but one of Cavendish's later works. See Cameron Kroetsch, "List of Margaret Cavendish's Texts, Printers, and Booksellers (1653–1675)".

10. *SL 1664,* p. 75
11. *SL 1664,* p. 63
12. *SL 1664,* p. 245
13. *The Works of John Dryden*, ed. H. T. Swedenberg Jr, Earl Miner, Vinton A. Dearing, George Robert Guffey, 20 vols (Berkeley; Los Angeles; London: 1956–2000), XVII, ed. Samuel Holt Monk, A. E. Wallace Maurer, and Vinton A. Dearing, pp. 8–81, p. 55
14. *SL 1664,* p. 246
15. *PL 1664,* sig. a r, sig. a1r
16. *PL 1664,* sig. b r
17. Grant, p. 201
18. *PL 1664,* sig. b v – b1r
19. *PL 1664,* sig. c r
20. See Susan du Verger, *Du Verger's Humble Reflections upon Some Passages of the Right Honourable the Lady Marchioness of Newcastle's Olio* (London: 1657)
21. For more on the elusive du Verger – who is thought to be an English Catholic who spent time in exile in France – see Jane Collins, *Susanne Du Verger* (London: Routledge, 1996)
22. *PL 1664,* p. 21
23. *PL 1664,* p. 18
24. *PL 1664,* pp. 40–1
25. *PL 1664,* p. 97
26. *PL 1664,* p. 97
27. *PL 1664,* p. 97
28. *PL 1664,* p. 137
29. *PL 1664,* p. 147
30. *PL 1664,* p. 192; for more on the "material" soul in response to dualism, see David Cunning, *Cavendish* (London: Routledge, 2016), pp. 62–5
31. *PL 1664,* p. 218
32. *The Conway Letters: The Correspondence of Anne, Viscountess Conway, Henry More, and their Friends 1642–1684,* ed. Marjorie Hope Nicolson and Sarah Hutton, rev. edn (Oxford: Oxford University Press, 1992), p. 237
33. *The Clarendon Edition of the Works of Thomas Hobbes,* eds Noel Malcolm, Simon Schaffer, Quentin Skinner, and Sir Keith

Thomas, 25 vols (Oxford: Oxford University Press, 1984–2014), IV *Leviathan: The English and Latin Texts* (i), ed. Noel Malcom, p. 34

34. *PL 1664*, p. 298
35. *PL 1664*, p. 298
36. *The Clarendon Edition of the Works of Thomas Hobbes*, IV, *Leviathan: The English and Latin Texts*, p. 34. For more on Hobbes, Cavendish, and witchcraft see Ian Bostridge, *Witchcraft and its Transformations c. 1650–1750* (Oxford: Oxford University Press, 1997), pp. 53–85
37. Lisa T. Sarasohn, *The Natural Philosophy of Margaret Cavendish: Reason and Fancy during the Scientific Revolution* (Baltimore: John Hopkins University Press, 2010), p. 35; PF, p. 1
38. *PPO 1655*, p. 6
39. *PPO 1655*, p. 6
40. *PPO 1655*, p. 21
41. *PL 1664*, p. 233
42. *OUEP 1666*, p. 101
43. Sarasohn, p. 9
44. *PL 1664*, p. 31
45. *PPO 1655*, p. 4
46. *PPO 1655*, p. 38
47. *PPO 1655*, p. 6–7
48. *PPO 1655*, sig. (a3)r
49. *GNP*, p. 241
50. *ODS 1662*, p. 303
51. Sarasohn, p. 35
52. Sarasohn, p. 36
53. Cunning, p. 21
54. *PPO 1655*, p. 119
55. Cunning, p. 24
56. *OUEP*, p. 167
57. Boyle, p. 32
58. Boyle, p. 31–2
59. Cunning, p. 16
60. Justin Begley, "Margaret Cavendish, The Last Natural Philosopher" (unpublished doctoral thesis, University of Oxford, 2016), p. 1
61. Cunning, p. 11–12; p. 16
62. Cunning, p. 9
63. Boyle, p. 34
64. Boyle, p. 33; John Rogers, *The Matter of Revolution: Science, Poetry, and Politics in the Age of Milton* (Ithaca, NY: Cornell

University Press, 1996); Neil Ankers, "Paradigms and Politics: Hobbes and Cavendish Contrasted", in Clucas, pp. 242–254

65. Sarasohn, p. 3
66. Boyle, p. 2
67. *The History of the Royal Society*, I, p. 3
68. Robert Hooke, *Micrographia* (London: 1665), sig. b r
69. *Micographia*, sig. b1r
70. *Micographia*, sig. a1r
71. *OUEP 1666*, p. 5
72. *OUEP 1666*, p. 8–9
73. For more on to what extent Cavendish trusted sense perception, see Cunning, pp. 37–43
74. Henry Stubbes, *The Plus Ultra reduced to a Non Plus* (London: 1670); *Campanella Revived* (London: 1670)
75. *OUEP 1666*, p. 11

Chapter 12

1. Virginia Woolf, *A Room of One's Own*, p. 65
2. *Letters 1678*, p. 5
3. *Letters 1678*, p. 72
4. *Letters 1678*, p. 111
5. *Letters 1678*, p. 113
6. *Letters 1678*, p. 99
7. *BL MS Sloane 1950* ff. 35r–38v, mentioned in *God and Nature in the Thought of Margaret Cavendish*, ed. Brandie R. Siegfried and Lisa T. Sarasohn (London: Routledge, 2014), and Whitaker, p. 319
8. *Pepys VII*, p. 309
9. *Evelyn II*, p. 33
10. *Evelyn II*, p. 31
11. *Diary and Correspondence of John Evelyn*, IV, pp. 8–9
12. *The Diary and Correspondence of John Evelyn*, IV, p. 9
13. John Evelyn, *Numismata* (London: 1697), pp. 264–5
14. *BL Add MS 75345*, f. 58r
15. *Pepys VIII*, p. 163
16. *Pepys VIII*, p. 196; p. 209
17. Andrew Marvell, "Last Instructions to a Painter", in *Poems on Affairs of State*, ed. George Villiers, Duke of Buckingham (London: 1697), p. 55
18. *Letters from Dorothy Osborne to Sir William Temple*, pp. 81–2; *Life and True Relation*, pp. 302–3

19. *Bodleian MS North c.4* f. 146
20. C. Willis and Philips Cunnington, *The Handbook of English Costume in the Seventeenth Century* (London: Faber and Faber, 1963), p. 170
21. *Life and True Relation*, p. 312; *BL Add MS 75345*, f. 58r
22. *Pepys VIII*, p. 186
23. See Corinne Thepaut-Cabasset , "Object in Focus: The *Mouche or Beauty Patch*", pp. 135–139, in *Fashioning the Early Modern: Dress, Textiles, and Innovation in Europe, 1500–1800*, ed. Evelyn Welch (Oxford: Oxford University Press, 2017)
24. *The Spectator*, ed. Henry Morley, 3 vols (London: George Routledge, 1891), I, No. 81
25. *Pepys V*, p. 281
26. Willis and Cunnington, p. 181
27. Willis and Cunnington, p. 163
28. Sandra Clark, "'Hic Mulier', 'Haec Vir', and the Controversy over Masculine Women", *Studies in Philology, 82* (1985) Vol. 82, 157–83
29. William Davenant and John Dryden, *The Tempest, or The Enchanted Island* (London: J.M, 1670), "Prologue"
30. *Hatton Correspondence,* ed. E. M. Thompson, 2 vols (London: Camden Society, 1878), I, p. 47
31. *History of the Royal Society*, II, p. 177
32. *BL Add MS 78357*, "Otiumn Evelyni", ff. 26r. For more discussion of this ballad – and its other very similar version, in *PRO, SPD 29/450*, ro2 – see James Fitzmaurice, "The Cavendishes, the Evelyns, and Teasing in Verse and Prose", *Quidditas* 16 (1995–6), 161–86
33. *Pepys VIII*, p. 243
34. *Pepys VIII*, p. 243
35. Grant, p. 194
36. Woolf, *A Room of One's Own*, pp. 65–6
37. Francis Bacon, *The Advancement of Learning, in The Two Books of Francis Bacon* (London: 1605), p. 17
38. *OUEP 1666*, "The Blazing World", sig. b*r
39. *OUEP 1666*, "The Blazing World", sig. b*v
40. *OUEP 1666*, "The Blazing World", p. 1
41. *OUEP 1666*, "The Blazing World", p. 13
42. Merve Emre, "How Leonora Carrington Feminized Surrealism", *New Yorker*, 28 December 2020
43. *OUEP 1666*, "The Blazing World", p. 56
44. Cristina Malcomson, "Christine de Pizan's 'City of Ladies' in Early Modern England", in *Debating Gender in Early Modern England*

1500–1700, ed. Cristina Malcomson and Mihoko Suziki (New York: Palgrave Macmillan, 2002), pp. 15–36

45. Hilda L. Smith, "Margaret Cavendish and the False Universal", in *Virtue, Liberty, and Toleration: Political Ideas of European Women, 1400–1800*, ed. Jacqueline Broad and Karen Green (Dortrecht: Springer, 2007), pp. 95–110, p. 97

46. For more on this, see Jacqueline Broad and Karen Green, "Fictions of a feminine philosophical persona: Christine de Pizan, Margaret Cavendish and philosophia los", in *The Philosopher in Early Modern Europe: The Nature of a Contested Identity*, ed. Conal Condren, Stephen Gaukroger, and Ian Hunter, pp. 229–54

47. Christine de Pizan, *The Book of the City of Ladies*, trans. Rosalind Brown-Grant (London: Penguin, 1999), p.6

48. de Pizan, *The City of Ladies*, p. 11

49. de Pizan, *The City of Ladies*, p. 107

50. *OUEP*, p. 3

51. Ruth Perry, "Radical Doubt and the Liberation of Women", *Eighteenth-Century Studies*, 18 (1985), 472–93, (p. 473); Katherine Rogers, "The Liberating Effect of Rationalism" in *Feminism in Eighteenth Century England* (Urbana: University of Illinois Press, 1982), pp. 53–84

52. de Pizan, *The City of Ladies*, p. 13

53. Broad and Green, p. 234

54. de Pizan, *The City of Ladies*, p. 9

Chapter 13

1. *CDSP 1667*, p. 255; passim thereafter for the whole of July

2. *Pepys IX*, p. 123

3. *CDSP 1667–1668*, p. 602

4. *King James Bible 1611*, I Kings 10.1–12

5. See note on Whitaker, p. 327; Anne Fanshawe, in her biography of her husband, repeatedly stresses her and her husband's "losses in the Royalist cause".

6. *CDSP 1667–1668*, p. 607

7. *PPO 1663*, sig. A2v

8. *NUL Pw 1/316*, f. 2

9. Grant, p. 232

10. *BL Add MS 70500*, f. 85; Whitaker, p. 330

11. *Pw 1/316* f. 2

12. *The Oxford Guide to British Women Writers*, ed. Joanne Shattock,

(Oxford: Oxford University Press, 1993), p. 312 ; Holly Kyte, *Roaring Girls* (London: HQ, 2019), p. 78

13. *PPO 1663*, sig. A2r
14. *PPO 1655*, sig. Av; *PPO 1663* sig. c1v
15. *PPO 1663*, p. 2
16. *PPO 1655*, p. 3
17. *PaF*, sig. A3v
18. *PPO 1663*, p. 5
19. See Elizabeth Scott-Baumann, "Margaret Cavendish as Editor and Reviser", in *Forms of Engagement: Women, Poetry, and Culture, 1640–1680* (Oxford: Oxford University Press, 2013), pp. 60–80; pp. 74–5, and Richard Nate, "'Plain and Vulgarly Express'd': Margaret Cavendish and the Discourse of the New Science", *Rhetorica*, 19 (2001), 403–17, p. 411
20. For a scholarly edition of the 1668 text see *Poems and Fancies with the Animal Parliament*, ed. Brandie R. Siegfried (New York: Iter Press, 2018)
21. *BL C.39.h.27* (1), sig. A8v, see Scott-Bauman, p. 60
22. *PaF 1664*, sig. A1r
23. *PaF 1664*, sig. A2r
24. *PaF 1653*, p. 46
25. *PaF 1664*, p. 57
26. *PaF 1653*, p. 110
27. *PaF 1664*, p. 134
28. *PaF 1653*, sig. A8v
29. Scott-Baumann, p. 65
30. *PaF*, Sig.A9r
31. Scott-Baumann, p. 66
32. Grant, p. 227
33. Whitaker, p. 343
34. James Fitzmaurice, "Margaret Cavendish on Her own Writing: Evidence from Revision and Handmade Correction", *The Papers of the Bibliographical Society of America*, 85 (1991), 297–307, p. 298
35. *GNP*, sig. A2v
36. *GNP*, sig. A3r
37. *GNP*, p. 1
38. *PPO 1663*, p. 5
39. *GNP*, p. 4
40. *GNP*, p. 6; p. 17
41. *GNP*, p. 241
42. *PPO 1663*, p. 32 ; *GNP*, p. 42

43. Whitaker, p. 311
44. *BL MS Egerton 607*, f. 119r
45. *PaF 1653*, sig. A8r
46. *Letters 1676*, p. 108
47. George Edward Briscoe Eyre, ed., *A Transcript of the Registers of the Worshipful Company of Stationers 1640–1708 AD*, 3 vols (London: 1913), II, p. 294; p. 277
48. *The History of the Royal Society*, I, p. 418, p. 425
49. *GNP*, p. 225
50. All details of funeral are taken from College of Arms, *MS I.31*, ff. 64–6
51. Costs of funeral to be found in *BL Add MS 12514*, ff. 282/90
52. "An Arundel Tomb" Philip Larkin, *Collected Poems* (London: Faber and Faber, 1988), pp. 110–11

Chapter 14

1. *PaF 1653*, sig. A3r; sig. A8v
2. *PF 1653*, sig. A4r; *WO 1655* sig. B r
3. *PF 1653*, p. 78
4. Woolf, *A Room of One's Own*, p. 66
5. *Plays*, p. 14
6. *BW 1666*, p. 96
7. *NP 1656*, p. 390 (mispaginated; this page number refers to the number that is printed)
8. *Letters 1676*, p. 153
9. *Letters 1676*, p. 158
10. *Letters 1676*, p. 158
11. *Letters 1676*, p. 165; p. 168
12. *Letters 1676*, p. 175
13. *Letters 1676*, p. 177
14. *Poems on Affairs of State*, ed. George Villiers, Duke of Buckingham (London: 1697), p. 209
15. Quoted in Whitaker, p. 355; *Bodleian MS Ashmole 36*, f. 186v; *Bodleian MS Ashmole 1463*, f. 62b
16. Gerard Langbaine, *An Account of the English Dramatick Poets* (London: L.L. for George West and Harry Clements, 1691), p. 390
17. Langbaine, p. 386; p. 384
18. Langbaine, p. 391
19. Giles Jacob, *The Poetical Register* (London: E. Curll, 1719), p. 191
20. Theophilus Cibber, *The Lives of the Poets of Great Britain and*

Ireland: to the Time of Dean Swift (London: R. Griffiths, 1753), p. 163. Authorship of this volume is debated, and it is sometimes attributed to Robert Shiells.

21. Cibber, p. 164

22. *BL Add MS 4244 f. 22r*

23. George Ballard, *Memoirs of Several Ladies of Great Britain* (London: W. Jackson, 1752), p. vi

24. Ballard, p. 305

25. *NUL Ne X 611*

26. *The Connoisseur*, 2 vols (London: 1774), II, p. 262

27. *The Connoisseur*, II, p. 263

28. Margaret Ezell, *Writing Women's Literary History* (Baltimore: Johns Hopkins University Press, 1993), p. 111

29. Samuel Egerton Brydges, *The Select Poems of Margaret Cavendish* (Kent: Lee Priory Press, 1813), p. 5

30. Horace Walpole, *A Catalogue of the Royal and Noble Authors of England* (London; Edinburgh: 1796), p. 183

31. Alexander Dyce, *Specimens of British Poetesses* (London: T. Rodd, 1825), p. 89

32. Louisa Costello, *Memoirs of Eminent Englishwomen*, 4 vols (London: Richard Bentley, 1884), Vol. 3, p. 212

33. Charles Lamb, *Essays of Elia* (London: 1823), p. 126 ; p. 28

34. Lamb, p. 191

35. Lamb, p. 83

36. Edward Jenkins, *The Cavalier and his Lady, Selections from the Works of the First Duke and Duchess of Newcastle* (London: Macmillan and Co., 1872), p. 7; p. 23

37. *PNBP*, "The Convent of Pleasure", p. 38

38. *PNBP*, "The Convent of Pleasure", p. 42

39. *The Poems of Lady Mary Wroth*, Sir Edward Denny, "To Pamphilia from the father-in-law of Seralius", pp. 32–3

40. Jenkins, p. 95

41. Eric Robertson, *English Poetesses* (London: Cassell and Company, 1883), sig. 'NOTE'

42. Robertson, pp. xiii–xvi

43. Margaret Cavendish, *The Lives of William Cavendishe, Duke of Newcastle, and of His Wife, Margaret, Duchess of Newcastle,* ed. Mark Anthony Lower (London: 1872), p.ix; Whitaker, pp. 361–2

44. Henry Ten Eyck Perry, *The First Duchess of Newcastle and her Husband as Figures in Literary History* (Boston, London: Ginn and Company, 1918), p. 1

45. Perry, p. 1
46. Perry, p. 4
47. Perry, p. 312
48. Perry, p. 174
49. Frank E. Manuel and Frizie P. Manuel, *Utopian Thought in the Western World* (Oxford: Blackwell, 1979), p. 7; Whitaker, p. 366
50. Woolf, *The Common Reader,* pp. 87–8
51. Ezell, p. 109
52. Woolf, *A Room of One's Own,* pp. 104–5
53. Jones, p. 180
54. Smith, *Reason's Disciples,* p. 75
55. Germaine Greer, *Slip-Shod Sibyls* (London: Penguin, 1996), p. xi
56. Greer, p. 98
57. Punctum Books are publishing *The Complete Works of Margaret Cavendish,* ed. Liza Blake, Shawn Moore, Jacob Tootalian
58. *A Princely Brave Woman: Essays on Margaret Cavendish,* ed. Stephen Clucas, p. 1
59. *WO 1665,* unpaginated "epistle" between pp. 134 and 137

Image credits

Page 1

The Picture Art Collection / Alamy Stock Photo

Page 2

(*top*) Artokoloro / Alamy Stock Photo
(*bottom*) Niday Picture Library / Alamy Stock Photo

Page 3

(*top left*) Margaret Cavendish, *Poems and Fancies* (1653) /
    Bridgeman Images / British Library
(*top right*) Margaret Cavendish and Abraham van
    Diepenbeeck, in Cavendish, M., Duchess of Newcastle,
    The World's Olio (London: Printed by A. Maxwell, 1671) /
    British Library
(*bottom*) Alan Reed / Alamy Stock Photo

Page 4

(*top*) Photo by Heritage Art/Heritage Images via Getty Images
(*bottom*) Album / Alamy Stock Photo

Page 5

(*top*) The Elisha Whittelsey Collection, The Elisha Whittelsey
    Fund, 1962 / The Metropolitan Museum of Art
(bottom) Photo by English Heritage/Heritage Images/Getty
    Images

Page 6

(*top*) © Look and Learn / Bridgeman Images
(*bottom*) © British Library Board. All Rights Reserved /
  Bridgeman Images

Page 7

(*top*) Margaret Cavendish, Abraham van Diepenbeeck, in
  Cavendish, M., Duchess of Newcastle, *Natures pictures
  drawn by fancies pencil to the life. Written by the thrice
  noble, illustrious, and excellent princess, the lady
  Marchioness of Newcastle.* (London: printed for J. Martin,
  and J. Allestrye, at the Bell in Saint Paul's Church-yard,
  1656) / British Library
(*bottom*) Margaret Cavendish, *The Blazing World* (1666) /
  British Library

Page 8

(*top*) Photo by The Print Collector/Getty Images
(*bottom left*) The Picture Art Collection / Alamy Stock Photo
(*bottom right*) © Dean and Chapter of Westminster

Acknowledgements

There are far more people who made this book a reality than just one name on the cover. Thank you to my endlessly supportive and utterly peerless agent, Sabhbh Curran. Thank you to Kate Appleton, Kathryn Colwell, Dan Jones, Anthony Cheetham, and the whole team at Head of Zeus for believing in Margaret Cavendish and being such a joy to work with. Thank you to Meg Shepherd for such a glorious cover. And thank you to Neil Belton for his wise and insightful edits, and for commissioning the book.

Thank you to all the libraries and archives who helped with research: everyone in the British Library manuscripts room, the College of Arms Archive, the London Library, the Bodleian Libraries, the Stationers' Company Archive, and the University of Nottingham Manuscripts and Special Collection.

Thank you to the many academics and historians who answered my questions about conundrums big and small (Ben Higgins, Sophie Littlewood, Rosie Harte, Peter McCullough), and to everyone who has written about Cavendish before me.

Thank you, too, to the wonderful academics and teachers who made me love literature and history. Amongst many others: Peter McCullough (again!), Timothy Michael, Harriet Soper, Jonathan Patrick, Julie Runacres, Phoebe Dickerson, and Joshua Newton.

Thank you to my friends and family who have been so understanding and helpful throughout the whole writing process. Thank you to my parents, Jonathan and Charlotte, for everything, and to my wonderful brother, Ed. A million thank yous (and frozen margaritas) to Betty, who is the best friend and housemate anyone could ever wish for. Endless love and thanks to Rosie, Kiki, John, and Nicole. And a special thank you to Benedict and Alastair, for graciously and patiently always answering my questions about seventeenth-century Latin and Greek.

Finally, thank you to Margaret Cavendish – for her fascinating writing, her endless contradictions, and her all-round brilliance.

Index